LETTERS FROM THE NEW ISLAND

Edited by Dermot Bolger

RAVEN ARTS PRESS

Letters from the New Island
is first published in 1991 by
The Raven Arts Press
P.O. Box 1430
Finglas
Dublin 11
Ireland.

ISBN 1 85186 090 8

Cover design by Rapid Productions. Design by Dermot Bolger. Printed and bound in Dublin by Colour Books Ltd., Baldoyle. Special thanks to Aidan Murphy.

CONTENTS

*For Adrian Munnelly
in appreciation of his work
for the Arts in Ireland.*

INTRODUCTION

Dermot Bolger

The *Letters from the New Island* pamphlet series came out of conversations with people in the summer of 1987, during which there was a general consensus that the number of forums for new ideas in Ireland was rapidly shrinking. Pitched between book size and the long magazine article (which was, in any case, becoming increasingly harder to place) the pamphlet idea appealed to the writers in question as both allowing them the maximum of freedom and choice and also (by the very broadside nature of the form) encouraging them to adopt an outspoken and often polemic approach to their theme.

The tradition of pamphleteering in Dublin goes right back to before Dean Swift and his famous *Drapier's Letters*, which were said to have been secretly printed in the grounds in Glasnevin where the Bon Secour hospital now stands. Although still at times an active practice today, they can often suggest a world of academics preaching to academics. In launching a new series we were anxious that they should touch on issues that affected people in a concrete manner, that a piece like Ferdia Mac Anna's brave exploration of the ostracisation within society of somebody with cancer should belong to the *Letters* as much as Colm Tóibín's examination of the links between metaphor and action in Irish life.

The initial three pamphlets by Fintan O'Toole, Colm Tóibín and Michael O'Loughlin were launched in that autumn, with three more in the following spring and summer – Ferdia Mac Anna's and Katie Donovan's which both quickly moved into the best seller lists, and Anthony Cronin's provocative *Art for the People?* Although the seventh in the series was launched that Christmas (a forum of sixteen writers with very different views of the Easter Rising) already we were beginning to see the problems that went hand in hand with the freedom of the pamphlet form.

These problems basically were in both size and price. A twenty page pamphlet, while an effective object in itself, is something which can get lost very quickly in a bookshop – especially when the bookshop is small, there is no room for cover display and anything without a spine is virtually condemned to limbo. The size also proved a great incentive for editors not sympathetic to the ideas of the series to ignore them. But more importantly was the fact that production costs were actually often not much cheaper (taking into account set up costs, covers, etc) than an actual small book and it made the collecting of the whole series expensive for the general reader.

It was our stated intention on the cover of the existing pamphlets to reissue them in book form and we decided that instead of releasing the next five in the series individually we would collect them together with the old ones, therefore, hopefully, bringing the whole set within range of a broad readership.

Each pamphlet began with the wording: *The views expressed by individual authors in the Letters from the New Island pamphlets are not necessarily those of the Raven Arts Press*. It was never our intention to provide a consensus, but instead, in a very small way, to help initiate a discourse about the rapidly changing society which is Ireland today. Thus, not only in the *16 on 16* pamphlet, but throughout the book you will find contradiction and disagreement as much as accord.

The changes, whether real or illusionary, in Irish society are especially striking in the different political landscapes (created in large part by the Mary Robinson Presidential election victory) in the first pamphlets written in the late 1980s and the new ones completed this year.

Fintan O'Toole's *The Southern Question* which began the series in 1987, examines the condition of the Irish Republic today in relation to the clichés which Southern politicians perpetually apply to the North of Ireland, and argues that "alienation" and "division" are as deeply ingrained south of the border, and that the reality of the state is equally "a failed political entity". He goes on to claim that the cure to these and other political and social problems must be found by change within Southern Ireland itself and not by linking them in as a side product to hypothetical aspirations.

Colm Tóibín's *Martyrs and Metaphors* deals with the curious relationship between literature and public life in Ireland now and examines the way in which our history has been governed by small acts of sacrifice which have served as metaphors for communal action in the same way as a poem or song will send out ripples to move people.

The Amsterdam based poet Michael O'Loughlin examines the life of Frank Ryan, one of the major figures in the post Civil War Republican movement, who died near Dresden in 1944. He examines the contradictions of Ryan's life, the relationship between Ireland and Europe, and claims that while Ryan was an obvious failure on one level, he still remains an important anti-hero and a more contemporary figure than, say, De Valera to a modern Irish nation frequently living in disillusionment, alienation and exile.

The perspective on Irish life in Ferdia Mac Anna's *Bald Head* could hardly be more contrasting. There are certain subjects which are taboo in any society. Chief among these today and among our greatest unspoken fears is cancer. At the age of thirty one Ferdia Mac Anna was diagnosed as having testicular cancer. As he writes in *Bald Head* "The word *cancer* has a powerful effect on some patients. Sometimes it was the word that killed people as much as the disease."

In *Bald Head* he sets out to demythify the word. In a raw and personal testament he details both his mind's fight with the word and his body's fight with the disease, examining his own coming to terms with the illness and also the changed reaction of people to him. Although a harrowing journey through a cancer ward, *Bald Head* is ultimately a story of survival and hope which has come to mean a great deal to a large number

9

of people since its publication.

Katie Donovan's *Irish Women Writers*, subtitled "Marginalised by Whom?" argues that attempts to present new female Irish writers as representing the emergence of the female voice in Irish literature for the first time, have obscured the very real achievements of Irish women novelists over the past century. Instead Katie Donovan sets out to detail the huge contribution of female novelists, since Maria Edgeworth, to mainstream Irish literature, and claims that to understand their full significance, their work must be examined as part of the whole tradition of Irish fiction rather than as that of a "marginalised minority."

Although of an older generation than the other writers in the series, Anthony Cronin occupies an important position in the tradition of writing which seeks to challenge conventional ideas. Often a lone voice, throughout the 1970s his *Viewpoint* column in *The Irish Times* was one of the few places where fresh and outspoken opinions were aired. Indeed, it was in part from the reading of one such column, while still a schoolboy, that the decision to establish the Raven Arts Press was taken.

The pieces in *Art for the People* are, with one exception, taken from that *Viewpoint* column, and in them Anthony Cronin asks certain basic questions about our response to poetry and the other arts. What do we expect or want from Art? Are the educational processes which are supposed to end "cultural deprivation" in fact major contributions to it? The answers offered in *Art for the People?* are provocative and, as one would expect from this author, original and controversial.

The pamphlet *16 on 16* already contains an introduction. In commissioning it, I had wondered just how relevant the topic would be today. As the response to both it and the 75th anniversary celebrations has shown, it is still very much a live issue. An interesting fact, both in the pamphlet and in recent radio and television discussions, is how two events were actually being discussed. For anyone who grew up in the 1960s, the Easter Rising meant 1966 and not 1916.

On Easter Sunday this year my wife, my child and myself formed part of a tiny crowd gathered in O'Connell Street.

Watching old footage of the 1966 commemorations that week, it was hard to believe this was the same occasion, a quarter century on. In one sense standing in O'Connell Street in 1991 was more interesting than 1966 in being closer to the original scene seventy five years before — a small crowd of curious onlookers, mainly unable to see what was happening now (apart from the glimpses of figures and a flag being raised) and unsure of what was going to happen next.

The answer was nothing. The flag was raised, the proclamation read and everybody in authority hurriedly scarpered, leaving the last few survivors (who were only given transport there as an afterthought following public pressure) sitting in the only chairs provided.

The question being asked then (and the question asked in *16 on 16*) basically is, can the Provos justifiably claim to be the successors of Pearse and Connolly? Later that Easter Sunday John Hume asked on the radio would the Provos tell him "if they really think Patrick Pearse would have gone out on the Strand Road in Derry last week with a machine gun to riddle a poor widowed lady who had lost her husband to the same machine guns? Would James Connolly have strapped a working class man to the seat of a car and turned him into a human bomb to kill British Soldiers?"

The answers to these, it seems to me, is that Pearse and Connolly who surrendered "least they bring too much suffering on their own people" would not have recognised their successors as those engaged in such genocide. The problem is that I don't think they would recognise their successors either in a Government which, the week before the 75th anniversary, was too scared of offending a major power, the Chinese Government, to even meet the Dalai Lama when he came to Dublin, that simple man whose stories of the oppression and torture of his small nation they would recognise only too clearly.

The five unpublished pamphlets or essays are all in different ways assessments of Ireland as we move into a decade of change, and are linked by common themes and events, if

11

frequently drawing differing conclusions.

Officially the perception of the state of the country has changed. As John Waters puts it in *Who's Afraid of Change?* "Through the medium of the Doheny & Nesbitt School of Economics...fiscal rectitude became big in Irish politics, and close links were forged between politicians, economists and journalists, who between them succeeded in hi-jacking the entire political and social agenda and making it a vehicle for the views which, though they ensured the immediate survival of those who promoted them, had little to offer in terms of the long-term well-being of the country as a whole... Cutbacks became the order of the day and the catchcry of the time. Needless to say, most of the cutbacks occurred in places far removed from the habitats of Dublin 4... The establishment congratulates itself on the latest inflation rates – proof, we are told, that the policy of fiscal rectitude is bearing fruit – but gives no thought to the cost of this abstract gain to the lives of the people who populate this economy of ours."

Although Waters is discussing the effects of these policies on the lives of people in rural Ireland, their effects have been heavily felt by that large (and increasingly invisible) section of Dublin's population who live below the poverty line. Aileen O'Mara has already received an A.T. Cross Journalism Award for her writings about social conditions in Dublin, and in *Women and Poverty* she details with devastating accuracy the hidden underbelly of our capital city. Although written about a whole class, the title *Women and Poverty* grew in the main from the fact that it is generally the women of the family who are left to "queue for a living".

As Mary Raftery points out in *The Irish Family* attempts by that section of the population to make ends meet by trying to "illegally claim the small amounts handed out on the dole are severely dwelt with, but to make off with millions while carrying on your business is ignored... The combination of archaic laws and a hopelessly undermanned Fraud Squad forces one to conclude that Irish business can make up its own rules."

In *The Irish Family* Mary Raftery examines the Gallagher

12

family, tying in their growth and eventual collapse with the changes in Ireland over the past thirty years. She moves from Matt Gallagher, who in the 1960's employed thousands in the building trade and who – with his friends in Fianna Fail "could feel together they were literally building the country", to his son Patrick who in the harsher climate of the 1970s laid off the workers and switched the company interests from building on their vast land bank to simple land speculation until his collapse with devastating effects for the ordinary account holders in the Gallagher controlled banks north and south of the border. Patrick Gallagher has been tried in a Northern Ireland court but has never faced charges in the South.

The dichotomy between the actual views of ordinary people and those of their politicians is touched on by Edward Mulhall in his study of the political writings of two Irish journalists who have recently died – John Healy and Breandán Ó hEithir. He explores the power of radio, which both men recognised the often unacknowledged importance of, as a barometer for the views of ordinary voters and a stumbling block for politicians, be it in Charles Haughey's acknowledgement that he was not aware of the state of discontent about the health service or Padraig Flynn's attempt to smear Mary Robinson which backfired on *Saturdayview*.

Mulhall examines the portraits that both men left of that generation of 1960s Fianna Fail politicians that Matt Gallagher would have known, and maintains that both Healy and Ó hEithir were among the first to articulate the real concerns of grassroots voters as against the issues which we, as a nation, are supposed to be engrossed with. Emigration is chief among these, and Mulhall examines the pain of this subject both in the past through Healy's books like *No One Shouted Stop: The Death of an Irish Town* and through both men's writings of the new wave of modern emigrants.

The bleakness of Healy's descriptions of Western communities devastated by emigration is echoed in Waters' *Who's Afraid of Change?* where he describes whole rural towns where "you will see nobody between the age of eighteen and twenty-five." Taking Mary Robinson's election as a call from ordinary people for a real change in Irish politics he writes, "The political process, while paying lip-service to the 'tragedy of emigration', is in reality quite happy to have the possibility of sudden and dramatic change filtered off by emigration. But nobody bargained on emigration having a radicalising effect on many of those who remained: Mary Robinson got the votes of Irish emigrants by proxy – their parents and friends voted in their place."

Attacking both journalists and politicians who have tried to write off the election result as being of no consequence, he examines how each of the main political parties is coming to terms with having to leave entrenched positions and face a changing electorate setting the agenda for the 1990s.

The series concludes with three open letters by Richard Kearney to three presidents, to Jacques Delors, Mary Robinson and Gerry Adams, in which he advocates ways forward for Ireland both internally and within a broader European context.

Looking back over time I notice that nine of the authors of individual pamphlets here (as well as the editor) were born between 1954 and 1960 – five inside Dublin and five outside the capital. This is a generation caught between two contrasting Irelands, a generation for whom emigration was often only black and white photos of uncles and aunts who had vanished in a past, and yet for whose younger brothers and sisters it was to be a normal fact of life again, a generation caught in time between the flames of the GPO burning in black and white in RTE's Insurrection, and the remote control world of European satellite television, the last generation to have clutched large green passports now being traded in for wine coloured EC ones.

No claim could be made that these pamphlets come close to reflecting the whole spectrum of opinion within Ireland today. But I hope that, in a small way, they will help to engage debate and argument in the present, and, at the very least, leave a record for future readers of what moved, provoked and interested a selection from that particular generation of Irish people within a society in flux, frequently in conflict with itself and very much vibrant, emerging and alive.

THE SOUTHERN QUESTION

Fintan O'Toole

That year, for a while, we stopped playing cowboys and indians. The ambushes from behind the garden wall, the shots fired from the safety of the stone lamp-posts gave way to barricades, house-to-house fighting, and the grim heroism of the lone sniper pinning down the alien advance. It being 1966, and the fiftieth anniversary of the Easter rising, we watched Hugh Leonard's *Insurrection* on television every night and played out the manoeuvers next day, blocking the stairs with matresses and chairs, ducking below the window of the front bedroom to reload and fire again on the British cavalry prancing arrogantly up O'Connell Street. Sometimes, one of us would forget and swoop at a barricade with a plastic tomahawk, hand to mouth in a fearsome whoop, and would be resisted by another with a plastic 1916-1966 badge — green shamrock on a white background with orange lettering — fixed to his cowboy hat. It helped that on the television the rebels wore hats that were like stetsons with one side of the brim turned up, and anyway the image was appropriate enough, for Crumlin was often thought of as a Wild West annexed to a nationalist republic. As one of its residents, Kathleen Behan, described it: "Crumlin, you know, is right out of the city, on the slopes of the Dublin Mountains. It would put your heart crossways, just looking at miles and miles of new roads. No lights. It was like the Wild West."

Just as the pioneers who drove west gave their new found lands the names of old world places — Dublin, Ohio; Paris, Texas — in order to convince themselves that this was still the world they knew, so the planners who pushed westwards towards the Dublin Mountains, named and shaped the ground

15

in the image of that Ireland they dreamed of. The centre of the corporation housing estate of Crumlin began to be built in 1932, the year of the Eucharistic Congress, so they built it in the shape of the Eucharistic Cross. Our roads were named after the ancient dioceses of the Irish Catholic Church: Leighlin, Clonmacnoise, Ferns, Kells, Bangor, Lismore, Clogher, Saul, Kildare. When they ran out of ancient monasteries and dioceses, they turned to the patriot dead, to Parnell and his estates: Aughavannagh, Glenealy, Rathdrum, the names conjuring up not only Ireland's most benevolent landlord, but also the soft, harmless hills and glens of Wicklow. Out here it was pioneer territory, a kind of Ireland, suburban and working-class, not known before. As if to magic away the uncertainty of what might emerge from these winding rows of pebble-dashed two-up-and-two-downs, the planners gave a ready-made history to a place that had no history, gave Crumlin the shape and names of the great guarantors of Irishness: land, nationality and religion, Wicklow villages, the patriot dead, the one, holy Catholic and apostolic church. In such a place there would be happy homes and happy families, with the huge vaulted church and the granite barracks-like police station to look down and smile. The nameless planner who named Aughavannagh Road may have thought of Synge: "Here and there in County Wicklow there are a number of little known places — places with curiously melodious names such as Aughavanna ...where the people have retained a peculiar simplicity...When they meet a wanderer on foot, these old people are glad to stop and talk to him for hours, telling him stories of the Rebellion, or of the fallen angels that ride across the hills." He may not have read on to Synge's description of the "three shadowy countries" that are never forgotten by the people of Aughavannagh: "America (their El Dorado), the Union and the Madhouse."

At Scoil Iosagain Christian Brother's primary school that year of 1966, a framed Proclamation appeared on the wall, and the school concert was to be a celebration of the glorious anniversary. We were kept in after school time to learn the songs and rehearse the actions, the brother's pounding on the piano mingling in a muffled echo with the tramp of marching feet on the bare floor of the hall. I was to sing solo, a sentimental ballad of martyrdom to a country-and-old-time waltz tune, called the The Black and Tan Gun. At a late stage, it was decided to make the number an "action-song" with the story of the murder of a pure young Irish hero by a Black and Tan to be played out in dumb show while the song was sung. A very large 8-year old called Fred was assigned the martyr's part, a mean, ferret-faced boy was to play the Black and Tan, and two weedy, scrawny kids were chosen as pall-bearers and instructed to drape Fred with the tricolour as the last verse of the song got into its stride, salute solemnly, lift Fred on their shoulders and carry him offstage.

I stood at the side of the stage in starched white shirt, tricoloured tie, green short trousers and green socks with golden stripes at the top, watched for the signal from the brother and began, as the assembled parents quietened to a hush "It was down in the town of old Bantry, where most of the fighting was done..." I could see nothing of the tableaux behind me. "It was there that a young Irish soldier, was shot by a Black and Tan gun." There was a bang, a thud and a titter, as Fred crashed to the stage, mortally wounded. I heard the pallbearers march on as the last verse waltzed its way towards a triumphant climax. "He turned to his comrades and said..." Ripples of adult laughter gathered themselves into a wave rushing towards the stage from the body of the hall. I looked down: my fly was closed. "Won't you bury me out on the mountains, so I can see where the battle was won..." The laughter had become helpless and hysterical and I turned my head to look across the stage. The pallbearers, having apparently failed at several attempts to lift Fred, had taken him by the heels and were dragging him slowly, the tricolour bunching around his neck and head, his head bumping off the rough boards, to the side of the stage. Land, nationality and religion had become a glorious farce.

That same month, April 1966, as part of the 50th

Anniversary celebrations, Charles J. Haughey, Minister for Agriculture, made a speech on the aspirations of young boys. "What finer end" he asked rhetorically "could there be for a boy who aspires to become a man according to Pearse's ideal than to follow the calling of the land? Little wonder that so many of the countless young men who fought for Ireland down the centuries came from farming stock, for there, on the land, so close to nature, the feeling of patriotism has ever been a living thing. The present and each future generation owe it to the men of 1916 to make well organised and intelligent efforts to improve the land of Ireland and exploit its resources." The rhetoric was in a direct line of descent from that of Fianna Fail's founder Eamon DeValera, full of the same appeal to sacred republican tradition, the same mystical belief in the virtue of the land as the essential Ireland, the same sense that the present generation remained a guilty debtor which had to prove itself worthy of the sacrifices of the past, the same Christian Brothers vision of aspiring boys.

But this 1966 was not only the anniversary of the Rising; it was also the year of Taca, of fortunes being made on property speculation, of rising tides and lifting boats. Whereas DeValera would have used this rhetoric to extol the moral virtues of frugality, Charles Haughey plugged it in to the new materialism: "That the members of (rural) communities should reach the highest level of material prosperity that our resources can make available at any given moment is also a basic requirement." It has been the achievement of the Irish political system, and of Fianna Fail in particular, to evolve a rhetoric which conceals more than it reveals, a language which paints out the reality of the Republic of Ireland. In its official imagery, the Republic of Ireland has been unable to conceive of itself, and a society which cannot conceive of itself is doomed to remain sterile. Not only has the Southern Question not been answered, it has not, officially, been asked.

The language employed by Ireland's major political parties

evolved from nineteenth century romanticism, combined with Christian imagery of suffering, sacrifice and resurrection, and has been sustained by the need to evade social realities and to maintain a political system that is devoid of overt ideological division. It is the common heritage of all those parties tracing their line of apostolic succession back to the Fenians. Fine Gael, as much as Fianna Fail, has made use of a set of abstractions which serve to make real divisions in society invisible. In December 1981, for instance, the Fine Gael Trade Minister John Kelly, speaking of the small entrepreneur, said that "this thrusting, forceful individualist is in a way the quintessential human being", an image in which all men become petty capitalist, and those who are not become inessential and invisible. And such rhetoric has served that party, too, to mask basic contradictions on fundamental issues of society and economics: in April 1981, for instance, John Kelly's leader Garret FitzGerald stated clearly that poverty could only be tackled by re-allocating newly created wealth, and not by a re-distribution of existing resources; later in the same year he said exactly the opposite — that the elimination of poverty could not await future economic growth. When large sections of the society have been rendered invisible by the prevailing rhetoric, the same political leader can say utterly contradictory things about them without appearing to contradict himself within the terms of that rhetoric. For it is precisely the point of the rhetoric that it acts to evade all contradictions.

The most important figure in maintaining the language and imagery of Irish politics into the eighties, however, has been Charles Haughey. He it was who straddled the paradox that, as Irish reality has departed further and further from the rhetoric, so the maintenance and refurbishment of the rhetoric has become all the more crucial. In the years before Charles Haughey's initiation into Irish parliamentary politics, before T. K. Whitaker and the *Programme for Economic Expansion,* there was a crisis in Irish political language. In the early fifties, Eamon DeValera, the man who had said that he had only to look into his own heart to know what the Irish people were thinking, looked at the lines of people heading for the cattle boats and confessed "I don't know why they are going". As Independent Ireland became a patent failure as a political entity, the fuel of its political rhetoric began to dry up, both anti-partitionism and the divisions of the Civil War running out of steam as sources of inspiration and aspiration. DeValera, the embodiment of the nationalist dream, began to say things about partition like "If I am asked 'have you a solution for it?'...I have to say that I have not and neither has anybody else" and "France was France without Alsace and Lorraine...Ireland is Ireland without the North". One of his most fervent followers from Civil War days, Frank Aiken, told the Dáil that, after all, "There are, in fact, very few differences between Fianna Fail and Fine Gael and they are differences only of personalities".

Ireland could be Ireland without the North, political leaders did not understand why their people were emigrating, anti-partitionism offered no solutions, the political system itself was based on a sham of opposition — these were dangerous words with the tang of reality to them, uttered in the gloom of despair. They were words which would, and would have to be, forgotten in the new dawn after 1958. The new direction of Lemass and Whitaker needed a national consensus to support it. It was Charles Haughey's task to bridge that gap, to take the old rhetoric into new horizons. Ironically, the things which made that new rhetoric more and more distant from reality — urbanisation, multinational capital, consumer culture — also made it all the more necessary to the survival of the political system.

Charles Haughey's career in political speech-making begins, on the threshold of the Irish Industrial Revolution of Whitaker and Lemass, by accommodating the traditional rhetoric of Fianna Fail — land, Christian values, nationalism — to the rising demands of consumerism, and ends up using that traditional rhetoric to disguise the increasingly obvious failure to satisfy those demands. In his maiden speech to Dail Eireann in 1957, he retains the outward elements of DeValera's idealistic zeal, calling for "a tremendous national crusade" and "a crusading spirit". He also brashly replaces Tone's belief that the link with England was the source of all of Ireland's troubles with the blunt statement that "the trouble with this country is that too many people are making insufficient profits". In keeping with the mood of the times, as Ireland is just about to launch on a jettisoning of Fianna Fail's stated aims of economic independence in search of multinational capital, the iron fist of right-wing economics is clearly visible beneath the velvet glove of mystical rhetoric. By 1981, however, when that courtship of multinational capital has proved itself a failure, he addresses the Fianna Fail Ard Fheis as Taoiseach, now using the crusading rhetoric to divert attention from the economic crisis: "I would urge the Irish people to look up from the temporary difficulties of the present and look forward to the sort of Ireland we have already set about creating." Somewhere between the profits and the prophecy lies the official political ideology of the Republic.

As a party founded on minute linguistic distinctions — the "empty formula" of the oath providing a stark reminder that words mean what we choose them to mean — Fianna Fail has been scrupulously careful with its choice of words. The Fianna Fail Coru (Constitution), in spite of the fact that it creates formal goals and structures for The Republican Party is careful to avoid the use of the word "party" wherever possible. That term is reserved for the parliamentary caucus, while the word "organisation" is used for Fianna Fail as a whole. The distinction is crucial: a party would be an expression of a particular class or interest group in a divided society; the organisation is merely the physical expression of the will of the people. Fianna Fail portrayed its stated aims — the ending of partition, the restoration of the Irish language and the achievement of economic self-sufficiency — as the national goals of the Irish race, its political machine as a national movement dedicated to redressing the historical grievances of the oppressed and dispossessed. It presented itself more as a

21

church than as a political party engaged in the sordid struggle for power.

In his memoirs, Todd Andrews recalls that Eamonn DeValera, too modest to wear the gold fainne reserved for accomplished speakers of Gaelic, had his secretary sew a fainne of thread onto a lapel of his jacket. "Cardinal Conway brought him some authentic cardinal red thread from Rome to enhance the job". The image of DeValera elevated to the status of cardinal for his modest austerity and dedication to the national aims is an apt one, for as head of Fianna Fail he was the nearest thing to a secular cardinal. As political scientist R.K. Carty has pointed out, the Irish Catholic church is "an anti-intellectual, male dominated, authoritarian, hierarchical organisation which rewards loyalty and faithful service." So is Fianna Fail. "Indeed, Fianna Fail's predominance in the nineteenth century tradition of there being but one Irish party, constitutes a secular caricature of the church's unchallenged position in society...TDs occupy, both in their relationships to their local clients and to their party much the same structural position as priests in the Catholic church, who so long acted as the Irish peasant's primary contact with external authorities."

Fianna Fail inherited something else from the church, too: the ability to divide the country into us and them, the damned and the saved, the true Irishman and the faithless traitor, a turn of mind greatly assisted by the identification through history of Catholicism and Irish nationality. Fianna Fail defined the people: those who supported the "organisation" were true Irishmen; those who did not became invisible. Claiming a difference of kind as well as of degree, Fianna Fail was able to distinguish itself from all other parties put together. The advantages were electoral as well as ideological. In an electoral system which practically invites voters to express their preferences for individuals across party lines, Fianna Fail voters have always been characterised by a very high degree of exclusivity and solidarity. Half of Fianna Fail votes become non-transferable when there is no Fianna Fail candidate left in the field. A steady 80 to 87 per cent of Fianna Fail transfers have remained within the party at every election in the last twenty years, an incredible record in a system in which geography and personality play such crucial parts. What this means is that not only has Fianna Fail managed to get its supporters to think of themselves — a steady 46 per cent of the population for the last fifty years — as "us", it has also got its supporters to think of themselves — as "not them". What has been excluded has been just as important as what has been included. Fianna Fail has been more than a catch-all party; it has been a subculture, resting on neither a genuine class base nor a set of affiliated organisations but on a psychological identification with the movement, a sense of community. In the political language of the Republic, the word "community" has become crucial, invoking a sense of warmth and tradition, while at the same time excluding those who are not visible. In the official language of Irish politics the more all-embracing a term — nation, spirit, nature, history, Ireland — appears to be, the more rigidly it is excluding someone from its embrace.

What is most obvious about Charles Haughey' ideology as it emerges in his speeches is his continual insistence that he has none. He paints himself as a pragmatist, a man equally concerned with profit and with social justice. Many of the key terms of political discourse in other European societies simply do not figure in the Haughey lexicon. "Class" or "social class", for instance, is mentioned less than half a dozen times in his collected speeches, *The Spirit of the Nation*, a book which contains over half a million words. The word "inequality" is used in three of the 245 speeches. The key words of both right and left are used relatively rarely and then always in a derogatory context. "Conservative", "right-wing" and "monetarist" are terms of abuse, the latter as much on nationalist as on intellectual grounds, since it is "not an indigenous but an entirely imported product". Socialism, as an "alien gospel of class warfare, envy and strife" is also inherently unIrish and therefore unworthy of a serious place in the language of Irish political debate.

This sense that politics should be above ideology runs

through Haughey's career, but it is best expressed in his 1981 speech to the party's 50th Ard Fheis in which he defines the reason "we adhere to Fianna Fail" as the fact that "it represents not this pressure group or that sectional interest, this class or that creed, but because in the board sweep of its membership and their faith and devotion to their country there resides what one can call 'the Spirit of the Nation'". The latter phrase, appropriately, comes from Thomas Davis who began the business of defining the authentic Irishman by conjuring an idealised peasant and identifying anglicisation with urbanisation, commercialism and mechanisation. In this *credo*, class, economic interest, the real divisions of southern society, give way to the religious virtues of Faith, Devotion, and Spirit. Politics ceases to be politics and becomes a cross between literature and religion. Political language becomes a flight into the abstract, politics the science of evading reality, life becomes art.

In his need to evade the categories of left and right, Haughey takes on much of the stock of semi-mystical imagery which 19th century nationalism bequeathed to DeValera. The latter used messianic language to cloak material deprivation, telling the Irish people that they were, by their very poverty, uniquely fitted"to save western civilisation". Faced with modernisation and the development of technology, DeValera sought to make it palatable by claiming it as part of a timeless Irish struggle. Technology, he said, could be harnessed to "help by truth to save the world", "calling modern science to the aid of Ireland's age-long mission". Charles Haughey, in a time of unparalleled modernisation in Ireland, used exactly the same rhetorical device. Thus in the heady sixties, when things are changing at what could be a bewildering pace, he tells his listeners that the new Ireland that Fianna Fail is creating is "the Ireland that our patriots have dreamed about for over a century". Into the eighties, he is still promising to achieve "the bright dreams that sustained our ancestors and were passed down to us" and claiming that "we are working to create the future of which the Irish people have always dreamed". While that Davis, Tone and Pearse dreamed of IDA advance factories, bungalow bliss and The Late Late Show, this rhetoric helps not only to disguise the abandonment of the Fianna Fail aim of economic self-sufficiency, but also to further the image of Charles Haughey, Man of Destiny, the patriot who has achieved what generations of patriots could only dream.

Charles Haughey's imagery serves to present himself as the embodiment of Ireland, the fulfilment of both time and space. As a long march towards Kinsealy, history, the dreams of generations of dead Irishmen, is eschatalogically fulfilled in the person of the man who is to make those dreams come true. (Thus Haughey's anger at those who would see history as something other than an unbroken chain leading to himself, or those who fail to pay proper respect to the patriot dead: "Nor are we prepared to acquiesce in any rewriting of Irish history or to ignore the anniversaries of historic events and achievements..."). And what is true of time is true of space also. The carefully cultivated image of the man born in Connaught of Ulster parentage, living in Leinster and taking his holidays in Munster ("Look at the dilemma I'm in" he tells his family over breakfast, discussing the All-Ireland football semi-finals in the television film *Charles Haughey's Ireland*, "Of the four teams in it, three of them are Dublin, Kerry, Mayo. I was born in Mayo, I live in Dublin, and I have my holidays in Kerry". Shortly afterwards we see him in Swatragh, County Derry: "As a child I used to spend my holidays here".) is an image of the dismembered country made whole, of the divisions between country and city, west and east, north and south, healed in the mystical body of Charlie. (The same image has been exploited by Garret FitzGerald who used his mixed Southern Catholic and Northern Protestant parentage to present himself as an embodiment of a unified island).

In the biography of Mr. Haughey at the front of *The Spirit of the Nation*, the nobility of nature is added to this transcendence of time and place: "(His) descent can be traced back to the Uí Neill, Kings of Ulster. Haughey in Irish means a horseman or knight as the Irish version Eochaidh is derived from the word

'Each' meaning a steed. The numerous O hEochaidh clan inhabited a wide area of mid-Ulster and were kings of Ulidia up to the end of the 12th century. One of the O hEochaidh Kings fought and fell with Brian Boru at Clontarf. Haughey's Fort is part of the Emhain Macha (Navan Fort) site near Armagh". Besides adding noble steeds to the myth, and *Charles Haughey's Ireland* is full of shots of him on, with or around horses, the image of descent from kings has long been one of the ideological barriers to class consciousness in Ireland. The late Roy Geary, director of the Economic and Social Research Institute, maintained wryly that there were no classes in Ireland since we are all descended from the high kings of Tara.

In this curious but brilliantly effective ideological construct, nature, the land and rural values are identified as the essential Ireland which Fianna Fail represents. Charles Haughey told the Dublin Institute of Catholic Sociology in 1964 that "Those who live on the land are in close harmony with nature and are constantly reminded of the basic spiritual values. Their work has a special dignity demanding many qualities...There is fortunately one great stabilising influence in our situation which underpins the whole structure of our society. It is the love of the farmer for his land and his abiding determination in spite of all difficulties and disadvantages to hold on if he can". And a leap is made from this identification of the land with spiritual values and with the essential Ireland to the identification of nature itself with Charles Haughey as the fulfilment of Ireland's destiny. For Christmas 1986, Charles Haughey, lonely ruler of the great nation, sent cards to his friends which featured a painting of eagles on a rocky island and the caption "Lonely Ruler of the Great Cliffs". The accompanying text identified the eagle with Irish Catholic tradition, with persecution, death and resurrection, and with great political leaders: "The eagle has, since earliest times, been used as a symbol of power and nobility. It was greatly favoured as such by the monks who produced our early Christian manuscripts...Two hundred years ago sea eagles were a common sight in Ireland and many places are still named after

26

them...Uncrowned kings of their domain they had no real enemies. Alas in modern times, they were hunted to extinction and disappeared completely from Ireland and Britain...Perhaps someday this great bird will once again glide silently and majestically over the sea and along the cliffs of our western coast". Mr. Haughey has been at pains to identify himself with nature, wildlife and conservation. In 1986 he announced his intention to re-introduce the Lonely Ruler of the Great Cliffs to Ireland — at his own holiday home on Inishvicillaune.*

The uses of this identification of himself with nature are, in practical political terms, twofold. In the first place, nature, the land itself, is an argument for a United Ireland. "Ireland is unmistakably a geographical entity" he maintains in *Charles Haughey's Ireland*, remarking on the similarity of a field in the South and a field in the North. His nationalism is founded on a belief that the natural shape of the land must be reflected in political institutions, claiming an authority for government, not just in the people but in the land which the most authentic of those people — the farmers who are "in close harmony with nature" — embody. In a speech of 1965, when he is, appropriately, Minister for Agriculture, he tells a London audience that "a United Ireland...is in the *natural order of things*". The second use of this politicisation of nature is that if the authority of government derives essentially from nature, as it does in Haughey's rhetoric, then those who are most in touch with nature, the denizens of rural Ireland, have a political as well as a moral priority over the working class of the towns and cities. While there are nearly forty mentions of Dublin and its problems in *The Spirit of the Nation* (and Mr. Haughey has represented Dublin constituencies for his entire political career) there are half as many again of the West of Ireland, "the remote but beautiful and tradition-rich places of the West".

Perhaps the most important abstraction in the Haughey rhetoric is "culture". Not only is there much more in his collection of speeches about the arts and culture than one would expect from any comparable politician, but the speeches on cultural topics are generally the most extensive, coherent, well-written and intellectually impressive of all. The role of culture is to act as a non-contentious sanctuary above the petty strife of conflicting interests, and as practical proof of the existence of the spirit of the nation. In debating with Conor Cruise O'Brien his proposal that BBC television should be broadcast in Ireland, he says of the term "national culture" that "it would be difficult and perhaps even dangerous to try to spell out exactly what was meant by it" and this resistance to definition is precisely its usefullness to a political ideology which depends on ill-defined abstractions for its effect. Standing in front of Newgrange in *Charles Haughey's Ireland*, he is impressed by the fact that it is "mysterious". A dainty quip springs to his mind: "Malraux claimed that all art came from our desire to defy our nothingness" before the real ideological meaning of the megalithic tomb comes into view. "It proves to me that I belong to a very, very old country, a people who had such a stable society that they could look forward for a long period ahead....To me that gives me a tremendous satisfactory feeling of continuity and permanence". In a sleight of mind typical of the complex ideological system, we have gone from mystery and nothingness to a stable society and a permanent 45 per cent of the vote without straying from the realm of "culture".

A more direct example of the use of history, culture and religion to bolster a political point is in his Saint Patrick's Day message of 1981: "Because Ireland at the time of Saint Patrick and for many centuries afterwards possessed a cultural unity transcending its petty political divisions, the partitioning of their land was and has remained an almost inconceivable eventuality to the vast majority of Irish men and women". In this sentence, the partitioning of Ireland seems to have taken place at the time of Saint Patrick, in the mists of holy antiquity, making it not an act of modern politics and economics, but a primal sin against a godly community of innocents. A contemporary political fact becomes a mystical and mythological evil. Reality, a reality with which "the vast majority of Irish men and women" have lived for sixty years,

28

becomes "inconceivable". In this rhetoric, the Republic of Ireland, created by that act of partition, cannot be conceived of.

The mysticism of the rhetoric is dropped only when there is a real threat to the interests of the ruling class. The Haughey disdain for ideologies of left and right is left aside when a real socialist challenge emerges in the shape of a seemingly radicalised Labour Party in 1969, and straightforward attacks on socialism go to the extent of telling an election press conference that "Manifestos have a Marxian ring about them so we will not be having one". The semblance of being above the fray is also dropped in 1974 when the appearance of a wealth tax prompts a warning that this spells the end of private property as we know it and a dangerously open acknowledgment that "I make no apology for stating here that only a private enterprise system can provide us with the economic development which we need to procure any worthwhile social progress". Only once do the hard-edged concern for profit and the soft-focus imagery of myth and history merge. Opening the Cork Film Festival in 1962, Mr. Haughey tells the assembled movie moguls that "I should like to say that I have always felt that our Irish history and mythology represent a rich storehouse of romance, legend and dramatic episode into which an enterprising producer might profitably delve…if you are short of a story we'll produce one while you wait".

Once upon a time, Patrick Pearse, father of militant Irish nationalism in this century, brought a cinematograph operator from Dublin to his beloved Rosmuc in Connemara, home of all the simple virtues which he so admired. He set up a film show in the local school. The people came in from the mountains, the wide moors, the lakes studded with islands, and Pearse showed them " beautiful rural scenes". The people had not seen a film show before, and were amazed to see the reality that lay all around them transformed into an image, a metaphor for beauty and simplicity. There was trouble, however, when one old woman insisted on getting behind the screen to see "the real people". The strained relationship between reality and image in Irish nationalist politics had commenced.

Pearse's cottage at Rosmuc appears early in *Charles Haughey's Ireland,* just after the Blasket Islands and Newgrange. It is the background for a declaration that Pearse "believed in the Gaelic nation, submerged by many waves of conquests, very old, uniquely Irish with its own modes and forms and attitudes, and, above all, its own language, and that these were Ireland's special contribution to the rest of the world". The imagery of the film is dominated by nature: landscapes, seascapes, red deer, horses, trees, hay-making, rivers. When people appear, they are generally annexed visually or verbally to the natural world. The first large-scale shot of young people, on the safe ground of Páirc Uí Chaoimh Gaelic grounds is a cut from a Paul Henry painting of fishermen pushing a currach into the sea and is accompanied by an assurance that the young are "Ireland's greatest *natural* resource", identifying them immediately with nature and with the land which is again the essential Ireland: "In Ireland we are a bit more conscious than most of how directly the well-being of mankind is linked to the land". A sequence shot in the UCC micro-electronics research centre cuts directly to the stone walls of Connemara and farmers shearing sheep. Nature takes the place of history: over a shot of Irish red deer we are told that these are "the direct linear descendants of the deer hunted by Fionn MacCumhaill and his warriors". A windswept Charles Haughey, intercut with the waves and the gulls tells us that "When the storm sweeps in from the Atlantic and the sea rages with awesome power, one feels very close the the centre of creation". What is the mere petty division of classes, the irritation of poverty and deprivation, when set against the centre of creation? "Yeats believed that certain things are beyond flux and time and change and so do I". The poor you have always with you.

Three things in Charles Haughey's Ireland are "unique":

Newgrange ("a unique and mysterious structure"), Dingle, represented by shots of men in currachs and a girls' pipe band ("this unique part of the western world") and Fianna Fail ("It sees itself as unique, a part of Irish history"). All three are bathed in a mysterious fog as Haughey links himself to each and to the wonders of time. His holiday home in Kerry "certainly has its own magical, mystical qualities". He fires a gun to start the Dingle currach race and it becomes "an occasion which is totally different to any other. Its origins are lost in the mists of sea-faring antiquity. I love it all and feel an integral part of it". This Ireland is a place where in a Dingle pub "the conversation will be brilliant and wide-ranging" (the snatch we hear is about a man drinking seven pints); where Dublin is a "safe and friendly environment where old people can live out their lives in familiar surroundings and where young people can have fun and enjoy their youth", where the toughest survivor of Irish politics, Charles Haughey himself, is "perhaps a little sentimental, even romantic in my loyalties to people. As yet, the iron hasn't entered my soul". It is also, we are told from the old House of Lords chamber in the Bank of Ireland, a place where "Irish nationalists turned away from nostalgia".

Apart from the General Post Office, where the statue of Cuchulain and Yeats' terrible beauty are the subject, Dublin does not appear in *Charles Haughey's Ireland* for almost an hour. Then we see the Ha'penny Bridge and the Moore Street market, the stock picture-postcard images of a quaint city. The latter is not, as might be supposed, a place to buy cheap fruit and vegetables, but "a place to come and relax and savour Dublin humour at its best and maybe even buy something". A shot of young people in Grafton Street is carefully offset with a voice-over of someone singing "I remember Dublin city in the rare oul' times" and is soon followed by a long, lingering shot of an old man driving a horse and cart, a folksy image of Dublin before Taca, before Sam Stephenson, before the suburbs. When Christ Church appears it is in a shot carefully framed to avoid the flats to the left, the carpark to the right, and, above all, Stephenson's Civic Offices behind.

There are two mentions of suburban Dublin. The only "problem" the city has had, we are told, has been "a tendency to push outwards towards the suburban perimeters and leave the centre to look after itself". Donnycarney, the working-class suburb which is at the heart of Charles Haughey's own constituency cannot be avoided, but it comes wrapped in a protective coating of acceptable imagery. There is no wide shot of the housing estate, the camera taking us immediately onto church property and into the after-Mass crowds. Sarah Haughey, aged mother of the presenter, is picked out. Others appear only in order to do homage to the leader. Church, Mother, loyal retainers — then a quick cut to green fields. The place is exorcised away by the power of traditional images. It is literally invisible.

Even at its most manipulative and deceptive, however, television has a way of throwing up inadvertent truths. In *Charles Haughey' Ireland,* two sly snatches of truth sneak in: Once, the Man of Destiny is at the wheel of his boat, the spray moistening the wind that blows into his face as he steers the ship of state with a steady hand. In the voice-over, he talks about the O Dalaigh brothers, last inhabitants of Inishvicilaune, the wise old men who initiated him into the ancient lore of the Gael and "taught us about island life". One of his sons touches the wheel of the boat. "Don't touch my wheel. Don't you dare touch my wheel". A second time, at the races, Haughey is talking about his horses and his racing colours. Larry Hagman, the actor who plays JR Ewing in *Dallas,* appears, got up as JR in a huge stetson. He shakes Charlie's hand, then reaches into his inside pocket, takes out a piece of paper and gives it to the once and future Taoiseach, the man who has told us that he has "a strong sense of heritage, of what has been handed down from one generation to the next, a feeling of continuity and belonging". The piece of paper is a dud thousand dollar bill with the face of JR Ewing on it.

Charles Haughey sums up his Ireland at the end of the film by telling us boldly that it does not exist: "When I talk about

32

my Ireland I am talking about something which is not yet a complete reality. It is a dream that has not yet been fulfilled". Reality is not complete; the country is only a dream. The language is starkly appropriate, for not only is the Ireland which we have been shown a patent fabrication, a country which does not exist, but the Republic of Ireland has never been able to imagine itself, to grasp its own realities as a society. Partition is not, as suggested by *Charles Haughey's Ireland* the reason for this failure. It is merely the excuse. It has provided a way of using words like "alienation", "division" and "failed political entity" without encompassing their real resonances within the Republic.

So long as Ireland remains unreal, an unfulfilled dream, so long will a recognition of its socio-economic realities be postponed. The rhetoric of anti-partitionism, a rhetoric which has very little to do with the reality of Northern Ireland and everything to do with the unreality of the Republic, raises the spectres of alienation, division and failure, but by associating them immediately with the never-never land of dreams, spirits them away, enveloping them in the occult mists of time. Socially and economically, the Republic of Ireland is more divided, has alienated more of its population, even to the extremes of exile, and is a worse failure as a political entity than almost any other in Europe. Only in recognising that it does exist, in waking from its unfulfilled wet dreams of union with an elusive and mystical body, can it begin to change, and only in change can it begin to create a society. That change has to be within the Republic.

There is a connection between political power and a sense of place, though it is not the one established by the mystical imagery of Fianna Fail. It is that the evolution of political power has always been predicated upon the existence of the polis, a bounded unit within which people live together and create common institutions. "The only indispensable material factor in the generation of power" says Hannah Arendt in *The Human Condition* "is the living together of people. Only where men live so close together that the potentialities for action are always present will power remain with them, and the foundation of cities, which as city-states have remained paradigmatic for all western political organisation, is therefore the most important material prerequisite for power". If real political power is founded on cities, then the writing-out of cities from Irish political culture is crucial to the underlying failure of the majority of Irish people to exercise political power. Unable to conceive of itself as an entity, Ireland has failed to act as an entity. It is this which has rendered genuine politics impossible.

Two things have happened to the Irish sense of place. When partition was important in the political consciousness of Irish people, as it has effectively ceased to be, Ireland could not be conceived of as an entity because a part of its mystical body had been lopped off. When, with the abandonment by Fianna Fail of its national aims and the opening up of the country to foreign investment, partition ceased to be the primary political issue, the new economic order militated strongly against the notion of Ireland, the Republic, as a coherent entity. Economics becomes the defining reality, but it has been impossible to see the national economy as a cohesive and self-contained unit. The multinational industries which were attracted to the country have been characterised by the fact that they form an enclave within the economy, only tenuously linked to Irish industry and Irish society. As early as 1972 a report for the National Science Council by Charles Cooper and Noel Whelan found that foreign plants were little more than "production platforms" with few links to the rest of the economy, and predicted that there would be a massive outflow of profits through the as yet undiscovered "black hole". Ten years later the Telesis Report characterised Ireland as a country with few high-skilled, high-technology enterprises, where indigenous exports were small and confined to a limited market, where Irish firms were not even linked as sub-suppliers to the foreign multinationals, where in other words, the industrial superstructure rested on shallow foundations. What

34

this means is the failure to construct an economic polis. Local areas within the Republic are, in terms of economic production, linked less to each other than they are to a global economy through the branch plants of huge corporations. In economic terms Tallaght or Castlebar are linked more directly with Denver or Pittsburgh than they are with the institutions of the Irish state. The state itself has been transformed into a local co-ordinator of international investment. There is no economic entity and hence there is no real political entity.

If, economically, Ireland has gone from the pre-industrial to the post-industrial without ever achieving a coherent industrial revolution ("The Irish industrial revolution" says Kieran Kennedy of the ESRI "must be judged unfinished") then so too its sense of place has been unable to achieve the condition where there are imaginable units within which democratic political power can be exercised. Moving from the pre-industrial to the post-industrial Ireland has also moved from the pre-urban to the post-urban. Instead of the foundation of cities, or even of towns and villages, both rural Ireland and urban Ireland have been physically converging on a state of placelessness. Rural Ireland has been "industrialised" by the placement of multinational plants in rural areas but because these plants have been so little linked to the local economy, they have formed no kind of centre around which an urban space can form and cohere. The characteristic mode of building in the rural Ireland of the seventies and eighties has been ribbon development straggling along country roads, resisting at all costs the formation of defined units of settlement. In Dublin, at the same time, there has been a development of the post-urban "motopia" in which the motor car is supreme and, as architectural critic Kenneth Frampton puts it, "we are no longer able to maintain defined urban forms". The characteristic of the modern Megalopolis dominated by the motorway is, according to Frampton, the absence of "any true public realm". The city ceases to be a political unit and becomes the locus of "an urbanised populace which has paradoxically lost the object of its urbanisation".

35

The crucial absence is that of defined boundaries: "Only such a defined boundary will permit the built form to stand against — and hence literally to withstand in an institutional sense — the endless processal flux of the Megalopolis".

The development of Dublin over the years of Independence has been precisely the process of a loss of definition. In 1922, urban Dublin comprised the area between the Royal and Grand Canals and along the east coast to Dun Laoghaire. About 400,000 people lived in this small, well-defined, high-density area. Today, the city spreads from the mountains to the airport, from the cost to Tallaght and Blanchardstown. While the population is only $2^1/_2$ times greater than it was at Independence, the urban area of Dublin is six times bigger than the compact city of 1922. Instead of building a city the planners have been developing ways of separating people from each other, of avoiding the construction of a physical entity. What is significant is that this development was fostered by the same ideology of the land and nature, of the rural over the urban, which is such a feature of Charles Haughey's Ireland. In the new suburbs of the sixties and seventies, it is wide open space which dominates. Whereas in successful inner city housing areas such as Pimlico, there is a density of 30 houses to the acre, in Tallaght there are 7 houses to the acre. Areas of parkland, large back gardens and above all the distance between houses, all contribute to a failure to dominate and enclose the suburban environment. Houses are dotted onto the agricultural landscape unlike the packed and thriving housing streets in the inner city where the house become the landscape. The planners decided that 10 per cent of the land area within the suburbs should be devoted to open space and that gardens should make up a further 35 per cent and be of a defined size. They also decided that land should be divided into zones separate from each other, thus effectively preventing the establishment of an urban entity. At the same time the vast distances created by planning for wide open spaces in the suburbs has made public transport impossibly expensive and cut the residents of the suburbs off from the city centre. They are denied both a new town and the old town, confined in a place that is not imaginable as a political entity.

What we have seen in Ireland since Independence, therefore, has been the failure to create a public realm. It is no accident for instance, that public political debate in the republic in recent years has been dominated by the private realm: the family, sexuality, marriage. According to Greek political thought, the human capacity for political organisation is not only different from, but stands in direct opposition to that natural association whose centre is the home and family. The foundation of the *polis* was preceded historically by the destruction of all organised units resting on kinship and the rise of a sharp distinction between the private and the public realms. If this is so, then the dominance of the family and the private realm over the public and the communal in the debates on contraception, divorce and abortion is merely further evidence of the failure to establish a political entity. And, what is more, this failure is encouraged by the political thinking of the New Right which has pittered through to Ireland. As Mrs. Thatcher maintained in October 1987, implicity adopting the terms of the Greek distinction but turning them on their heads, "There is no such thing as Society. There are individual men and women and there are families". In the rhetoric of the international New Right, Ireland's failure to form a society is not merely defensible, it is ideal.

Not only has there been a failure to achieve a public realm in the Republic, but the great achievement of the political system has been to prevent its emergence. Irish politics are the great exception to all of the worldwide rules because they have managed to preserve peasant forms long after the disappearance of a peasant society. The characteristic of political organisation in peasant societies is clientilism, the system whereby the highly personalised nature of social relationships leads to a belief that the authorities can be approached only through intermediaries of position or influence with whom one has direct, personal contact. The form of this political organisation is a machine based on "transactional relationships between

37

voter and politician". In clientilism, politics exists essentially outside of the public realm, in the domain of a private arrangement between voter and politician. In the language of political science, "Clientilist politics are characterised by particularistic, ascriptive and individualistic orientations to action, rather than values of universalism, achievement, and collectivism generally associated with modernity...As long as the underlying peasant social order persists, clientilism remains the dominant pattern of politics. As collectivist orientations develop, the claims of secondary associations representing interests in the wider society grow, mass parties defining the public interest in terms of collective goods emerge, and the disintegration of clientilism seems inevitable". But in Ireland, the inevitable has not happened. "With the increasing modernisation of Irish society has come, not a group politics organised within this party system, but a strengthening of conservative parochial clientilist politics". This strengthening has been a result of the failure of the Republic to conceive of itself and a triumph for the imagery and language of Irish politics.

As the abstractions about the nation and its spirit have become less and less effective as a way of binding the Republic together, as the sense of connection with the political centre of the country has been dissipated by the arrival of multinational industry, as each locality has become more fractured and ill-defined, so a sort of local nationalism has arisen in which the "community" has replaced the "nation" as the governing abstraction. In a detailed study of the adaptation of the towns of North Mayo to industrialisation Lorelei Harris found that "community" became a key word in maintaining the ideal of classlessness in the face of the actual emergence of a working-class and a bourgeoisie: "'Community' has become a local level proxy for 'the nation'. It is a basic component of the Irish mythology of industrial development: the story of how local consensus is achieved in a fragmented national context". The ideal of community could be used to exclude as well as to include: strikers being quickly defined as "troublemakers working against the interests of the community". "'Community' exists only insofar as consensus in relation to the balance of local class power is maintained...the entrepreneurial middle-class have appropriated power by forging alliances with other classes on specific issues which are often dressed up as furthering 'community interests'. Of these alliances, the most notable have been those with industrialists and farmers". Just as at national level the idea of the nation has been used to exclude the working-class, so at local level, in an increasingly fragmented country, the appeal to the local community has played the same role.

Within Dublin, too, this notion of community has been a powerful factor in the occlusion of the suburban working-class. By allying 'community" with the old city and with the past, the suburbs have been effectively excluded from its remit. The ideology of the "rare oul' times", of which Charles Haughey's view of Dublin is a part holds that "community" was a compensation for poverty and squalor and associates it with the fallen Eden of the Georgian tenements. Brendan Behan, one of the few important literary figures to have come from Dublin since 1922, spent most of his life in Crumlin, but never wrote from or about it. As his mother Kathleen explains, he continued to identify with Russell Street and its tenements: "He thought the empty drab streets of the housing estate were cold comfort after the street. He missed all the hallways. You know, children learned more about the facts of life in a hallway like that than they ever would out on the foot of the Dublin Mountains. That's why Crumlin was so cold — it was on the slopes of the hills. There again, Brendan missed all his friends from the street. He would go over time and again, but it was no use — the street was finished. The old houses, dirty and all as they were, he loved every brick of them. Cities change, I told him — like people they have to renew themselves. But he never really got over the move". "Dublin" wrote Dominic Behan of Brendan "was the only *country* in the world for him". As "nation" has weakened its grip as a governing abstraction, so a sentimentalised sense of local place, fragmenting the conception of the Republic even further.

It is appropriate that this Dublin nationalism should find its most complete political expression in Sinn Fein. Its anthem The Rare Oul' Times speaks of the "rebel liberties" and its closest expression in popular culture is in the Wolfe Tones playing the Wexford Inn, mixing pro-IRA songs with "rale Dub" rhetoric. The folksy local history which has gone with it, confining itself very largely to the old city, has been the work for the most part of another Sinn Fein supporter Eamon MacThomais, a former editor of An Phoblacht, and much of that history itself has been a local version of the 800 years of oppression that used to be taught at primary schools. By substituting a nostalgic notion of place for the real and potentially subversive division of urban and rural, it neutralises the growing consciousness of Dublin as a city which has never found its true place in Irish life. And it ensures that the times which are neither rare nor old remain underground in the political culture.

On the day of the second great PAYE demonstration of the early eighties, when conscious working-class protest emerged on a large-scale for the first time since the War, 7,000 workers took to the streets of Ballina and closed the town's businesses for the afternoon. Many of the women who took part, however, "attempted to disguise their identities with sunglasses, hats and scarves in order to avoid recognition and the possibility of their photographs appearing in the local papers". If proof were needed that Irish political culture has rendered much of the population invisible, this was it. Those workers were transgressing against the spirit of the nation and could not bear to be seen doing so. What the system and its chosen imagery have managed to render invisible is its failure. The Republic of Ireland is a failed political entity twice over. Fianna Fail failed in its initial set of aims on national unity, the restoration of Irish and the achievement of economic independence. It has now also failed in its second, more pragmatic, set of goals for the state: the provision of jobs, the achievement of a standard of living on a par with the rest of the western world, the ending of emigration. Taken over the whole period of Independence, no other economy in the whole of Europe, socialist or capitalist, has achieved such slow growth in its Gross National Product. Even in terms of per capita income (where statistics work in Ireland's favour because our population has grown more slowly than any other European state in the last 60 years) we have fallen much further behind every other state except Britain that was ahead of us 60 years ago, and far behind every state that was at the same level then. Every state that was behind us then has either narrowed the gap significantly or overtaken us. We have failed to achieve the average European growth rate for any sustained period since Independence, including the sixties, which, according to Ken Whitaker, has "come in retrospect to be regarded nostalgically as a sort of Paradise Lost".

Both in terms of establishing a stable base of industrial employment and in terms of its supposed egalitarianism and meritocracy, the Whitaker/Lemass programme has been a spectacular failure. There are fewer people at work in Ireland today than there were in 1951. There are even fewer people at work in manufacturing industry today than there were in 1951. There has been a boom in production and export of manufactured goods, but it has provided few jobs overall and its profits have been exported. As Kieran Kennedy puts it "Manufacturing production in Ireland is now four times higher than in 1960, and has replaced agriculture as the dominant source of exports...The industrial revolution in other countries brought about a large rise in manufacturing employment. This did not happen in Ireland, even though employment creation was the chief goal of industrial policy. The share of manufacturing in total employment in 1985, at less than one fifth, is only a little higher than it was in 1960, and is far lower than in most industrial countries at the same state in their development". And the evidence is that this process of rising output and falling employment is, if anything, accelerating.

41

Since 1983, there has been a recovery in manufacturing output but most of it has been concentrated in a few "sunrise" industries, electronics and pharmaceuticals in particular, that have very low employment in relation to their total sales. At the same time, the indigenous industries have either collapsed or shed huge numbers of jobs. Guinness, long the country's best employer, now has one-third the number of Irish jobs it had in 1960.

The other major goal of social policy has been the elimination of inequalities of opportunity among the population. In fact, there has been what Christopher Whelan of the ESRI has called "a remarkable stability in the distribution of privilege". In short, Ireland is probably the most divided society in Europe, with the most rigid class system and the least mobility between classes. While there have been some improvements in the standard of living of most of the Republic's population since 1960, the differentials between the top and the bottom of the class hierarchy have been unchanged. Those who were rich in the 1950s were able to secure the same level of privilege for their children in the supposedly meritocratic age of the sixties and seventies. Ironically, state spending on education, which increased rapidly in the sixties and helped to provide a socially progressive gloss for the men in mohair suits, actually served to copperfasten class privilege. In spite of "free education", state spending on education overwhelmingly benefitted the better-off. While the number of 15-year -olds at school increased from less than 50 per cent in 1965 to over 85 per cent in 1979, those who went on to Leaving Certificate and to third level education were of the same social background, as they had been before "free education". There has been virtually no change in the social backgrounds of students at second and third-level over the last 25 years. Nearly half the children of unskilled workers still leave school with no qualifications, compared with only one in twenty of the children to the self-employed. Boys from professional backgrounds are at least six times more likely to sit for the Leaving Certificate than are unskilled or semi-skilled manual worker. They are also thirteen times more likely to enter third-level education. In a country where education remains the key to inclusion in the privileges of society, the chances of children from an unskilled manual background graduating from a university are five times less than their chances of receiving treatment at a psychiatric hospital.

The dream is over, and we must wake to a fundamentally unchanged reality. With the end of the dream, so too comes the dispelling of its hazy miasma of rhetoric. Faced with division, alienation, and failure, as emigration rises again to the levels of the 1950s when a third of those between 15 and 30 at the start of the decade had emigrated by the end, even the pleasant, warming abstractions of Irish political imagery have begun to show their nasty side. The image of Ireland as a realm of nature has given way to John Kelly's darker natural imagery in his description of the Irish young as piglets feeding off the state. Charles Haughey's image of the young as a natural resource has been inverted into a metaphor of exclusion. In his recent statement that the island was too small to contain its population — "After all, we can't all live on a small island" — Brian Lenihan took Fianna Fail's traditional rhetorical identification of the people with the land, the sense that our political destinies are decided by the physical nature of the island, and used it as a way of telling the young that the country has no place for them. In *Charles Haughey's Ireland,* the present Taoiseach used the land itself as the foundation for political authority, its geography as his only argument against partition. In Brian Lenihan's use of geography, it is the land — not political or economic failure — which is rejecting its young. An image which seemed broad and all-embracing has been revealed as narrow and exclusive. The spirit of the nation has begun to rattle its chains.

1987

*Note: After this pamphlet was first published, an American eagle strayed into Ireland. Mr Haughey was at great pains to be photographed with it. Unfortunately, at the photo-opportunity, the eagle attacked the Taoiseach.

MARTYRS AND METAPHORS

Colm Tóibín

I.

We hold our breath during that moment in the movie when the camera pans slowly up the hill to find an Indian staring down at the white man from behind the boulder. We know that now there will be drama: there will be battles and fires, death and destruction, war-cries and bare-back riding. On one side, the Indian will have a strange and aboriginal relationship with the land where his ancestors were born. On the other side, the white man will have reason, technology, need.

The landscape will be wilder and more extreme in its contours than what the white man has previously known. He will never cease to fear it, to fear the boulder and the presence behind the boulder. And so we watch the movie: the play between the essential elements in the colonial drama.

No one can easily escape from the orbit of that drama. The woman around the camp-fire who sings of love will find that her song with its notes of yearning begins to move the listeners to think of other things they yearn for, like the time before the white man came and the time in the future when he will not be there.

When disentangling the strains between those who know the land and those who use it – the tribe and the settler – the song becomes a way of simplifying the divisions, just as history itself becomes as widely disputed as the very ground it happens on.

Everything centres on this dispute, the dispute over ground, over history, over the future. There is no escaping it. Every time we move away it follows us. Writers, in taking up the subject, in conjuring with it, or in evading it, have an extra burden forced on them in the countries where this dispute has taken place. The ghost at the boulder will not go away.

II.

The thing we used to call our history, but could more correctly call our mythology, is a series of short stories, full of moments of great bravery and daring, immense tragedy with blood everywhere and tears in every eye, but there is no connection between the stories in the fiction we have been given as our history, no continuity and no legacy.

Irish history, then, is that set of moments in the Proclamation of 1916 when "in every generation the Irish people have asserted their right to national freedom and sovereignty; six times during the past three hundred years they have asserted it in arms". Six small, local insurrections, all failed.

Six short stories, six lyric poems in a country where history wiped out any hope of us forming a cohesive, safe, secure, well adjusted, class-ridden society. We were left instead with something broken and insecure, a post-colonial society which remained in sprit part of the one-time mother country, and part of America, and part of its own invention.

III.

How can the novel flourish in such a world? The novel explores psychology, sociology, the individual consciousness; the novel finds a form and a language for these explorations. We require an accepted world for the novel to flourish, a shared sense of time and place.

Our whole history is a form of fiction, full of love stories with ill fated lovers, one noble and true, faithful until death, far from the land, shall die with a smile, so daring and sweet his thought.

Our history is a ballad, a drawing room song by Thomas Moore sung by John McCormack. Those central moments in

45

French history are communal and urban; the crucial moments in Irish history resemble more a nineteenth century novel in which the individual, tragic hero is broken by the society he lives in: Wolfe Tone, Robert Emmet, Daniel O'Connell, Parnell. We have no communards, no rabble being roused in the streets. Instead, we have the men of 1916 made into literature by themselves and then by Yeats, just as Thomas Moore had immortalised Robert Emmet into song. We have personal sacrifice, as a metaphor for general sacrifice. No little streets being hurled upon the great.

It is striking how much this activity resembles literature. A poem may move the reader, influence the reader, strike a chord with the reader. So too with a song, or a story, or a novel. So too with Irish political action from Wolfe Tone to Bobby Sands. Martyrdom is a stone thrown into a pool so that the ripples may cause action. The take-over of the GPO and the publishing of a poem are similar forms of action

IV.

We live in the shadow of those who died young: the virgin dead. There is a quality of sexual innocence about those who led the Easter 1916 Rising which lent it such subsequent reverence and respectability. Not even the brothers Pearse reached the dizzy heights, however, scaled by Joseph Mary Plunkett whose marriage – he was allowed marry on the night before his execution and spend a brief period with his wife – so typifies the whole enterprise of 1916 and Irish martyrdom in general in that it allowed very little to stand for a lot; it established metaphor almost as an end in itself so that what 1916 stood for – a revolution in Ireland – could be ignored by subsequent politicians and all the attention could be focussed on its glory as metaphor.

We are left, then, with a legacy of martyrs and metaphors, with versions of the individual pursuit of truth and beauty, with speeches over graves and from the scaffold high.

46

The most influential figure in shaping the Irish political psyche over the past two hundred years has not been a politician, a martyr, a revolutionary, a priest or the man who founded the GAA. The most influential figure in shaping the Irish political psyche has been Thomas Moore, the songwriter, who left Ireland at the age of twenty and seldom came back.

He was the one who gave us the sense of the Irish landscape as starkly beautiful and full of doom. He was the one who gave us the equation between the Irish landscape and a deep melancholy, which fills volumes of Irish short stories. He was the one who made Emmet a Romantic figure and a hero and paved the way for martyrs to be seen as poetic, doomed and lost. Without Moore, it is likely that the 1916 leaders would have changed their tactics, written less poetry and been less prepared to lose.

Without Moore, it is likely that the sense of defeat in the state which was subsequently created would have been tolerated to a lesser extent. Without Moore, it is likely that the Ireland of cities and towns would have become more official and less hidden.

V.

Because Ireland is built on such dreams, there remains no fixed, formed place where one could stand and say: this is Ireland. There are so many versions of reality in this country, so many visions of where the centre of gravity lies. Although there are monoliths – Fianna Fail, the Catholic Church, the GAA, to take just three examples – these cannot offer fixity or fusion. The business community and the poor can both offer loyalty to these organisations because they represent interests with the rhetoric of ideals. There is no society in Ireland as there is elsewhere: no sense of continuity, tradition, legacy, except one that is jagged, broken.

What Tone's suicide, the execution of Emmet, the failure of O'Connell, the fall of Parnell, the Rising of 1916 resemble are the worlds of Balzac, Zola, Dickens, Flaubert, Henry James rather than those of Bismarck, Garibaldi, Abraham Lincoln, Lenin, the world of serious political action. What they have in common with fiction is the male individual consciousness confronting and shaping its destiny and the destiny of others. But our events offer only a last chapter to such novels, the dramatic ending which the reader so longs for, which takes its bearing, both in truth and in fiction, from the Crucifixion in the New Testament where all is fulfilled.

The New Testament failed to do what the novelists have done: to fill in the first thirty years of our hero's life, throw light on the place where he was born, his parents, how money was made in the society, his connections with other individuals, the drama of growth and development. So much, of this, too, is missing from Irish fiction.

What we have come to treasure instead are those small moments in our literature known as short stories. This is the legacy we have chosen to take from Joyce, not the vision and word play of *Finnegans Wake*, but the glimpses of life as it is truly lived in *Dubliners*, the sharpness of the realism, the precision, the detail, the ending of each story in pathos and bitter wisdom and purple prose, the individual in relation to landscape and memory.

Short stories occur in a limited time and a limited place. In our post-colonial societies, it is a perfect form: we need not deal with the bitterness of the past, the confusion of the present or the hopelessness of the future. We can offer merely small instances unassociated with other instances, just as Emmet's Rebellion had no association with O'Connell's mass movement. A short story is pure and simple, like a sacrament.

In a society such as ours with no real core, no past which stretches back in identifiable ways, where there were no fixed festivals until the 1950s except religious ones, where there is mass emigration at each slump in the economic life of the country, in a society which is inexact, chaotic, defensive, nervous, only slowly beginning to form, the writing of short stories is a suitable solution to the writer's dilemma.

VI.

The gift which Joyce offered to Ireland was the novel *Ulysses*, which made the city of Dublin into a fixed, formed and stable world, which each character in the book could brush against. He made Dublin into a city.

What Ireland took from him was his story *The Dead*; what Irish writers took from Joyce was the famous poetic ending of that short story, how it seemed to express and imply in its rhythms the long sufferings of the Irish people, the ennui of modern man, the sheer sadness of life, what the late Bishop of Ferns used to call the *lacrimae rerum* when he preached in Enniscorthy Cathedral.

The last section of *The Dead* offers a new let-out as well as a new language to the Irish writer. "A few light taps upon the pane made him turn to the window. It had begun to snow again. He watched sleepily the flakes, silver and dark, falling obliquely against the lamp-light. The time had come for him to set out on his journey westward. Yes, the newspapers were right: snow was general all over Ireland. It was falling on every part of the dark central plain, on the treeless hills, falling softly upon the Bog of Allen and, farther westward, softly falling into the dark mutinous Shannon waves. It was falling, too, upon every part of the lonely churchyard on the hill where Michael Furey lay buried. It lay thickly drifted on the crooked crosses and headstones, on the spears of the little gate, on the barren thorns. His soul swooned slowly as he heard the snow falling faintly through the universe and faintly falling, like the descent of their last end, upon all the living and the dead".

There is no sex in that passage. They go home from the aunt's party. What Gabriel has on his mind is sex, he may muse on about the snow and the West and the ghost of Michael Furey, and indeed the dead who play the title role in the story, but the rest of us know that what has Gabriel in this state is the fact that his wife has gone asleep.

He has been drinking a bit, they're staying in a hotel for the night, and he has a right to feel like – does he not? – a certain amount of conjugal bliss when his wife suddenly decides she wants to talk.

And when she's finished talking she falls asleep and Gabriel takes to looking out at the snow. In the years after Joyce in the new Irish state what remained unmentionable was not snow or sleep but sex. *The Dead* was the perfect model. It is tempting to feel that de Valera had a hand in writing it.

The writers discovered, to what one can only imagine was their glee, that if you wrote short stories you didn't have to mention sex, you could end in the bedroom with the spurned husband contemplating the snow.

Irish landscape and Irish failure became synonymous, the fields and the horizon seemed in their stillness and serenity to reflect the very dullness of the country, the sheer beauty of our failure to form a society in post-colonial Ireland. Snow was general all over Irish fiction. Sean O'Faolain would end *The Planets Of The Years* with: "How gently the lighted snow kept touching that window pane, melting and vanishing, and, like love, endlessly returning across the planets of the years".

Frank O'Connor ends his story *The Babes in the Wood* with the following passage which also takes its tone and phrasing from *The Dead*: "She put her arms around him and he fell asleep, but she remained solemnly holding him, looking at him with detached and curious eyes. He was hers at last. There were no more rivals. She fell asleep too and did not notice the evening train go up the valley. It was all lit up. The evenings were drawing in".

Indeed. Just a few paragraphs previously she "sedately smoothed her frock about her knees". (No wonder she did not notice the evening train go up the valley!) Now she is content in sleep, and sexlessness, in child-like togetherness. The only thing missing is the snow.

VII.

Story after story about childhood. Joyce started it in *Dubliners*, the depiction of the great beauty and simplicity in a child's mind and a child's perception, a cross between Dickens and Walter Pater. Patrick Pearse wrote over and over again about children, praising their mute sadness and cute innocence. Yeats in "Easter 1916" identifies the 1916 leaders as children, names them "as a mother names her child", reduces their activities to "limbs that had run wild". De Valera's ramblings about comely maidens and athletic youths seemed to propose that life in Ireland was going to be one long children's game.

We look back at what happened in Ireland this century: the Great War, 1916, the Black and Tan War, the Civil War, the Cosgrave government, the long shadow of de Valera, the church's stranglehold on the society, the poverty and emigration, the abandonment of the North. We look as well at the sort of fiction we have produced; we find that, except in a few short stories by Frank O'Connor and Sean O Faolain and a few novels by Liam O'Flaherty which deal with the excitement of war, almost nowhere between 1920 and 1960 is this society and its relationship with the individual destiny seriously examined or dramatised, explored or exploited in works of fiction.

Instead, there are all those brief moments of defeat, novels about the lives and loneliness of priests, the decay of the Big House, a stagnant world full of pathos and set scenes.

Those who succeeded as novelists did so in a manner which was experimental, personal and innovative. Francis Stuart created a world of mysticism, religion, personal memory and disassociation from the public world. Others such as Aidan Higgins and Kevin Casey descended into silence or near silence. The worlds created by Samuel Beckett and Flann O'Brien are rich, modern and self-conscious, are almost hermetically sealed in the study of the possibilities of language itself, raising questions about communication and silence, about the comedy

51

of consciousness, the desire to be through with history, to deal with states of mind rather than states of Ireland. There is, in their writing, and that of others such as John McGahern and John Banville, a sense of desperation in the prose, a sense that the language is being worked for all its worth because there is nothing else, there is no world outside, nothing to lean on except the personal voice and the literary tradition.

In the Irish novel from *Ulysses* to Sebastian Barry's *The Engine of Owl-Light* we have a deliberate elusiveness, each novel seeming to have a built in reader as well as a writer. In novels such as *At Swim Two Birds*, *Birchwood*, *The Pornographer*, parodies and pastiche are thrown in for the narrator to amuse himself with, as though no actual reader existed outside the pages of the book. While employing this and other such strategies, Joyce, Beckett, Flann O'Brien, John Banville and John McGahern may take their bearings from formalism and the development of the modern novel and may mirror what was happening elsewhere, yet it is remarkable that the mainstream tradition in the Irish novel over a period of sixty years, unlike elsewhere, took on experiment, formal trickery, parody and built-in readership.

There was no audience here for such books. It was not just that Ireland did not offer a shelter between history and destiny for the novelists to pitch their tents, thus causing them to write at one remove from what was happening. But there was no one to read the books, no set of educated, curious, open-minded, literate people. It should not be assumed that censorship did not deeply affect what was written and in what style it was written during this period. The result was a tradition of the novel which was clever, inventive and self-obsessed.

John McGahern, and to an extent Francis Stuart, have used in their work the sense of Ireland as a fractured society which cannot offer a satisfactory habitation to the individual. Their work has exploited this sense of the individual's isolation and alienation in a hostile Ireland.

Nowhere in their work is this hostility softened or idealised. Their characters do not find solace in the landscape. McGahern removed his characters and concerns from the world of the short story to a world where the fate of the Irishman becomes the fate of all mankind: alone, lost, in search of some whole, unbroken place which may have existed in the past, which will be possible in the future only in a personal and intimate way, but which will probably not be possible at all. The Irish Free State, the Republic of Ireland, so full of dull habit, poverty of the spirit, insecure authority, becomes the whole world. McGahern writes about a place which has settled down for the first time: the land is held once and for all and peace has broken out, but there is no sharing, or sense of community, only pain and isolation.

The last to assume that Ireland was a public place with shared instincts and values was W.B. Yeats, whose public utterances and public poems, with their elaborate rhetoric and vast store of radicalism and self-importance, fell on deaf ears.

Meanwhile in England and America each move was being charted by the writers as much as the movie-makers, each social change and social nuance was being seized upon; hardly any single cultural experience was left untouched so that those of us who have not been to the United States can conjure up, without much difficulty, what it would be like to live one's life there.

VIII.

We have, as Kavanagh says, lived in important places. There have been riots in our very streets. Some of us have seen history happen in front of our very eyes, the little streets being hurled upon the little streets; the figure behind the boulder emerges with an Armalite in one hand and a petrol bomb in the other.

Some of us have written poems about this, and plays; some of us have even written pamphlets about it. What is strange about all this is that the only two successful pieces of serious fiction – Eugene McCabe's *Heritage* and Mary Beckett's *Give Them Stones* – both close to the novella or the long short story in form – have been written about what has been happening in the North since 1969.

53

It is as though the community in the North has been concerned with its own defence rather than its destiny that no novel is possible.

We can put the violence on the stage as Graham Reid and Martin Lynch have done; we can find metaphors to describe it as Seamus Heaney has done; but the moral perspectives and political consciousness which a novel requires have been found only in the recent novels of Brian Moore, *Black Robe* and *The Colour of Blood*. Moore, like the poet Michael O'Loughlin, has searched elsewhere, in Canada and Poland, for ways of examining and dramatising the question of Ireland.

Exile, for him, has been fruitful. For others, it has served to remove them from the reality of what is happening in the North, without liberating them from realism. The Belfast they describe is a dream city with unreal armies and implausible events.

In a recent anthology of South African writing edited by Andre Brink and J.M. Coetzee the generation of writers who went into exile in the 1950s and 1960s are excluded: "for them history froze when they departed: they can no longer be said to give voice to contemporary South Africa". It is unlikely that any of these people would write about the current activities of the ANC for example, or life in South African prisons.

Violence lies close to the surface now in so many places that the novel of manners, the English novel on the Booker shortlist seems irrelevant, outdated, unnecessary. So much of the power in the novel now, both formally and thematically, lies in the work of novelists like V.S. Naipaul, Mario Vargas Llosa, Nadine Gordimer, Chinua Achebe. All of them have worked as journalists and commentators. The recent work of Gordimer (*July's People, A Sport of Nature*) has been set in the future, her novels enter the world of prophecy as they also become technically more experimental; her novels are not journalism, they play with notions of language, form, voice, tone and perception. Yet they remain exact, close to the actual.

Vargas Llosa in his recent novel *The Real Life of Alejandro Mayta* has also conjured with the future, a social and political

54

breakdown in Peru. And, like Nadine Gordimer's South Africa and Chinua Achebe's Nigeria, his Peru is a real place, he is not using an idea of Peru to explore the novel form or the human character. The place will not go away in his work.

The sense of time and place in all these novelists' work is overwhelming; not just each corner turned, each bar, each sunset, each stretch of scrub or desert, but each change in the structure, each shift in the way power works.

In Ireland we have no such exactitude and those who use what is happening in the North have done so either playfully or without precision.

It is as though writers like Nadine Gordimer and V.S. Naipaul had created a taste for work from places where the earth's crust is thin, where violence is close to the surface, and Northern Ireland was forced to join in, despite the fact that so many writers from there had been in exile for so long and knew so little about the structures in the society which they were writing about.

The figure behind the boulder has become interesting now. His world of displacement, cultural deprivation, violence, post-colonial deracination and all the other things which were put into train the moment the white man came riding down the valley have become the material for a great tradition in fiction. A fiction in which the country itself, Ireland, South Africa, Peru, Nigeria, lurks between the lines, nagging at the characters, a strange and insistent protagonist. It is a fiction which we have yet to explore seriously in Ireland.

FRANK RYAN
Journey to the centre

Michael O'Loughlin

In his biography of Mozart, Wolfgang Hildesheimer spends page after page complaining of the impossibility of biography, our inability to know an historical personage. But, in a way, his argument is irrelevant. We only have to place a record on the turntable and we have as much Mozart as we need. With political figures it is more difficult; but they also have their monuments, the outward form of our everyday reality. As for the ordinary nameless masses, they exist under the palimpsest of our daily life, in its structures, in our language, in our flesh and bones.

But what about Frank Ryan?

He blows through Irish history like a ghost, leaving no stone turned. In his self-appointed mission, he was an almost total failure. His view of Ireland's place in the world has had no noticeable influence on the policy makers of Iveagh House. His contribution to Irish politics was to poll a few hundred votes in Dublin City South in 1937. Now Ireland has her border and her social problems still, because the politics of Frank Ryan's kind makes nothing happen. And yet there is no denying Ryan's strange presence in the minds of many Irish people. He is a footnote, but as has been said, the history of our times may be found in footnotes.

That Ryan had a presence in the minds of his contemporaries also is obvious from writings from that time, memoirs and biographies. He occupies an amount of index inches completely disproportionate to his concrete political achievements. He made an impression on everyone he met, from Irish politicians to Spanish prison warders to German intelligence agents. He possessed what we commonly call charisma, something which by definition can not survive death. Reading about him we cannot experience his personality, any more than we can hear the voice of a nineteenth century diva. After his death, what continued to fascinate is the bizzare, and ultimately tragic, narrative of his life and death. This can be seen, both physically and symbolically, as a journey to the centre. But also as a journey to the margin, to the edge. It is this ambiguity, I believe, which makes him so important to a certain concept of Irish identity, and also completely irrelevant. Ryan is a kind of national hero, which means that his narrative is woven into another narrative, what they called, in the early years of this century, "The Story Of Ireland". "The law of this life, for which one yearns, is ... that of narrative order", wrote Robert Musil. A nation is a story that it tells itself, and I think the case of Frank Ryan can tell us something about the nature of the story we are now telling ourselves. Paradox creates a space in which freedom can exist, and I want to investigate what kinds of freedom the paradox of Frank Ryan makes available to us.

Seen solely in terms of the "the story of Ireland", Ryan's life is a journey from the centre to the margin, and literally, right off the edge. It begins, in the standard way, with Ryan being born and brought up in what a certain type of narrative would call "a strong nationalist household". He was just old enough to participate in the war of independence and the Civil War where he was lucky to escape death. It is easy to imagine him dying at this stage, becoming another name on a roll call central to the narrative. A photograph taken at this stage shows him to be like a thousand others, one of the shadowy Homeric heroes of a nation's birth, its epic age. But Ryan survived the Civil War in another way too. For many people, it was a defining experience, though meaning different things to different people. Some, like Ernie O'Malley, would never quite recover, but would live their whole life like Ossian *i ndiaidh na fianna*. For others, like Sean O'Faolain, it led to a kind of maturity. Still others were to internalise it: they managed to balance the past conditional with the future tense in such a way as to obscure their real nature in the present – and these were the people who gained political power, and could claim to be the mainstream of Irish life. Those who were unable to balance those two tenses were to some extent disenfranchised, and these people for whom independence and the Civil War were little more than inconveniences in their daily lives, would always remain outside "The Story of Ireland". After the Civil War, Frank Ryan begins in this mainstream. There is a photo of him in the UCD Gaelic Society with De Valera and Douglas Hyde. Here, he is a nationalist *pur sang*. The man we meet in these years through letters and photos is not a very attractive figure: dogmatic, fanatical, intolerant ("No free speech for traitors!"). We can easily imagine him taking part in the Abbey riots, making speeches full of Pearse-like rhetoric, affirming the necessity of "the restoration of the Irish language". However, he was unable or unwilling to take the steps taken by De Valera, in order to gain real political power. And during these years, he is becoming increasingly marginalised, like the other republicans who did not join Fianna Fail. But something else is happening too. He becomes increasingly aware of social issues, and of an international context for his ideas.

What it was exactly which turned the green one red we do not know; but it would be nice to think that it was his observation of the everyday wretchedness of life in Dublin in those years. This personal transformation was to have the result of marginalising him even more. The hazy dramas of those years ended in total failure. He had a vision of Ireland, but he could not achieve it, perhaps because it was impossible. By 1936 he had nothing to show for long years of agitation, propaganda, organisation, effort.

Then came Spain.

The Spanish Civil War has continued to fascinate, not because it was a sordid war fought in a backward country, but because it was a crucial event in European intellectual history. The man who is one of the greatest, and perhaps the most representative

58

poet of our century, Cesar Vallejo, wrote that if Spain fell, then the world fell. It did, and it did. The fall of Spain was a kind of death, the beginning of a loss of innocence, a process completed by Hiroshima and the holocaust. For the Spaniards themselves it was, to some at least, a clear issue; as the poet Machado put it, a struggle between a Spain which wants to be born, and one which is dying. For the European intellectual it was equally clear-cut, a battle between good and evil, the past and the future. In Spain, words like "Libertad", "Cultura", even "La Idea", had, and perhaps still have, an aura of primal innocence. They could be uttered without equivocation, without irony, without distancing, without sinister overtones. Vallejo's great poems about the war could not have been written in English. When Auden quickly withdrew from Spain, it was not a case of *trahison des clercs*, but its opposite. As a poet, as a living guardian of the language's core, Auden saw correctly that Spain and the Civil War was no place for the English language.

Frank Ryan's motives in going to Spain were no doubt the same as those of other European intellectuals and political activists. Ryan and the other Irish people who went to Spain were predictably criticised for leaving unfinished work behind them to fight in a foreign war. By going to Spain, never to return, Ryan was abandoning the central concerns of Irish political culture; and thus becoming irreversibly marginalised in Irish life. But he was also moving from the margin into the centre. He went to Spain to fight for a political culture which had not taken root in Ireland. Ryan's language was Dutch to Irish politics; it was the lingua franca of Republican Spain. If we read his letters and look at the photographs from that time, we see a change. Gone is the young gunman, the political outsider. He looks at ease, relaxed, matured. He has come home. In Spain, he found a common language — he writes to his sister. "It would be funny if I were to be on the winning side for once". He achieves high rank, has important responsibilities. But all along, in the background, a tragic aspect is waiting and Frank Ryan, like the rest, has begun to lose his innocence. In June 1937 Ryan was back in Ireland, wounded, and talked all night confidence to one of his former comrades about the nightmare that Spain had become — the treachery, the splits, the political manoeuvres, the death of idealism. It is easy to imagine his loneliness; there can't have been many people who could believe, if they could even understand, what was going on in Spain. With immense courage, Ryan returned to Spain, knowing that he was facing defeat. The world had become a very complicated place. He is captured, and begins a long period of imprisonment with fellow Spanish Republicans. An "Irish" note appears briefly in the narrative, like a hornpipe in the filmpit orchestra when Barry Fitzgerald appears on screen; Ryan does not share his fellow-prisoners' anti-clericalism, confusing his guards. From here on, the narrative acquires a special character; we know all the facts, but they are so surprising and implausible that there is always an aura of suggestion around them, that there is some other secret narrative in which they figure in another light. Attempts are made to secure his release, through a number of channels, without apparent success. Despite the paranoiac attitude to Communism in Ireland, the Catholic church, even, seems to be involved in these, not to mention the men who are supposed to be his direct political enemies. At this stage, the war has begun, and Ireland is officially neutral. The Spanish authorities will not release Ryan. German intelligence expresses an interest in working with him. So, he is unofficially allowed to escape into France, and the custody of the Germans. All this unbelievably takes place under the supervision of the Irish ambassador to Spain. When Ryan "escapes" from Spain there is an identity crisis. How can a man of socialist principles be working with the Germans? Who is he? A citizen of a neutral country offering neutral advice? Secret liason man? Adventurer? And who is the enemy? The Germans are fighting against England. The Soviets are their allies? Ryan was not alone in his sense of disorientation. a few years earlier Robert Musil had written of his hero: "A whole man no longer stood against a whole world, but was a human something moving in a diffuse culture-medium". When thinking of Ryan, we must keep this formulation in mind, over and above

60

questions of passports and protocols.

Ryan's actual position at this stage, working in Germany with German intelligence can be seen from the point of view of a number of narratives. One is "The Story of Ireland", and this provides the tragedy. We perceive tragedy when we, believers in free will, see a man locked into a narrative which is inexorable, which will not release him, we feel pity and terror. Frank Ryan in Hitler's Berlin is like a nightmare rerun of Wolfe Tone in Napoleon's Paris. Frank Ryan in his U-boat is like Casement, is like Tone on his French ship. But the context has changed. He is like one of those cartoon characters who run off the edge of a cliff and keep running in mid-air till they drop like stones. His role here is the Irish political exile, working with a friendly foreign power (Spain, France, Germany), believing that "England's difficulty is Ireland's opportunity". And this is what he does for the next, the last years of his life. A man of uncertain status in the centre of a disintegrating empire, involved in various half-hearted schemes to further German interests in Ireland. Sometimes merely offering his interpretation of Irish affairs. A citizen of a neutral country.

The other narrative is a more complicated one; it involves Ireland's relationship to Europe, the notion of exile, and the question of neutrality. To begin with the last one, this is a question which has been the subject of much discussion recently. A minimun consensus by commentators would seem to be this, limited as it is; those in favour claim that it was the only possible course for a nation so weakened by recent history, so precariously held together; those against claim that our neutrality was only made possible by Britain. It could be argued that it was morally wrong; but there are few examples of a nation entering a war on any other grounds besides that of self-interest. However, all agree that neutrality had a unifying and healing effect on the Irish State, confirmed it in its nationhood, and incidentally, reinforced partition. It is also claimed that it cut us off from the mainstream of European culture. Running through these discussions, however, there is a note which I can only call the 'amateurism' of being Irish; as if Irish identity is an

61

Irishman's hobby. It appears because Irish history is usually seen as being the history of Irishmen *in Ireland*.

Once Hugh O'Neill has climbed into his little boat in Lough Swilly, he vanishes from the pages of Irish history. The wild geese are lamented, but not encouraged to return. The tradition continues: hundreds of thousands of Irish people live abroad, but can not even vote in Irish elections, the radio does not broadcast to listeners abroad.

This is linked to the peculiar Irish notion of exile. I have always found it amusing to hear people, including literary scholars, refer to James Joyce's "exile". Exile from what? By leaving Ireland he found readers, publishers, collaborators, patrons, a sympathetic milieu. If he had stayed in Ireland, that would have been a true exile: exile from himself, from the James Joyce he became. There is a real issue here which characteristically, was pinpointed with unerring instinct by Brian O'Nolan, in his portrait of James Joyce in Skerries. But his humourous treatment has led people to miss the tragic point he was making, as in some of the *Irish Times* columns which refer to the war, and coat despair in bar-room facetiousness. The themes of exile, amateurism, and neutrality come together in a well-known humourous anecdote from the war. An Allied plane is on a bombing mission to Berlin. The bombardier is Irish, and is having a furious argument with his British colleagues, who are criticising Irish neutrality while he defends it. As the plane drops its bombs and pulls away, the Irishman, in exasperation, points down to the inferno beneath them, and shouts: "Say what you like about De Valera, but he's kept us out of all of this!" When I think of this joke, I see Francis Stuart a few thousand metres under the Irish bombardier, writing this poem:

IRELAND

Over you falls the sea light, festive yet pale
As though from the tree hung candles alight in a gale
To fill with shadows your days, as the distant beat
Of waves fill the lonely width of many a western street.
Bare and grey and hung with berries of mountain ash,

Drifting through ages with tilted fields awash,
Steeped with your few lost lights in the long Atlantic dark,
Sea-birds' shelter, our shelter and ark.

Berlin, 1944

The bombardier in his plane; a few thousand metres below him, Francis Stuart and Frank Ryan; in occupied Paris, Samuel Beckett; James Joyce, a dead refugee in Zurich. And neutral Ireland. Who are the Irish? Which one is the "real" Ireland? For a long time now, the standard answer to that question has centred around the rural and catholic inhabitants of the island. A writer who is relevant here is Patrick Kavanagh. All the questions mentioned above come together in his long poem Lough Derg, a poem which I believe sheds much light on Ireland's relationship to Europe. The theme receives a number of different treatments in his work. One famous poem, "Epic", is often mentioned in the context of Kavanagh's paradoxical theory of parochialism. In this reading, the "local row" of the Duffys and McCabes is contrasted with the "Munich bother", and deemed to be more important. But what Kavanagh is actually saying is that the "local row" is more important than the "Munich bother", for his literary purposes. A more relevant treatment of the subject is in the poem "I had a future" set in nineteen forty. It ends with a striking image:

It is summer and the eerie beat
Of madness in Europe trembles the
Wings of butterflies along the canal.

O I had a future.

This is interesting for a number of reasons: Kavanagh clearly sees an organic relationship between political events in Europe and the very fabric of everyday life in Ireland. An idea which contradicts the notion of neutrality, and fits in with the numerous testimonies to the effect that the war had a debilitating effect on culture in Ireland for years afterwards. Kavanagh himself seems to associate this image with what he thinks of as his own "failure". The image also calls up a whole galaxy of associations around the idea of the centre and the margin, and their relationship. In the poem it is clearly Europe which is the centre and Ireland which is the margin. Ireland receives the fall-out of bombs detonated elsewhere. On one level this interpretation might seem to contradict Kavanagh's notion of the parochial — unless we take it as referring simply to a practise in literature, a technique, rather than as a critique of culture in general. That Ireland is on the margin in this sense is self-evident: it is literally, physically on the edge. It is also marginal in the sense that it does not have any major military or economic contribution to make to Europe. The recent referenda and economic crisis have shown how precarious our grip on a European way of life really is. We will always be an outlying province of an empire whose centre is elsewhere. It is only by accepting this fact that we can begin to investigate what freedom is still allowed us. And the dialectic between the centre and the edge is by no means straightforward. Look at Berlin, or Byzantium. Today's frontier outpost is tomorrow's Rome, and vice versa. Empires begin to break up at the edges, not the centre. It has recently been convincingly argued that Australian art, for example, is the most advanced art of our time, the one most expressive of a post modern sensibility. Its apparent naivety, in the view of the centre, of which Irish art is also often accused, could be due to a freedom, a clarity of vision, accorded by its distance from the centres of power, whose propinquity, if you like, can be both blinding and soothing. If Ireland is at this margin, what is at the centre? As I suggested earlier, the usual answer to this question involves notions of Irishness closely linked to the rural way of life, catholicism, the survival of ancient patterns of feeling and perception, a survival made possible by remoteness. Part of this has led a separate life in a fascinating example of dialectic between the edge and the centre: I mean the episode of the Ossianic material, itself once very much of the centre, surviving in the marginal areas, reintroduced back into continental Europe, where it marks the beginning of the Romantic age, which in turn, came back to Ireland as nationalism and the celtic revival.

Lough Derg is an attempt to deal with these questions. It is a difficult poem to talk about, in some ways, because of the textual problems associated with it. The text we have now is obviously unfinished, supposedly because Kavanagh could not bring himself to, due to the sensitive theological nature of the material. I prefer to believe that he abandoned it because it contains a number of ambiguities which he was not capable of resolving; it says, perhaps, more than he wanted it to say. On the other hand, he was aware of its existence and made no attempt to destroy it, knowing that it would be published after his death. In a way, it is his testament to us, a glimpse of the innermost workings of life and consciousness in Ireland in nineteen forty two. Almost all of its 639 lines are devoted to an exploration of a peculiarly Irish catholic form of spirituality, what Kavanagh calls "Ireland's secret". This is centred around a pilgrimage to Lough Derg, and various representative characters are explored. On this level the poem is remarkable for a number of reasons, mainly, as Paul Durcan has said, for its understanding of the fact "that ordinary people undergo mystical experiences". However, if this was its only message it would be a far less vital poem. The instructive ambiguities begin even in the title: for Lough Derg, now one of the navels of Irish rural catholicism, was once a node on the spiritual power grid of medieval Europe, and is said to have inspired its central document, Dante's *Divine Comedy*. while undergoing this personal mystical experience, the poet's mind, like the butterfly's wings, is vibrating to the madness of Europe, its chaos and its bounty. At a number of points in the text, it breaks through the simple prayer-like tone, and totally subverts it.

The imagination which is forming the poem sees the events in Lough Derg in a European context. At one point he seems to discuss this directly:

Then there was war, the slang, the contemporary touch
The ideologies of the daily papers

65

They must seem realler, Churchill, Stalin, Hitler,
Than ideas in the contemplative cloister.
The battles where ten thousand men die
Are more significant than a peasant's emotional problem.
But wars will be merely the dry bones in histories
And these common people real living creatures in it ...

To which one might add, if the battles take place at a comfortable distance from the peasant with the emotional problem! It may be true of Waterloo, but not of Hiroshima. Somehow, the contrast here seems too facile, a facility betrayed by the rhythm, and of course they seem to contradict the more profound grasp of the relationship between everyday life in Ireland and the situation in Europe, which Kavanagh displays elsewhere. But for me, the poem is centred around a line which, once read, emblazons itself on the mind forever:

All Ireland that froze for want of Europe.

To me this line is the heart of the poem, and the root of its difficulty. Kavanagh is plainly disgusted and repelled by the spiritual poverty he sees around him — a spiritual poverty which he explicitly links to an historical poverty. But if Ireland is frozen for want of Europe, a judgement shared by many of his fellow artists, then the kind of life he sees around him, and which he seems to value for its deep spiritually, "Ireland's secret", must be deeply flawed. Either Lough Derg represents all that is most malign in Irish life — subservience, sexual repression, and worst of all, economic and political failure — something which Kavanagh explicitly points out:

The middle of the island looked like the memory
Of some village evicted by the Famine,
Some corner of a field beside a well
Old stumps of walls where a stunted boortree is growing
These were the holy cells of saintly men —
O that was the place where Mickey Fehan lived
and the Reillys before they went to America in the Fifties.
No this is Lough Derg in county Donegal —

So much alike is our historical
And spiritual pattern …

— Or it represents a kind of spiritual superiority, unaffected by
the events to the east. Kavanagh's self, perhaps, tells him one
thing, and his supremely sophisticated imagination tells him
something else. He manages to hold the two together in the
poem, and that is what gives it its power and tension. It is not
surprising that Kavanagh was shocked by his own poem, once it
was finished and could not bear to see it again. It expresses
perfectly the ambiguity of Ireland's position, like the Irish
bombardier above Berlin. Kavanagh could not resolve it, but
merely join the contradictions together in a kind of tableau, a
portrait with one deliberate flaw which betrays a whole new
perspective, as in a painting by Velasquez. It is a profoundly
political document, showing the moral price that had to be paid
for neutrality.

In *Lough Derg*, Kavanagh re-wrote Pope's line:

Only God thinks of the dying sparrow
In the middle of the war.

If God and the imagination are one, as Wallace Stevens
believed, then the imagination working beneath the surface of
the poem, or the imagination forming the narrative, can lead us
to that dying citizen of a neutral country, in Berlin. From
Ryan's 'escape' from the Spanish prison, to his death, his life
becomes more and more unimaginable. What exactly his
position is in Berlin is difficult to figure out. While technically
working to help overthrow the government of his neutral
country, that government continues to take a semi-benign
interest in his welfare. It is both moving and somehow shocking.
We, the spectators, feel that if only we can get him out of that
hell and back to Ireland, we can work something out; perhaps
his stated intention is the overthrow of the state, but after all, he
is an old comrade of De Valera, etc. If we can get him back to
the ark, he can survive the deluge. As Ryan pursues his

oblivious of what is going on around him. His deafness seems to be a touch added by a stage director, to emphasise his relationship to the world around him, as opposed to his sensitivity to the Irish situation. But that is only the Frank Ryan of the narrative. The real Frank Ryan, no longer an Irish revolutionary, is becoming more and more a "human something", moving in an increasingly "diffuse culture-medium". Francis Stuart describes him thus:

"He would sit in a cafe with a cup of Ersatskafee in front of him, or, as I remember him remarking with one of his grimaces, line up in a queue at the hairdresser's simply in order to know what was happening".

On June 9, 1944 Ryan travelled by train from Berlin to Dresden, through the heart of Germany, along the same tracks which were carrying millions of people to their deaths. He was accompanied by a young German girl. Attractiveness to women was, like military prowess, one of the classical attributes of the hero which he possessed. The next day he died, ending his personal suffering. He was buried near Dresden, a city soon to become its own funeral pyre, under a cross which bore the names Proinsias O Riain and Francis Richard. It is fitting that he was buried under these names: Proinsias O Riain, Gael, citizen of Eireann, and Francis Richard, Irish revolutionary working with the enemies of England. Neither of these was Frank Ryan, citizen of Ireland. Frank Ryan's narrative ends there. And so does "The Story of Ireland". It peters out in the blacked out heart of Europe, shouting incomprehensible orders in a mixture of Irish and Spanish. Ryan's Irish nationalism was soluble in total war. "The Search for the Republic" in Sean Cronin's phrase, had come to its logical conclusion.

I would like to point out some more aspects of the "Story of Ireland". In its broad outline it is familiar to us, most easily seen in a schoolboy's history book. But to see it in another light we can look at some curious texts, which are strangely never discussed in this context. If we want to know what story of Ireland the Irish really believe, we should look at the books the Irish read, rather than the books about them. A few years ago an

American academic sniped at the Irish for being obsessed with writers they don't read. But what about the ones they read? I am referring here to the large corpus of memoirs dealing with the War of Independence and the Civil War. These books have a surprising, almost underground, currency, as can be easily seen by examining how often they have been re-printed, always by small Irish publishers. They range over a broad spectrum of 'literary' styles, from Ernie O'Malley's sophistication to Dan Breen's simplicity, but showing a profound structural similarity. All of these writers are eager to tell their story — one which is identical in structure to the others — so we can assume that this structure is the way that the Irish perceived the events happening around them. It must be then, "The Story of Ireland". At that time, these people experienced what was happening around them as a narrative, and one in which they had a very clearly defined role to play; this was, to liberate Ireland from English rule. This narrative pattern had occurred many times before in Irish history. The difference this time was that the narrative came to an end. Instead of ending in failure, to be repeated again in fifty years time, it ended in success, or semi-success. The books all follow this pattern: it begins with the hero slowly becoming aware of his role, becoming an Irish nationalist. None of them begin as this. Tom Barry is in the British Army, in 1916 Ernie O'Malley almost takes the other side, with his friends in Trinity College. After a kind of latent period, they begin their fights against the British. This leads to a kind of heroic phase, the Anglo-Irish war; however this period, rather than independence, is actually the climax of the narrative. After this it runs into a crisis. The Treaty and the Civil War disintegrate the narrative: the heroes become fallen angels. In almost all the texts from this time we get the impression of the writer suffering a kind of concussion, running up against a brick wall, just as he is about to enter the Promised Land. We encounter a silence which to me is eloquent of many things. What is interesting is that after these narratives end, there is nowhere to go — except to the Ireland which has just come into being. What is evident from the Civil War is that the

69

limited amount of independence which was granted was enough to bring the narrative to an end, but not conclusively. It was to go on repeating itself in the void, growing progressively weaker and fainter, to the stage where, according to one recent newspaper report, in terms of "The Story of Ireland" there is only one man living who can be regarded as the legitimate elected representative of the Irish people. Ernie O'Malley seems to have been consciously aware of this "Story" aspect, when he divided his seemingly autobiographical books up into sections named after literary styles. Like *Lough Derg* and *The Man Without Qualities,* his work remained unfinished, and perhaps unfinishable. Man may long for narrative order, but reality evades it.

This narrative was prolonged in people like Frank Ryan, and I have shown how it ended. But it was also used as a vehicle to political and cultural power by elements in Irish society. To what extent this was conscious or unconscious is difficult to say. As recent historical studies of people like De Valera have made plain, it is unlikely that they even knew themselves. What is obvious is the result that it has had.

So, what is the significance of Frank Ryan?

As I have suggested, Ryan died in the grip of a dead narrative. But he was also consciously involved with another narrative, one which led through loss of historical innocence to maturity. His journey to the margin was simultaneously a journey to the centre; and somewhere their intersection forms a starting point. He is a footnote to Irish history of the last fifty years, a footnote to our minds; but one which casts a strange light upon it, which calls it into doubt. It is clear that an Ireland which could not accommodate men like Frank Ryan, Joyce and Beckett, was a country in exile from itself. An Ireland which was not yet Ireland. Frank Ryan's career suggests that Irish culture, in the broadest sense of the word, took a wrong turning in the nineteen twenties. What we took to be the continuation of a narrative was merely its dead echo surrounded by a silence. The story of the Ireland which exists outside this "Story" begins in a vacuum. Some aspects of the main text have recently been highlighted again. It has once again become clear that emigration is a structural factor in Irish society, the most important subject on our hidden curriculum. Its continued existence undermines the entire basis of Irish culture, and reduces questions of Irish identity and traditions, Anglo-Irish and peasant, Planter and Gael to the status of a sideshow, a divertissement, and not always an innocent one. Joyce showed tremendous insight into this problem when he made his hero a jew, thus short-circuiting all the tedious arguments which would still be raging more than half a century later. The essential point is that Irish culture and society, in one way or another, can not accommodate all the people in it. Its continued existence is contingent upon placing itself in exile from its own people, by sending them abroad or by making them 'inner emigrés'. This confirms its own ambiguity, its amateurishness. War-time neutral Ireland had an army of 100,000 men, but more Irish men than that were in the allied armies. As I have suggested, the roots of this ambiguity are in the period around the Civil War. If we are to return from exile, we have to re-examine the assumptions which have been dominant since that time. Any assumption about Irish culture and society which sees it, in the present, as being the direct continuation of "The Story of Ireland", must be mistaken. It is time to start listening to the silence after the narrative ends. I have given some indications, in dislocated images, of how that new narrative might appear. But is that kind of narrative really necessary any more? Or possible? All narratives have their beginnings as a kind of justification and explanation of the society which produces them. At this stage, the Irish narrative can not be reduced to a simple tale with a beginning and end, recognisable heroes and villains, closed in between the covers of a green book with the title stamped in gold (such as the one which infuriated Beckett, containing his 'Murphy'). These kind of narratives create borders which are no longer acceptable. No one aspect of Irish culture can be singled out as central to the detriment of another. Irish culture since the Civil War, has, largely, been based on the lie that certain kinds of Irish people are more Irish than other, certain kinds of music,

71

certain kinds of sport etc. This is no longer possible. The end of the narrative in its falsely continued form, has been shown in literary works like Dermot Healy's. And yet it is the nature of the human mind to want to keep inventing new narratives, new Irelands. This is a task which has recently begun in Irish culture, taking as its starting point the silences of the last fifty years, the void in which all narratives begin.

Frank Ryan remains a footnote.

A number of images occur to me, with which to end this consideration of the meaning of Frank Ryan's career. The first one is a concert hall in London, New Year's Eve, 1985. There is an audience consisting of hundreds of young people, waving Irish flags. On the stage, a group of young men with Irish names and English accents are singing a song called "At the Sickbed of Cuchulainn", which contains the following lines:

"You pissed yourself in Frankfurt and got syph down in Cologne
And you heard the rattling death trains as you lay there all along
Frank Ryan bought you whiskey in a brothel in Madrid
And you decked some fucking blackshirt who was cursing all the
Yids".

The other image is an image from a narrative, its beginning. People stand on a short, about to turn inland, to colonise their own country. They have pushed a burning ship, an ark, and emigrant ship, out to sea. Perhaps on board, is the body of the last Irish hero.

The biographical details of Frank Ryan's life are drawn from Seán Cronin's *Frank Ryan*, Enno Stephan's *Spies in Ireland*, Michael O'Riordan's *The Connolly Column*, and Francis Stuart's *Frank Ryan in Germany*.

BALD HEAD
A Cancer Story

Ferdia Mac Anna

In summer 1986, I was working as the Arts Editor of the Dublin Evening Herald. I reviewed films, edited two pages of book reviews, compiled an arts page and a What's On section and wrote occasional features. For a person with my interests, it was the world's most perfect job. My wife Kate, an American, was a journalist with the Irish Times. We'd married in 1984 and had been living in Dalkey, Co. Dublin, since March 1986. The following events began in the summer of 1986 and ended in August 1987. I had just turned thirty-one.

...

Nobody told me I had cancer. I had to figure that one out for myself.

In July it was just a swelling in my left testicle. No big deal. Most of the time I wasn't even aware of it. There was no pain, just a vague discomfort. I decided it was the result of a kick or a bump and ignored it.

By early August, the swelling had increased to the size of a golf ball and turned a bluish-red. Now, it was as hard as a stone and a constant irritation. There was still no pain. But sitting down was awkward and crossing my legs a bit of an ordeal.

For a while, it seemed as though the extra weight in my pants was causing me to veer to one side when I walked – it was a lot easier to turn to the left than the right. Sometimes, I felt like the drunk in an old Charlie Chaplin silent comedy. It was an embarrassing situation, so I didn't tell anyone.

I kept on playing Machoman, and reckoned it would go away of its own accord. It never occurred to me that it could be serious. It was just a swelling.

But Kate was worried. She persuaded me to see our local G.P., which I finally did – thinking it was a waste of time and mortified that I had to submit to a humiliating examination. The G.P. diagnosed "Epididemitis" and prescribed anti-biotics.

A week later the swelling was down. But the discomfort remained.

Throughout the week of the 2nd Dublin Film Festival – which I attended as part of my job as a film critic, viewing twenty-nine movies – I was forever shifting in my seat, fidgety, uncomfortable no matter how carefully I arranged myself. It was like trying to deal with a rock in your underpants. People sitting behind me must have thought I really hated the films.

Around that time, I met my friend Richie in Bewleys. We drank coffee while I told him of my condition, in a schoolboy's whisper so the man sitting across the table couldn't hear. Richie thought it was funny – as I explained, I did, too. A swollen ball? Epididemitis? It sounded so ridiculous. How could anything bad come from a name as silly as that? We laughed and dismissed it. The man opposite got so pissed off with our juvenile giggling that he dropped his half-eaten bun into his coffee and left.

But next morning the testicle had expanded again, and its pinky colour had changed to dark blood red. I could barely get out of bed. Getting dressed was no fun at all.

I saw another doctor. This time I was advised to have the problem examined by a specialist. But that week the discomfort eased. So I didn't bother. Machoman would solve his own problems. Besides, it was going away.

The following Sunday things suddenly got serious. Kate and I were walking up to the swimming pool in the Killiney Castle hotel. I had the Sunday papers under my arm and was doing all right until I got to the corner at the foot of Killiney hill, where I had to stop. The rock had changed into a basketball. Everytime my leg brushed against it there was pain.

"I can't walk anymore", I told Kate and stood like a flagpole,

74

until she led me to the bus and brought me home.

That night Kate called our G.P. but he was away. His stand-by came over and examined me. He recommended that I go into Vincent's straight away to see the specialist.

Kate and I took a taxi to Vincent's. On the way we held hands in the back of the taxi. We were both scared, and scarcely said a word. Stupid to feel like this, I thought – it's just a pain in the balls.

...

A year before, I'd suffered a brain haemorrhage, from which I'd been extremely lucky to recover. I'd been having dinner at my friend John McKenna's house and had crumpled abruptly to the floor on my way to the bathroom.

John and his wife Sally had thought I was just drunk and fooling around, until they saw the blood coming out of my ear. Kate phoned an ambulance immediately. Her action probably saved my life. The funny thing was that one of the ambulance-men recognised me – from my time as a rock and roll singer with the stage name of Rocky De Valera. He too, thought I'd had too much to drink and leaned over reassuringly as I lay babbling on the stretcher.

"Don't worry Rocky, I won't tell anyone", he said and winked. I should have known that it was impossible to have even a brain haemorrhage in peace in this country, without someone dragging up your past.

Going to hospital again so soon brought back some bad memories, particularly for Kate who'd spent that weekend waiting around in casualty to see if I was going to make it.

I made it. But it had taken over three months for my brain to heal, and for the shock to wear off. It had been a hard time, much worse for Kate than for me.

I'd been lucky; I could have died, or been left paralysed down one side of my body, or had my memory erased. Instead, I made a complete recovery except for my sense of smell, which has never returned and probably never will. It was a small price to pay I reckoned; if I'd been asked to trade any of the senses for a second chance, then smell was the one I'd have chosen.

Now, I was on my way to hospital again. At least this time I was conscious.

Just before we reached St. Vincent's, "Maria" from "West Side Story" came on the car radio. Something bad was coming, we knew. The same song had been playing on John McKenna's stereo the night I'd fallen over. It wasn't the kind of number you hear every day — it was becoming the theme to our personal disaster movie.

In Vincent's, the night orderly examined me. At one stage he put on a plastic glove and inserted a finger into my rectum. My gasp woke up people who'd been dozing on the chairs in the waiting room.

After prodding and poking me around the chest and neck, he made an appointment for me to see the specialist next morning. Going home in another taxi, I was too stunned to talk much. Kate tried to cheer me up. But there's not much you can say when you're not sure what's going on. I asked the taxi driver to switch off the car radio, just in case some D.J. was on a "West Side Story" binge.

Next morning, I got to the private clinic early. The specialist was a gruff sturdy man with the rumpled face of a bloodhound who'd seen it all. His face had only one expression — extreme dissatisfaction. He worked me over thoroughly. Then he arranged for me to go into hospital that night.

"We're going to open you up and have a look", he said. "It's a ninety per cent chance there's nothing there".

He wasn't the sort of guy you questioned or argued with.

As I was dressing, he phoned the private hospital to reserve a time for surgery. I remember his turning away from me, cupping his hand over the mouthpiece like a village gossip as he spoke softly: "It's probably epididemitis, but there's a possibility of a tumour".

I heard, but it didn't register. When Kate asked me how it went I told her I had to go in for a straightforward examination. No big deal. I even felt relieved — if there'd been something seriously wrong Dr. Bloodhound would have told me.

That was Monday. On Tuesday morning I was on the fourth floor of Vincent's private hospital, waiting to be wheeled down to the theatre. They had given me strong drugs to knock me out and I was having one hell of a good time, joking with the nurses.

As the medication took hold I was left in the care of the older ward sister, who sat across from the bed and kept a steady eye on me. We discussed the great success of U2, my work as a journalist, and good movies I'd seen at the film festival. The last thing I recall is her wide friendly dark eyes through her big round glasses as she slyly studied my face for any sign that the drugs were hitting me the wrong way.

Afterwards, I woke up in the white bed. There was no fuzz in my head at all. Everything was clear and still. Sunlight splayed out from the large windows and bathed the whole room. I lifted the top sheet and looked down.

There was a large gauze bandage on my groin. I put my hand down and felt my right testicle. But the left side was numb, and my fingers couldn't penetrate the bandage. God, I thought, don't let them have whipped off one of my balls – it must be under the bandage, with a big plaster on it. For a second I had an image of my left ball in a sling.

I picked up the phone by the bed and dialled my home number. Kate answered. There were sniffles in her voice. I didn't beat around the bush.

"I lost one, didn't I?" I said.

"Yes love, you did".

Then she told me they'd found a tumour, a bad one, which had had to come out. I thought about it for a moment. My mind made slow connections. I recalled Dr. Bloodhound's phone conversation the day before.

"A tumour? That's cancer, isn't it?"

Kate said it was, but that I was to rest and take it easy and she'd be in to me very soon. After that the whole day seemed to just slide away. I don't remember much except holding Kate's hand when she came in and making jokes to try and take the tight

77

look off her lovely open face. I don't think it worked.

Days later, Kate told me that our G.P. had let her know of the possibility that I had a tumour. But it was highly unlikely he said, it was sure to be just an infection. Besides it was a billion to one chance that a man my age – just turned 31 – could have a brain haemorrhage and cancer in the same year. He said he'd call her as soon as he heard from the hospital. So Kate waited at home, while they opened me up.

But the second she saw our doctor's car pull up outside the apartment, she knew. When he came inside and told her she cried. Her mother had died of cancer in America in 1980. Now, her husband could go the same way. First a brain haemorrhage, now cancer; her Irishman was coming totally to pieces. Kate called my sister, Fiona, who came over immediately with a bottle of brandy.

Kate was still crying when I phoned from my hospital bed. She tried to put a brave face on it, but she knew I could feel her distress. As soon as Kate put down the receiver, Fiona said:

"That was the greatest performance of your life".

I'm not sure what I felt after that. It stunned me that I had guessed what was wrong; I'd always presumed that a whitecoated doctor came to your bed and gave it to you straight. Either that or a nurse told you. I didn't know that it was medical policy to tell the loved one, and let the loved one inform the patient.

Now, I was confused. Had the cancer gone completely or was there some still left inside me? I didn't understand how it had happened. I figured I was being punished for something. It made so little sense that I gave up thinking about it, and concentrated on what I could see, and hear, and do, and say – the real world, as I saw it then. I'd never heard of testicular cancer. The name had a nasty ring to it. So I pushed it out of my mind. I had cancer: that was enough to be worrying about.

When Kate visited the next morning, I joked that there was someone out there with a voodoo doll, sticking pins into my most important parts, doing it systematically. First the brain, then the left ball. Next would come the right ball, followed by penis... I tried to think who it could be; a former girlfriend? someone I'd let down? One of my enemies? Whoever it was had properly banjaxed Machoman now.

"I'm going to have a badge made", I said to Kate "Back to Mono".

She gave a tiny laugh.

I didn't think it was very funny, either.

...

I was never really Machoman. But no man likes to feel that there's anything wrong with his genitalia. Confronting cancer is bad enough, but the possibility of having your manhood taken away is too scary even for nightmares. I didn't know how to face up to either. So I made jokes, deflected my fears with humour.

For nearly four days after the operation, I couldn't piss. I was in a private room with my own bathroom and toilet and I spent hours standing over the toilet bowl trying to urinate. Nurse Mary had given me a little plastic cup to fill but I couldn't squeeze a drop out of my poor wounded self. From time to time she would call in on me to see how I was getting on, but all I could give her was a silly grin.

So I passed some of the time examining myself in the bathroom. With the puffy-white groin bandage and the quaint little elastic jockstrap which held my remaining testicle, I looked like a gladiator who'd had a really bad day in the arena. I could feel stitches through the gauze.

The waste fluid was building up in me, but nothing would move it. I tried everything I could think of: running tapwater: gentle massage: alternating dips into cups of hot and cold water: even reasoning with it in what I hoped were smooth, encouraging tones. Nothing happened, except for a feeling that I was about to burst.

On the morning of the fourth day I tried all the ploys at the one time, one immediately after the other. It worked: My urine stream was a beautiful golden-brown in the orange bathroom light. It went on for a long while too, which was a great relief, so much so that I forgot about filling the little plastic container. After that, there was no problem: I could give urine samples almost at will. The only trouble was that now I needed to urinate at least a dozen times a day. In the mornings, my bladder felt like a water balloon, splashing from one side of me to the other. But it was somehow reassuring. It meant my private parts were functioning again.

I was in hospital for two weeks. There were examinations, tests, blood samples, scans and X-rays. It looked pretty good the doctors said, there was no trace of cancer in my blood, or anywhere else in my body.

Dr. Bloodhound came to see me. He gave me his usual no frills examination and asked me how I was feeling. "Fine", I said. He nodded grumpily and pointed at my groin. "It was very bad. It had to go, had to go".

I learned later that Dr. Bloodhound in a gruff mood was a good sign. It meant that he was pleased with the patient's progress. If he was nice and smiled a lot, you were in big trouble.

As the shock of the operation wore off, I began to accept the situation. I had lost one. I still had one. Everybody assured me there would be no problem. All I had to do was get my strength back and I could resume my life. Kate was optimistic but she knew there was a chance that the cancer could reappear.

I kept the news of my operation and stay in hospital as quiet as possible. My father had a weak heart, so I didn't want my family to hear of my condition. I told only my editors at work and my friend Richie. Kate and sister, Fiona were just about my only visitors.

But it's hard to keep secrets in Dublin, especially if you've had a high profile for the past few years as I had.

There were rumours: I'd had a recurrence of the brain haemorrhage; another said it was heroin addiction. One guy told everyone he met that he'd heard I had Aids. Someone else said it was all of the above.

Finally, I had to make phone calls from my hospital bed to ask some people I knew to please shut up. Most did. But one man seemed to delight in walking up to my friends and acquaintances in pubs and informing them of my illness, and then speculating as to what it might be. It was just pubtalk, but it hurt me at the time.

Somehow, we managed to keep the news away from my parents. I would tell them afterwards I figured, when I was better and back at work.

The two weeks went slowly. Now and again I would find myself thinking about having cancer. Then I would just grow numb, and immediately switch to thinking about something else: it was too mysterious and frightening a topic to deal with.

Besides, I thought it was all over. All I had to do now was recover.

During the days there were long visits from Kate. She would tell me what was happening outside, how her work was going, what the doctors were saying. We held hands and I made her laugh. Sometimes, she stayed so long I'd have to throw her out myself in order to get any sleep.

When it came time for her to go, I would escort her to the fourth floor elevators, kiss her goodnight, and then dash back to my room to wave to her from the windows. It felt a little like old–style courting, except in reverse. She made me feel very special, and very loved, I suppose I made her feel she was married to a disaster area.

At night, I watched pop music on Sky TV, talked with the nurses who were always great fun, and read until I got tired. Then I'd take a sleeping pill and slowly black out. I don't recall having any dreams at all.

I was discharged in early November. Kate had built new bookshelves in the front room of the apartment and rearranged the stereo and tape collection. There were flowers in a vase on the kitchen table. It was like walking into a Japanese garden. It made me feel like a Prince.

It never occurred to me that the cancer would come back. The doctors had assured me that the problem had been caught in time. The cancer was gone along with my left ball.

I could live with that.

...

I went back to work. Things went well. I felt good. But I could sense that Kate was tentative, worried – the doctors had told her a lot more than they told me. Deep down, I had a feeling that there was more trouble coming. Every blood test was like an omen.

At Christmas, I bought Kate a beautiful black leather satchel bag, and as many nice things as I could afford. I wanted to shower presents on her, give her a brilliant Christmas – just in case.

It was a good time. We went out to dinner, saw friends, took it easy. We spent as much time as we could at home, cuddling and watching TV and going for walks and snuggling up in bed. We made love for the first time since the operation,
and I began to feel like a young man again instead of a lone-ball, brain-damaged cancer survivor.

At work, there was plenty to do, book pages, film reviews, articles for the arts pages, compiling the Friday "What's on" section of the paper, sorting out poetry submissions for the New Verse slot, catching up on the work I'd missed. Most of the time, I forgot all about hospitals and cancer.

In February, I went back to Vincent's for three days of tests. On Friday morning, I went straight from hospital to work. In the afternoon, Kate phoned me. Her soft voice was unusually light and carefree. For some reason, there was nobody in the office but me.

"I've some startling news", she said.

I knew something dreadful was coming because "startling" was not a word she ever used. She told me the cancer had come back. There were specks on my lungs and lymph nodes. It was more likely I would have to have some treatment. But I wasn't to worry she said, it meant we'd have a couple of days in Liverpool out of it: there was a really fine sperm deposit clinic there and we could fly over tomorrow or the day after.

One side of my face became hot, as though it had been slapped. I didn't know what to say about anything. The numb feeling returned. Kate and I talked quietly for a few moments, she soothing and loving, almost crying. But I was too confused to reason things out and was mean and surly with her. I told her I'd phone her back.

I went to the window and opened it. My office was on the first floor. A van was spewing smoke as it chugged off from the pavement below, where it had been making a delivery. The only coherent thought that came into my mind was that fucking fumes from those fucking vans had probably given me cancer. For a few moments I despised all van-drivers.

I got through the rest of the day by tearing into my work. I remember telling my colleague Colm, who'd looked after my work load and arranged to have my mail delivered to me in hospital, that "my little problem had returned". Then I told my editor. Both were calm and reassuring. If they were shocked, they didn't let on. I was shocked enough for all of us.

At home, Kate and I sat up and tried to talk the whole thing out. I was still upset and she had to take a lot of shit.

Gradually, I improved. But I couldn't cry, even though I knew it would unclog a lot of fear, and the savage anger rising in me that was seeking someone or something to blame. I felt that I'd somehow brought it all on myself for the way I'd lived in the past; in my wild youth, my student drinking period, my crazy rock and roll days.

Kate disappeared into the front room and played one of our favourite records, Peter Gabriel's "Don't Give Up" which features a moving duet with Kate Bush. The song's fragile optimism and message of love took me by surprise, and I cried.

It all gushed out. Kate held me while I sobbed into my hands. I didn't want Kate to see me bawling like a baby, so I kept my palms over my face until the wetness made them stick to my cheeks.

I cried for an hour. All the selfish fears were in my tears: I was going to die: I was going to be taken from Kate: I was never going to write the books I wanted, or achieve any of the goals I'd set myself: we were never going to have kids, raise a family, buy a house, take holidays, move to America, explore Paris again, kiss, make love, have dreams, giggle, cuddle in bed, go out, make dinners, have fights and make up, buy presents for each other, celebrate our love affair and all its little anniversaries, hold hands... why did it have to happen to me? Someone was messing with the voodoo doll again.

I remember that I remained seated at the kitchen table, my elbows gouging into the wood. Kate stood beside me all the while, holding me into her and talking softly, telling me to cry and keep on crying, that there was nothing wrong with crying and that we were going to be alright. She told me it was unfair, but that we'd beaten the brain haemorrhage and we were going to beat this too.

When I couldn't cry anymore we made coffee and talked. The cancer was spreading very fast, the Oncologist told Kate. Treatment had to begin within a few days. There was a chance I'd be infertile afterwards. So we had to decide quickly about Liverpool.

We argued for a while. In the end, I decided that I was going to need all my strength to kill off the cancer: going to Liverpool to leave a sperm deposit would be like admitting I might not make it through. As well as that, I didn't think you could make beautiful babies by going into a room and jerking off into a tube. We'd have babies, I promised her – I knew it and felt it.

As far as I was concerned, I was going to win. From now on, everything was going to be positive. I wanted to have treatment immediately – whatever it turned out to be – and start fighting. Kate accepted that. We were going to beat this disease, together.

We rang doctor Maeve, who'd been in touch with Kate earlier that morning. She was glad to hear I was ready for immediate treatment. "We're looking at chemo-therapy", she told me.

The prospect of chemo scared me more than cancer. What did it do to you? I'd heard it was months and months of agony. It made all your hair fall out, that was for sure.

While we were considering all this, two friends arrived unexpectedly – they were in the area and thought they'd drop in. We met them downstairs in the hall and explained the situation and they apologised and went off.

But their visit calmed us – it brought back the everyday babble of life, where people called in on you, phoned you up just to gossip, communicated about the normal things. It made me feel like an ordinary person. It helped us get through that night.

...

My mother knew something was wrong when I arrived unannounced at her door in Rathmines. She led me into the livingroom and sat down while I remained standing. My sister Darina was sitting on the sofa smoking a cigarette, looking calmly lost.

Keeping my voice as sharp and steady as I could, I told my mother that I had something to say to her but that I didn't want her to start crying or shout or get hysterical or anything like that. She said she wouldn't. Then I told her I had cancer.

I told her that I was being treated but that I didn't want any visitors at all, except for Kate. Most important of all, I wanted her to promise me that she wouldn't tell Dad. I'd tell him myself, later. She promised, then sat and gazed at the floor for a while before asking me if I'd like a cup of tea.

No thanks I said, I have to go, and I left as quickly as I could.

...

Professor Fennelly was the Oncologist in charge of my case. He was a big, bustling man with an easy, friendly manner. He was also refreshingly straightforward.

He told me Testicular cancer was one of the most treatable forms of the disease. The incidence of this particular cancer had doubled in Ireland during the past couple of years – no one knew why.

But it wasn't all bad news. If caught early enough, over ninety per cent of cases could be totally cured. The main problem was that some guys didn't heed the swelling in their testes and carried on for six months or a year before seeking medical help. By that stage, it was often too late. The cancer would have spread, affecting the vital organs.

Once that happened, treatment was both intensive and difficult, with no guarantee of success. A lot of guys had played Machoman with fatal consequences. Nearly a third of Irish men who contracted testicular cancer died.

Mine had been caught within the first four months. Fennelly was optimistic about my chances.

Fennelly's assistant was Doctor Maeve, a bespectacled young woman with long blond curls who seemed always to be under pressure. She too, reckoned I had a better than average chance of being completely cured. She told me not to fret about "chemo" it wasn't half as rough as it was made out to be.

The "regime" – as my course of treatment was termed – would last twelve weeks. Each Thursday or Friday I would be treated in the Day-Care centre on the second floor. But every third weekend I would have to check into hospital for four or five days and be hooked up to a continuous drip. It was the most intensive course of its kind.

The talk with the doctors reassured me. But I was still scared, though I tried not to let it show. I decided to arm myself.

The day before my first full weekend session of chemo-therapy I bought myself a Sony Walkman. We had very little money at the time, but I figured that music was a life-enhancing investment: whenever bad thoughts invaded, I could drive them away with Bruce Springsteen, Tom Petty, Creedence, The Bangles, John Lee Hooker, Sonny Boy Williamson, Fats Domino, Joe Jackson, Sade, Mink Deville, John Fogarty, even the Beach Boys – anything that made me feel good.

I arrived at Vincent's for my first session on February 17, with a briefcase filled with tapes, books, jotters, biros, toiletries and batteries. My first ever pair of pyjamas were in there too, along with a nightshirt, slippers and folding toothbrush – all of which Kate had bought for me during my first stay. It was like preparing for a short war. Everything I packed was going to help me win.

I told my friends I was going in for chemo-therapy. Most were shocked. Some wanted to know what kind of cancer I had, but

I was afraid to tell them the truth: "testicular cancer" sounded so shameful, as though I were about to lose my private parts altogether through some fault of my own. I didn't want people to think I was about to become a eunuch. I didn't care to think about it too much myself.

For a while, I told people I had abdominal cancer. It was a more serious form of cancer, but somehow, it sounded less immediately threatening to my manhood.

I was also reluctant to tell people about my operation. It was just too intimate, and the experience still terrifyingly fresh in my mind. It seemed to me that I'd barely had a chance to recover from the shock of losing a testicle before having to face up to a battle against cancer. Now, I had to deal with chemo-therapy as well. So I lied about that too.

In a short time, I adjusted. When people asked, I told them the truth − mostly. To disguise my anxiety, I said I'd gone from stereo to mono with one foul swoop of the surgeon's blade. It was the unkindest cut of all, I said.

...

Everyone in Vincent's referred to chemo-therapy as "chemo", like a nickname for an old pal. The nurses assured me I'd handle it easily.

"It'll be no bother to a fine big fella like yourself", nurse Val told me.

"You're a lot luckier than a lot of people", nurse Mary said.

For my first weekend session, I was put in a six bed, semi-private room on the fourth floor. My bed was nearest the window, overlooking a smooth green golfcourse. Some of the beds had screens around them. Those that were open contained patients who were asleep most of the time. From time to time, someone would be wheeled to and from the operating theatre. There was very little chat, just the squeak of beds.

Doctor Maeve hooked me up to drips attached to tall, mobile stands on either side of the bed. It took a while to get accustomed to the discomfort, to the awkwardness of having to

87

manipulate two steel hatstands dragging behind whenever I wanted to go to the bathroom.

Next morning, the drips were changed. While doctor Maeve was inserting the delicate butterfly needle into one of the veins in my right hand, a large man in the bed opposite began to mumble complaints through an explosion of black beard. He was lying fully-clothed. One of the nurses asked the Irish Rasputin if he'd like a cup of tea.

"I'd rather have a nice big creamy black pint", he whined, and winked at me.

I didn't return his wink. As soon as I was hooked up, I slid the earphones over my head and pressed the play button.

Rasputin spent a day roaming the ward, moaning to whoever would listen. He affected a good humour, but I could feel his pessimism. He seemed to be trying to bring people down to his own level of despair.

That weekend, I instinctively avoided all those patients with long faces. If a gloomy type approached I made sure to be deep in Walkman Nirvana. It wasn't that I was cold or uncaring, it was simply a question of survival: I needed all my strength to fight my own battle. As long as I was optimistic, I could beat the cancer.

...

The word "cancer" had a powerful effect on some patients. I heard about sufferers who were diagnosed and gave up the fight immediately. There was a story going around about one man who'd died within three weeks of being told. Sometimes, it was the word that killed people, as much as the disease.

That was not going to happen to me. I would never give up and just slide away.

I used everything I could – music, books, paintings, humour to keep myself in a positive state. It was crucial to stay "up" and be optimistic. The "chemo" would kill the cancer, but I felt that it needed help from the patient.

Whenever I sagged the nurses kept my spirits up. Nurse Mary – with whom I'd made friends during my first stay – reminded me that willpower was important.

"I've seen people beat cancers that were a lot worse than yours. They just kept on fighting", she told me.

In between offering advice and telling me stories, nurse Mary liked to borrow books from me. She always read them in a night and returned them the next morning. Before the end of the first full session, I was loaning her books in batches of three or four.

At night, I would lie back in the sheets and imagine swarms of coloured video game Pacmen rushing along my bloodstream gobbling up all the cancer cells. I put all my repressed anger and hatred into the jaws of those little Pacmen.

But it was difficult to get a full night's sleep, even with the use of sleeping pills. Four or five times a night I would have to rise, organise my trailing dripstands, and pad over to the bathroom to relieve my supersensitive bladder. To get in, I would nudge open the door with a combination of head and knee, then trundle everything past.

It was like being inside a spaceship, waiting to lift off. The room glowed with orange light and there was a dull hum from underneath. Squatting or standing, I couldn't hear any of the snores, or sobs, or sighs, or occasional long dribbly farts from the ward.

By the fourth night, I was sufficiently adept at manoeuvring my medical appendages to be able to leave the cumbersome dripstand outside. By gently resting the door against the tube, the steady flow was maintained. I sat there with my arm straight out in front of me so that the needle wouldn't pop out of my vein.

Most of the time, I got back to bed without yanking the tube out, or clogging it with blood.

...

At first, I resisted making friends with the patients in the same ward. It wasn't hard. There were a lot of new patients and I rarely saw the same face twice.

In Day-care the following week, it was easy to remain immersed in a book or listening to music. I arrived at nine, was hooked up to the drip by eleven, and absorbed in my own little self-contained universe by mid-day.

The following Friday, I found myself next to the bed of an old lady, who sobbed and muttered softly to herself. The screens were around her most of the time, even when visitors came. She had a lot of visitors. She gave them all the same detailed account of her ailments and symptoms and told them that it was the will of God that she was still going. For some reason, her faltering voice cut through the music in my earphones. In between visitors, her sobs made everyone in the ward restless and uneasy.

After a while, most of her visitors made their excuses and shot from the room like arrows from a strongbow. When my treatment finished and I was getting ready to leave I could hear her frail, trembling voice telling its tale of woe to one of the nurses. The nurse calmed the old lady down, humoured her, made her laugh, gave her hope.

During my second weekend session, one of the nurses introduced me to a lively young woman who'd been on "Chemo" for a month. The woman was losing her long hair in tufts, but she wasn't worried.

"I'm going to buy a wig", she joked."Which do you think, a red or green one? I've always wanted green hair".

She said she was going to buy a special wig catalogue and pick the most hideous. She'd come and show me, she promised.

When Kate visited, Professor Fennelly and doctor Maeve told us that my bloodcount was near normal. The "Chemo" was working. It was wiping out the cancer.

Kate was excited and relieved by the news. I was glad too, but it didn't mean as much to me: I remembered the way I'd felt in the office the day Kate had phoned to tell me the"startling news". I didn't want any more shocks. When the treatment ended, I'd see about feeling euphoric.

...

I didn't really know what to expect from "Chemo". The first few sessions were easy. The only immediate effects were slight weakness, numb toes, and a lot of wind – sometimes, walking along, I belched like an old toad.

But I was warned I would soon be very weak and nauseous, possibly depressed: it affected everyone differently. The only sure thing was that my hair was probably going to fall out.

That was something I could handle.

One lunchtime, shortly after my first full "Chemo", I called to the Dublin Barber – on the quays next to the Virgin Maga-store and requested a "crew-cut, U.S. marine-style".

The Dublin Barber who turned out to be an exuberant young Belfastman – burbled with delight.

"Great. I've always wanted to do one of those", he said.

A couple of weeks later, I was taking a bath at home when I noticed a lot of black hairs in the water. The hair on my scalp was brittle. It cracked in my fingers like dry spaghetti. Soon, there were swamps of it floating beside me.

At lunchtime next day, I was back at the Dublin Barber's.

"Shave it all off", I told him, "every bit".

"I've been waiting years for someone to say that", the Dublin Barber said.

...

For the first few weeks of baldness, I wore a black beret whenever I went out. It made me look a little like a French hitman, but it covered my bare skull and made me feel secure.

At work, I kept it on indoors at all times, I was too embarrassed to meet people without it. At first, few of my colleagues knew what was wrong with me. Many were puzzled by my wearing a cap indoors. Others thought I'd flipped. Those who knew said nothing.

Some had their own theories, Once, descending the back stairs, I overheard a conversation between two men below.

"That MacAnna fella was always a pretentious bollocks", one guy said.

His pal agreed. But they were both wrong: after the operation I was now technically a bollock.

I passed them by and said nothing. I'd never seen either before.

It was hard to get used to being hairless all over. Even the beret didn't disguise the absence of eyebrows. Catching sight of myself in mirror windows on the street, I was often shocked by the pale shadowless face under the headgear. With the beret off, I looked like an escaped psychopath.

But I sure saved a lot on razors.

After a while, I came to terms with being a baldhead, but I could never get used to being tired all the time. Chemotheraphy kills the fast producing and mutating cancer cells. But it also kills off a person's energy. The simplest physical task became a major trial. Walking from Tara street Dart station to Independent House in Abbey street took nearly everything I had. Typing a film review left my fingers numb and my arms dangling. It took a huge effort to interview a person for the arts page. My mind was agile as ever, but my body performed in creaking slow-motion and quit easily.

The full extent of my new weakened state was brought home to me one day, six weeks or so after treatment began. I was walking home in a strong wind, carrying a newspaper. At the corner of my road, I dropped the paper and it began to flutter, I tried to run the couple of yards to stand on it and prevent the pages blowing away, but I couldn't. By the time I'd walked over and bent down most of it had blown away. Shattered, I watched the rest fly off and went home.

So I learned to ration my time and energy carefully. If I grew overtired at work, I simply went home. When I was too exhausted to walk, I took a taxi. I worked in short, productive bursts, followed by long recuperative pauses.

Travelling anywhere by Dart or bus was wonderful, because all I had to do was sit and watch and think. Walking was an ordeal, but the accomplishment of getting someplace lifted me.

Work was a great therapy, too. It made me feel that I was still in control of an important aspect of my life. Getting through a working day meant I was beating the cancer, kicking the shit out of it.

At home, I took up to three naps a day, and went to bed at eight o'clock. It was the only way I could continue to function. All I had to do was rest my head on a pillow and I was gone. I will never forget the crushing emptiness of being the first home to a dark, cold apartment and being too exhausted to do anything except conk out on the sofa. At night, I had no dreams. Rising in the morning was a real monster movie.

On our days off, Kate would drive to the Killiney Castle hotel and we'd go swimming in the heated indoor pool. In the water I forgot my bald, hairless state. It was easy to swim and splash about. It required a lot less effort than walking, or typing an article.

In the upstairs changing rooms, I would towel down in the corner with my back to the other men so that nobody would see I had only one testicle.

One day, I noticed a small boy staring severely at me. The boy put his finger in his mouth and tugged at his father's togs.

"Da, look at yer man, he's a skinhead".

"Ssshh", the father said and looked mortified.

The boy chewed his finger for a few moments. "God, I'd hate to look like him", he said.

I smiled at the father to show him that I wasn't going to throw his son out the window — though I wanted to. The father made sure his boy kept his beak shut after that, in case I changed my mind.

Driving home, I told Kate about the incident and we laughed. It doesn't do to take yourself too seriously all the time, no matter what's wrong with you. Kids are a great leveller.

...

Word got out about my illness. At work, certain people began avoiding me. Occasionally, I would turn a corner and catch a glimpse of one particular guy diving into a doorway, any doorway, or hastily about turning on the stairs to zoom back the way he'd come. I got the impression he didn't want to catch cancer from me, or whatever he'd heard I had.

But mostly it was fine. People saw I was fighting and let me get on with it. For the most part,I was left alone. It was good to feel trusted. I wasn't given anything extra to do, just my normal workload – which was as much as I could handle.

Some afternoons, Richie and I would meet for coffee. We usually chose Sherries or somewhere quiet where we wouldn't run into people we knew. He would tell me what was going on in the world. I would describe the horrors of Chemo-therapy. I got the better deal.

Once, walking back to work through the alleyway next to Wynn's hotel, I pulled off my beret and joked that I'd lost all my hair, my eyebrows, my sense of smell, my left ball and nearly all my dignity.

"I must have done something terrible in a previous in-carnation?", I said.

"What do you mean in a previous incarnation?", Richie said.

...

As the weeks went on, I began to look forward to the long stretches in hospital. In a way, they relieved me of the responsibility for my illness. There, I always felt surrounded and buoyed up by good will; as if every single doctor, nurse, sister, orderly and admin-secretary was rooting for me to make it and be cured.

"You look crap, what's up with you?", Nurse Val asked me one day. I told her I'd been feeling weak and a little nauseous.

"Ah, you'll be alright, there are lots worse off than you".

Nurse Val was right. There were many people with more severe illnesses. I saw them in the hospital corridors every day, and sometimes in the next bed to mine. They made me feel lucky that my cancer had been caught in its early stages.

One of the best things about being in Vincent's was that I could talk about cancer without feeling guilty or paranoid. In hospital, I didn't feel like a freak.

Outside, it was almost impossible to discuss my problem. At the mention of the word cancer, people grew uneasy and either changed the subject or found an excuse to leave. It got to the point where I began to feel ashamed for having cancer. My cancer was dirty, uncivilised, bad manners, impolite, disgusting, contagious, fatal ... unpleasant: it reminded some people of their own frail mortality. It made me avoid people, whenever possible.

Eventually – through no effort of mine – I became friends with Shay, another cancer patient. Shay just wouldn't be put off by my coolness or attempts to seclude myself in books or Walkman.

"Lost a bit on top, I see", he said, the first time we met. I laughed and said I had, but that his own thatch didn't look too safe.

Shay had lymphoma. This was his second bout of "chemo". His fair hair was standing out in wispy tufts, but he didn't want to shave it. His kids would pull it out for him, he said, and save the price of a barber.

Shay was a gentle, optimistic guy. It was good to talk to someone in the same predicament, who was good-humoured and hopeful. He made me feel foolish for having isolated myself so much.

At Day-Care treatment, I usually took the bed across from Shay. We'd discuss news and events and swop tapes; he gave me jazz and classical, I gave him country-rock and blues.

On the long weekends, I chatted to the nurses and began to open up with the other patients. When I got tired though, I hid in music or books.

Whenever I was placed in a window bed, I watched the golfers on the course outside. They tee-ed off from a spot directly below, with a clear view of the flag across rolling, uninterrupted green. They couldn't miss. The only obstacle was a small clump of trees to the extreme right.

I lost count of the number of golfers who shot into the trees. I would lie on my bed and giggle, watching these frumpy incompetents in loud jackets and striped shoes whacking around

95

in the branches with their clubs, searching for their lost golfballs. The golfballs usually stayed lost.

On my third long weekend in Vincent's, Joe was admitted and given the bed next to mine. Joe was in for tests. There was something wrong with his lungs but nobody knew what exactly. A special oxygen mask was attached to the wall beside him. Every couple of hours he had to place it over his nose and mouth and breathe in and out. He made gattling, clanking wheezes, like a Knight in armour climbing stairs.

Joe was a quiet Dub with a thick black moustache and a freckled earnest face. He worried a lot about his family, his health, work. I lent him books and told him funny stories about my bald head.

His family came in to see him every day. They were as gentle as he was. I never saw the kids run or heard them shout or raise their voices. His elegant, dark-haired wife sat by his side, speaking with him in a soft unhurried voice. The kids too, sat by their Dad's bed for as long as visiting hours would allow. They couldn't have their Dad at home, so they brought their home in to him. When visiting time was up, they left quietly, and without fuss. Joe always got up and walked them to the elevators.

Joe was fascinated by the drips going into my arm, and hand, and by the dripstands. He couldn't get over the fact that I had to drag these monsters behind me when I left my bed, or went to the bathroom.

One morning, he told me that he'd suffered dreadful nightmares since arriving in hospital.

Until one night, he woke to see my bald dome emerging from the bathroom in striped nightshirt, with gleaming steel dripstand behind: in the orange glow of the open doorway, I was Frankenstein's monster rising from the cellar.

After that, Joe's nightmares went away – they just couldn't compete with reality.

...

At work, I avoided the canteen and ventured upstairs to the main news and features subbing areas only when I had copy to deliver.

Initially, I wore the beret indoors, as if it were a magical shield.

After a while though, I decided it was stupid and cowardly to wear a disguise. I got into the habit of taking it off once at my desk. I was bald and odd-looking but so what? So were other people. At least I had an excuse.

But the "chemo" had made me weak. I was also super-sensitive. The casual slights of life got to me in a way they never could before.

One afternoon, I was talking to a friend in the street outside my office building when a Designer Anorak with a receding hairline – who knew of my condition – came around the corner.

"Ah, come out of the closet have we?", he said good-humouredly and slapped me hard on the back as he bustled by.

I was shocked, but also hurt and angry. What fucking closet? Did he mean I should stay at home and not show my bald head and hairless face until I was cured – or dead?

"At least my hair's going to grow back", I yelled as the Anorak scooted around another corner.

I don't think he heard. But yelling after him made me feel good. As soon as I calmed down, I realised that he hadn't really meant any harm. He was just one of life's jolly-natured insensitives.

...

At press screenings, I took my usual place in the front. I kept my beret on while the film was rolling: I was worried that my dome would gleam in the projection flicker. It was almost April before I got the confidence to sit through a movie with the cap off.

Most nights, I got home from work too knackered to do much except nap and watch TV. Cancer cropped up everywhere.

Former champion jockey Jonjo O' Neill was interviewed about his cancer on a BBC awards programme. He was now a baldhead, and he was still on "chemo", but his calm resolution cheered me.

Dr. Vicky Clement-Jones appeared on the Wogan show. Five years ago she'd been diagnosed as having terminal cancer and given two months to live. She was still going strong. Her gentle philosophical spirit gave me great hope.

To amuse Kate, I'd sing along with the TV jingles. The Bisto kids were my favourite. It was childish carry-on, but it brought me joy. Anything that brought joy was fine with me.

...

The only major outing I made during "chemo" was to Paul Simon's "Graceland" gig at the RDS. Richie arranged the tickets and my colleague Frank picked me up at home and drove me there. Inside the enormous dark hall, Frank stood close in case I fell over suddenly, or exploded, or lost an arm or a leg.

It was uplifting to be in the midst of an excited crowd. Such a big deal to be out in the world, doing something as normal as going to a concert.

At one stage, I went off to buy cokes. A rock concert is one of the few places on earth where odd looks and a beret don't look out of place. Nobody stared or commented as I queued up at the drinks stand. Getting back to Frank and Richie and Colm, with the cokes was a big achievement. Just a simple everyday thing, but it meant a lot to me.

Paul Simon sang with delicate sincerity. I could feel the music filling me with strength. Every couple of numbers or so, Simon gave up the stage to the South African artists and musicians he'd collaborated with in the making of his album, "Graceland". Some of the audience were disappointed. They wanted Simon to sing his own hits all night.

I couldn't understand that. I had never seen an act as appealing as Ladysmith Black Mambaza, a ten-piece accapella group who sang with captivating precision and style. They moved and harmonised with such simple joy, they made me want to dance

– which would have finished me off.

Towards the end of the evening Hugh Masekela came on. He spoke and sang with gravelly authority, and played glorious shrilling trumpet on "Coal Train", the story of the tragic plight of the black miners in South Africa. It was powerful, and passionate. It was not the music of despair or defeat. The music lifted me.

I had a wonderful time. It was the only occasion where I almost forgot I had cancer.

Just before the encores, I grew suddenly very tired and had to leave. I told Frank I'd catch a taxi outside, but he insisted on driving me to my door.

"Yarrah sure, I was going that way anyhow", he said in his soft Cork burr.

...

My life became extremely simple.

Everything was reduced to basics. I let my instincts influence my dealings with people. Pessimists were bad; optimists were good. If someone annoyed or disturbed me I stayed away from them. If someone was kind I lapped it up, and added it to my reserves of strength.

It didn't matter that occasionally someone would look at me with stone-dead eyes, dismissing my chances. I had Kate to comfort me, and there was still good news from Professor Fennelly about my blood tests and X-rays. The cancer had been gone since mid-March. It should be well and truly killed off by the time "Chemo" finished in early May.

Home days and nights were quiet. The phone rarely rang. People left us alone. Some were scared, many didn't know what to say to a person who had cancer. There were a few – like the people who gave me the stone-eyed looks, who believed that anyone with cancer was a goner: I might beat it this time, but it would be back for sure: To them, I was a "Dead man".

I went for walks as often as I could. Short walks. To Bullock Harbour and to Dalkey town, both ten minutes from where I lived. I loved to stand on the pier at Bullock and toss coins into the sea. I'd wish for good things, and ask God to help me beat the cancer for good.

On Fridays, I'd stroll into Dalkey and browse through the secondhand books in the Exchange bookshop. Afterwards, I'd buy a Herald and go to Georgina's delicatessen for coffee and a danish.

Simple adventures. But they made me feel good.

My last session of "chemo" was rough going. I suffered from nausea and vomited often into the silver dish beside my bed. My veins had all but collapsed. It took a great deal of patient and meticulous struggle to insert the drip needle into my arm.

On my last treatment in Day-Care, a young doctor had just managed to complete the difficult process of hooking me up when there was a sudden thunk on the window. A golfer had accidently tee-ed off at the hospital. The young doctor was unperturbed.

"Happens now and again, I wouldn't worry about it", he said.

Later, one of the nurses told me that the year before a golfball had crashed through a third floor window. I had a vision of beating cancer only to be assassinated by a lunatic golfer: I'd end up a bizarre headline in my own newspaper.

At the beginning of May, I was pronounced "cured". Professor Fennelly told me that I was now in full remission. I was what was termed "96 per cent cured". It meant I had a 96 per cent chance of never having cancer again.

I wrote it in my diary at work:

"96% cured".

By Christmas, Fennelly told me, I should have a full head of hair.

...

Like an eejit, I thought it really was all over.

Back at work, I told people I was cured and plunged into my job. I even left the beret at home.

But my strength didn't return and I grew paler and more

100

nauseous by the day. Within a week I was having trouble walking. My weight was down and I had headaches all the time. I couldn't understand it. What was happening to me? I certainly didn't feel particularly "cured".

On Wednesday, May 18, less than two weeks after my final "Chemo", I finished my film reviews early and left work, feeling feverish and drained.

Next morning, I couldn't hold down food and had violent eruptions of pains in my sides and back. It was like being stuck with hot needles. My bowels felt like bricks. I couldn't drink a glass of water without puking. I couldn't eat, couldn't crap, couldn't even walk.

For the first time since I'd fallen sick, I actually considered the prospect that I was not going to make it.

Kate had to send for a doctor again. This time he sent me to hospital immediately. While I was packing my pyjamas, the doctor told Kate that he thought the cancer may have spread to my liver, which meant it was terminal. Kate didn't panic or cry. She organised me and led me to the car. Baldhead knew he was banjaxed again, but didn't know why. He was too sick to even think about it.

At the hospital, the nurses couldn't believe I was back. Some didn't recognise the pale skinny hairless lurching ancient in the dressing gown and slippers, who had to be helped from the car into the elevator.

I was put in bed and one of the nurses drew the screens. I didn't object. The fever was making me dizzy and I had almost no strength to talk.

I had no funny cracks for the nurses, none for myself. I just wanted to stop being sick. My back and chest had broken out in small, sore red spots which wouldn't let me get comfortable in the bed. Whenever I made a sudden move, my sides exploded in pain.

To make matters worse, doctor Bloodhound came round to visit me and was polite to me. That's it I thought I'm finished now.

One of the nurses gave me some pills to ease the fever. Then Professor Fennelly came around and examined me. He examined the area around my liver and told me I'd be fine. He seemed relieved.

Then He took Kate outside to the corridor for a private chat.

When Kate came back she had a tight look on her face again.

"You'll be fine, love", she told me, "you're just completely run down".

I didn't believe a word. I thought I was a "dead man".

...

I didn't have liver cancer.

But I did have pneumonia, pleurisy and chronic anaemia, as well as a stack of minor aliments. The "Chemo" had seriously weakened my immune system and I'd been attacked by everything that was going. I'd tried to resume a normal working life too soon after my "cure". Now, I was paying the price.

My body was very seriously run-down and I needed complete rest.

The brain haemmorrhage hadn't killed me.

Neither had the cancer.

Nor even the "Chemo".

But the side effects were having a fair shot at it.

It didn't seem that I would ever be well again. I was a practical joke. Whenever the Gods of health had a medical experiment to conduct they choose me to be the guinea pig. It was humiliating.

I didn't even make cracks about voodoo dolls anymore. I just wanted it to be all over.

The next morning they gave me intravenous antibiotics, which lasted a couple of days and nights. Soon, I felt a lot better. My colour returned. The brick in my bowels dissolved. I started eating. I didn't puke or feel nauseous. By the afternoon, I felt re-born. I could feel the summer coming.

"Good times on the way", I told Kate, and sang her the Bisto Kids ad.

I spent two slow, easy weeks in hospital. Then I took a month off work. There was no stress anymore, no pressure. I dawdled

102

about at home, went for walks, visited Georgina's and drank coffee. I read books and watched a lot of T.V. Jonjo showed up on a BBC sports programme and looked well. Vicky Clement-Jones appeared on a late-night discussion show on Channel 4, but seemed uninterested and tired.

Kate and I made plans to take a long summer break on Cape Cod. I was alive. We deserved a holiday. We needed one.

My Dad came to Dalkey to see me. He was softly curt and stone-faced as always. He sat on one of the wobbly kitchen chairs, a great dark sprawl of presence with cigarette ash trickling from his shoulder. He studied me with a softer, more inquisitive gaze now, as if he were discovering certain new features about the face and eyes of his troublesome son. He gave me money to help with the holiday and I thanked him.

"Don't thank me", he said, "just buy your mother and me a castle sometime".

Then he borrowed as many books as he could carry to the car with him and drove off.

...

On August 3, Kate and I boarded the Aer Lingus jumbo bound for Boston.

I had grown a spiky crew-cut, U.S. marine style. For the first time in nearly a year, I felt healthy. Kate ordered Champagne from the stewardess and I drank Ballygowan.

While the jet's engines idled, I read through the English papers. On page 2 of one of the British dailies, a small one-paragraph news item announced the death from cancer of Dr. Vicky Clement-Jones.

As I was showing it to Kate, the plane began its take-off.

Epilogue
It's never really all over.

Once a cancer survivor, always a cancer survivor. Some patients make the adjustment back to normal life without too much trouble. At first, I was sure I would.

103

But I didn't expect to have depressions which dogged me for weeks, often arising from petty frustrations, or repressed anger at a nasty remark or slight.

Nor did I anticipate being so vulnerable in my dealings with people, especially those who had little understanding or sympathy for what I'd gone through. It's taking me a long while to shake off the cancer hangover.

But I'm getting there.

Fighting off depressions is something I can handle. I tell myself that I got through a brain haemorrhage, cancer and "Chemo", so the present problem seems minor by comparison.

And I'm always aware that there are many others far worse off.

There is still the fear that the cancer will return – the monthly blood test is a constant reminder. But that fear is lessening as time goes by. Once a year is past, the doctors say, it's virtually certain that I'll be clear for the rest of my life. 96 per cent certain.

I'm over nine months clear now, and I've never been healthier. No matter how depressed I sometimes get, I never feel that the cancer is going to come back. I know too, that the depression will pass in time.

I've been noticing Baldheads on the street ever since returning from holidays. Some go bare-headed. Others wear hats or berets, or even wigs. But the lack of eyebrows is a dead giveaway.

A couple of weeks ago, I saw a young Baldhead standing in the queue for the Pass machine, outside the Bank of Ireland on the Bridge end of O'Connell street. He was bare–headed, with tiny blonde fluffs dotted about his scalp. He wore a long green mac, and had an anxious expression on his sharp young features. He seemed to be daring people to look at him.

I passed and said nothing, though I felt a strong bond with him. I wished him good luck and a strong will. I hoped he was lucky enough to have someone who loved him, as I'd had and have still.

Ferdia Mac Anna.
Dublin. Feb 1988.

IRISH WOMEN WRITERS
Marginalised by whom?

Katie Donovan

"It is not feminism, but the merest common sense to insist that women's contribution to fiction can only be judged in relation to their opportunities."
Dr. B.J. McCarthy, **The Female Pen**

Dr. McCarthy introduces a critical work on early women novelists with a protective stance. Ever since the novel germinated out of the diaries and letters of women in the seventeenth century, female fiction writers have had obstacles to overcome because of their sex. McCarthy argues that women writers must thus be judged as a special breed apart, who cannot be evaluated alongside their more privileged brother authors. She has a point, and her view is in keeping with many current feminist publishing houses and critics, who have recently sought for the publication and criticism of women writers under an isolating spotlight. This drive to offer more recognition to women writers of genuine talent has had several beneficial effects, not the least of which has been the publishing and reprinting of books by women which may otherwise have been ignored, or left to moulder out of print. Aspiring female fiction writers today can now see a whole network of strong role models behind them. Alice Walker gives voice to this heartening discovery: "I had that wonderful feeling writers get sometimes, not very often, of being with a great many people, ancient spirits...eager to let me know...that indeed, I am not alone."

Yet isolating women writers into a single category has the self-defeating effect of further marginalising them from the literary mainstream. If their claims to be given an equal place alongside their male peers are to be taken seriously, women writers must be pushed into the flood, there to sink or swim on their own merits. Self-proclaimed feminist publishing houses today place their protegees in a custom-made pool where they hover, maternal life-guards, ready to buoy up their charges. Such books will be bought by other feminists — a converted audience — and will not reach the audience amongst whom they might effect some of the attitude-changes they desire. Although women writers now experience less sexual discrimination than before, this hothouse effect results in reviewers comparing several "women's books" in one column, while weighing up male writers elsewhere, as though the two sexes needed different scales. Even the reviewing of women's novels is usually given to a female reviewer.

Women writers have been marginalised by obviously biased male critics too often to risk self-marginalisation in this way. Sexist remarks like this from a recent American author have been common for too long: "Literary women lack that blood congested genital drive which energises every great style." (William Gass.)

This equation of literary prowess with the possession of the male sexual organ is more suited to the wall of a public toilet than to serious literary analysis. Yet by retreating behind the skirts of feminist publishing houses and minority literature studies, women writers seem to yield passively to such accusations of impotence. It's tantamount to saying: "Yes, you're right, we'll go off and publish quietly on our own, you needn't pay us any more attention." Notice how no-one is stopping this potential retreat. In fact academics seem only too pleased to accommodate women writers in such an unthreatening way — relegated to the literary outhouse of minority studies. There they can rub shoulders with other "minorised" writers such as the Afro-Americans or the Anglo-Indians, not to mention the Anglo-Irish. One can imagine these men thinking: "Now that we've given that whining lot a little

106

room to call their own (which is what Virginia Woolf asked for, after all), they'll keep quiet and let us get on with the important business of studying the major (male) writers."

Joyce Carol Oates, a prominent American fiction writer, expresses her annoyance at being categorised and thus confined under the label "Woman writer".

"How am I to feel when discussed in the *Harvard Guide to Contemporary American Literature* under the great lump "Women Writers", the only works of mine analysed being those that deal explicitly with women's problems – the rest of my books (in fact, the great majority of my books) ignored, as if they had never been written? What would any serious woman writer feel? Insult ... hurt ... anger ... frustration ... indifference ... amusement? Or gratitude for having been recognized at all, even if it is *only* as a "woman writer" (and I stress the "only", though not with much reproach)."

Our own poet Nuala Ní Dhomhnaill, has expressed similar sentiments: "When people say to me, "Are you a "postfeminist"? I think, who the hell cares? I don't want to be used and taken for a feminist."
The word "used" is important here. A writer can be inaccurately represented and condescended to by terms – "feminist"; "woman writer" – which were invented initially to have the opposite effect.

To focus the discussion on our own literary tradition, as previously mentioned, Anglo-Irish literature (that is, Irish literature written in English), is a favourite "minority subject" in English and American universities. With the ever-increasing academic appetite for fresh blood, new literary categories (marginalisations) are being invented all the time. One can imagine the advent of the study of "Irish women writers". This would have the advantage of highlighting some of the Irish women writers who are still languishing (like many of their male peers) under the shadow of internationally feted brothers such as Joyce. Yet how can we reach any conclusion about the Irish woman writer's merits if we examine her in isolation, as though comparison with her male peers might be an exercise too

107

rigorous for her slender talents to endure? If Irish women writers are to be recalled and examined with more credit and understanding than they currently receive, they must be taken from the outhouse and ushered into the centre of the Irish literary tradition. Only then can we get their special talents, their representative traits, their inter-connections and variables, into some kind of realistic perspective.

Only then can we begin to see where the differences and similarities between our major writers are determined by sexual identity or other factors.

It is to fiction that Irish women writers have made their largest contribution. This genre seems to have more appeal for women writers in general, as while poetry and drama have been the claimed arena of male writers for centuries, the novel or short story is a relatively new form, and women have figured large in its development. The novel has been defined as the portrayal of "the self in process", and it grew out of the letters and diaries of the leisured bourgeois women of the seventeenth century. These women were attempting to chronicle their own development through such communicative channels, so the step from letter to novel must have been fairly straightforward. Most early novels are in the epistolary form, and tend to follow the development of a female "self in process", such as Samuel Richardson's *Pamela*.

An advantage of the novel as a medium of self-expression for women was that it needed a minimum of formal education, and no training in literary technique, unlike the writing of poetry or drama. Literary "apprenticeship" in the writing of poetry or drama would not have been readily available to women, and, in any case, they didn't want to draw attention to their literary aspirations, fearing ridicule. With its open form and straightforward chronology, the novel could be written on the sly, picked up quickly and dropped again when the writer's privacy was invaded, just like a letter. It was in this fashion that Maria Edgeworth wrote her masterpiece *Castle Rackrent* (1800).

Castle Rackrent was Edgeworth's first attempt at fiction, and is now considered to be "the first real Irish novel of any quality", as well as one of the first novels of merit within the literary canon as a whole. Being of the Anglo-Irish Ascendency, Edgeworth possessed the advantage of an education, a wealthy family, and the opportunity to travel. Although her father was her self-appointed mentor, his enthusiasms tend to overshadow her work after *Castle Rackrent*. This first and most successful novel was written, as previously mentioned, without his knowledge. While it is distinctive and unique, her later novels, such as *Belinda*, contain a more self-consciously moral tone and follow such set forms as the courtship novel.

Like Joyce's *Ulysses*, *Castle Rackrent* broke new ground in the evolution of the novel. It is considered to be the first regional novel in English, and one of the first novels wherein regional English dialect is recorded in an accurate and appropriate fashion. It is also seen as the first socio-historical novel, where recent social history is presented through the lens of a fictional narrator. The creation of a narrator who is both observer and three-dimensional participant was also a new narrative technique.

Edgeworth's narrator is one Thady Quirk, loyal peasant retainer to the hapless Rackrents, landlords originally descended from "the Kings of Ireland", but, during Thady's lifetime, sadly reduced by drink and other excesses. Edgeworth discards responsibility for the telling of the tale in any other capacity than that of "Editor". She thus masks the source of her own informative wit and keen ear, surreptitiously instructing us about the lives of both retainer and landlord in the Ireland of the mid-eighteenth century. Two generations later, William Carleton, a notable exception to the trend of pulp fiction writers in nineteenth century Ireland, published his *Traits and Stories of the Irish Peasantry* (1830-3). Carleton was from peasant origins himself, and he offers an insider's view of his own people. His achievement is a valuable piece of social documentation, presaging the trend of social realism in twentieth century Irish fiction. As a record of his people and time, it is comparable with *Castle Rackrent* yet his narrative perspective is quite different from Edgeworth's. While Edgeworth effaces herself from her text, behind the figure of Thady, Carleton never abdicates from the role of narrator and observer/commentator, offering his own judgements and conclusions with regularity and confidence. Edgeworth allows herself some marginal comments, in her self-appointed role of Editor, but otherwise she uses the hidden subtext of irony to highlight what she wishes us to notice as absurd or unjust in the world she portrays. Even her irony is not partisan, as Thady's canny pragmatism puts the whims and self-delusions of his employers in an unflattering light, while his solid loyalty to such a succession of losers throws the joke back on himself.

Edgeworth's perspective is deliberately that of the personal and domestic "biographer" rather than that of the "historian", which she considers to be public, and therefore mannered and false: "... that love of truth, which in some minds is innate and immutable necessarily leads to a love of secret memoirs and private anecdotes. We cannot judge either of the feelings or of the characters of men with perfect accuracy from their actions or their appearance in public; it is from their careless conversations, their half- finished sentences, that we may hope with the greatest probability of success to discover their real characters." ("Preface", *Castle Rackrent*)

Thady's constant presence within the intimate and domestic arena of the Rackrent abode renders him a perfect narrator for Edgeworth's purposes. Carleton, on the other hand, seems to espouse the perspective which Edgeworth would dub the historian's, as he records the public rituals of his people such as their love of fighting, their superstitions, their attendance of wakes, their education in hedge-schools. He sees his role in a public sense, as one who portrays his people's way of life with "tenderness" and "mirth" in order to "furnish them with a pleasing encyclopaedia of social duty ... as will force them to look upon him as a benefactor." This reminds us of the public perspective of the nineteenth century Ascendency male poets, such as Mangan, Ferguson and, to a certain extent, Yeats, whose work is largely and overtly concerned with the nationalist cause.

Edgeworth had her own public theme in mind as she wrote *Castle Rackrent* – that of the imminent Act of Union with Britain – yet she refrains from making a public stand on the issue. Instead her book illustrates a private and subtle protest against all forms of "absurd authority", of which the British Empire may be considered the most obvious and public manifestation, therefore it has no place in the private and domestic world of her novel. Instead she highlights the demise of the absurd authority of the Rackrent landlords, whose last representative, Sir Condy, drinks himself into ruin and is bought out by Thady's own son. Edgeworth herself abdicates from the authorial role in favour of Thady, thus allowing her tale at least a semblance of independent life.

This dichotomy in perspective which we have noted has to do with the sex of either writer. As Virginia Woolf reminds us: "The essential difference lies in the fact, not that men describe battles and women the birth of children, but that each sex describes itself."

The male Irish writer, especially in the nineteenth century, would have perceived his role as part of the larger arena of public life. This is in keeping with the usual male definition of self as one who has agency within, and a voice which will be heard by his society. Carleton took on the part of the traditional seanachai, by telling stories about his community and earning his living from his efforts. Edgeworth, on the other hand, had no intention of publishing *Castle Rackrent* when she first wrote it, and when she did, she published it anonymously. Her experience as a woman would have taught her not to expect an attentive audience in the public world, not to expect a socially acceptable role for herself as a writer, not to see herself as an authority in anything, least of all public affairs. When she did not take the role of obedient wife, she was forced to take the next most approved role for a young woman of her class, that of obedient daughter. She had no socially sanctioned excuse for writing, as she didn't need to earn her own living. Her experience of life would have been, like most Irish women up to the present day, limited by the four walls of the domestic

111

sphere within which she was given leave to express herself on set terms. This explains her concentration on the private canvas, and her self-effacement, which is indicative of her lack of assurance in the traditionally male authorial role. This self-effacement allows her to make certain subtle but effective protests without showing herself to be the source of anarchy, which was the best that a woman could hope for in terms of airing her opinions to the public. Her choice of Thady as narrator now seems less unlikely, as we remember that Thady, as much as a woman like Edgeworth herself, represents those who have heretofore been denied a platform on which to share their vision of their world, in which they usually exist as domestic satellites around their masters, achieving private disobediences simply because these tend to go unobserved. Edgeworth, despite the constrained circumstances of paternal supervision in her other novels, still manages to continue this quietly rebellious trait.

Edgeworth received deserved acclaim for *Castle Rackrent* – Scott raved over it, and used it as a model for his historical novel *Waverly* – yet even now the full implications of her achievement have not been realised. Perhaps if she had been less self-effacing and less smothered by her well-intentioned father, she would have left more of a stamp on the archives. Joyce, in the face of ridicule and censorship, remained sure of his genius, alone and uncompromising. He is now considered the giant of twentieth century fiction. Edgeworth's sex was against her in this instance.

The nineteenth century closed as it began, with the emergence of another distinctive novel from the female perspective of the Anglo-Irish Ascendency: *The Real Charlotte* (1894). Somerville and Ross are well known to us from their popular sketches in *Some Experiences of an Irish R.M.* (1899). These episodes convey, like *Castle Rackrent*, their protest against British authority by portraying the chaotic romp of the Irish and Anglo-Irish populace, beautifully undisturbed by British efforts to impose order. *The Real Charlotte* is arguably their best novel, where they use their wit in tandem with a deeper psychological portrait of their protagonist, Charlotte. In Charlotte we have the personification of a number of uneasy blends: gentry and peasant; independent opportunist and romantically inclined spinster; passionate impulse and devious manipulation. The magnitude of her nature (she is always described in terms of large dimensions) is distorted by the cramped opportunities in her society for a woman to define herself. Because of her hybrid status within genteel society, which includes her age, unattractive looks and intractable temper, Charlotte is denied the socially approved route to self-expression for women: marriage. She compensates for this perceived loss by her eccentric devotion to her cats, and, more seriously, by her passion for accumulating property and good social connections. Charlotte is seen to be most at home amongst the Irish peasantry, who converse honestly and colourfully, and allow their women ample opportunity to express the wildness and ferocity of their feelings, as exemplified by their abandoned keening at funerals and the sharpness of their tongues in general. Yet Charlotte's desire for self-improvement means that she must angle her way into the accepted ranks of the gentry, and this means underhand dealings and hypocrisy. There is no socially sanctioned, straightforward method for a woman to improve her lot, unless through marriage.

In Charlotte's niece, Francie, another "almost gentry" Catholic without social connections, we see Charlotte as she might have been: fifteen years younger, naive, and very pretty. Yet, unlike Charlotte, Francie does not have to learn to look after herself. She is courted by men to the extent that she sees herself as the passive being whose fate will be defined by the one who eventually wins her hand in marriage. As a result she is bullied and manipulated by both Lambert and Hawkins, who are motivated by sheer physical desire. She ends as a victim of her own passive indecision between the two. Whatever about her morals, Charlotte's determination is a good foil to the typically passive heroine/victim exemplified in Francie, trotted out far too often in nineteenth century fiction.

Beneath the deceptive neutrality of their humour, Somerville and Ross show us the bleak quality of the options available for

Charlotte in their portrayal of the fate of the other women in her circle, each of whom is a passive victim, in one sense or another. With these spectres in mind, we can see why Charlotte does all in her power to escape a similar fate, in spite of the damage to others and to herself which this involves.

George Moore's *Drama in Muslin* (1886) is a self-professed "realistic novel", which traverses similar ground to *The Real Charlotte*. He also introduces two Catholic Ascendency women, one plain and one pretty, who must make their way in the world within the limited terms of their society. His is also a plea for the plight of such women in a landscape almost bereft of socially approved swains, whose only option for self-definition is that of wifehood.

Yet Moore's perspective is different from that of Somerville and Ross, in the same way as we have noted between Edgeworth and Carleton. In Edgeworth's terms, Moore takes on the role of the impersonal historian, while Somerville and Ross are the domestic biographers. Moore's novel concentrates on causes in conflict, rather than a glimpse into the psyches of individuals. His novel is set at a time of great public turmoil, the Ireland of the 1880s, and Moore makes frequent references to the general conflict between landlord and peasant, and its political ramifications. Moore is also interested in certain moral and philosophical trains of thought current at the time, such as the nature of religious belief. The two sisters at the centre of the novel are merely illustrations of his theory that pretty women are by nature silly and frivolous, while plain women are the opposite pole of sense, prudence and intelligence. The speech of both is often unnaturally heavy with stereotyped phrases of unutterable foolishness or unbelievably articulate reasoning respectively. Moore's other characters are no different, yet his aim is not to give them individual life, but to use them as representative puppets to illustrate his views of current Irish society.

By interpolating his own views and conclusions with regularity, Moore also defines his narrative role in a public way. This is unlike the self-effacing nature of Somerville and Ross, who, like Edgeworth, rarely tell the reader what they wish us to conclude. Instead they illustrate, with their light touches of wit and psychological observation. Their focus is on the private and domestic canvas, and their novel is not set at a time of public strife. Public or political events intrude only when they are seen to be a natural and intimate part of the lives of their characters. Thus the Land League is mentioned, the decline of the Anglo-Irish gentry and the rise of the Catholic middle-class is portrayed, but at the same time the characters are seen as people who are living their own lives in a unique and personal way. This dichotomy of perspective can be seen as the result of Moore's public life of travel, political involvement, property ownership, and writing to earn a living, juxtaposed against the more settled, domestic lives of Somerville and Ross, who had few such opportunities.

Moore's concern for the cause of his "muslin martyrs", because overstated, misses its mark and descends into paternal condescension. His plain heroine, Alice, is supposed to be a representative type, yet he gives her the unusual fate of a happy and humble marriage and the role of a successful novelist in London. This is clearly the work of a partial author and self-appointed moralist, who rewards his well behaved protagonist and punishes her empty-headed sister (who falls ill after a botched elopement, and can't ensnare another wealthy husband). Even within the terms of the novel, Alice never gets beyond passivity, for her literary career is fostered by a man, and her escape from Ireland can only be achieved through marriage. Somerville and Ross, in their portrayal of Charlotte, never offer her as a heroine. They convey her deeply flawed personality as humorously and tolerantly as those of their other characters, whether gentry or peasant. Charlotte benefits from no authorial machinations in her favour. Neither does she benefit from the favours of anyone, man or woman, within the novel. Yet she will not be passive. She tries to "make it" alone, and in her own distinctive rather than quasi-representative way, manages to take revenge for the lot which society in general and one man in particular has given her. Somerville and Ross allow the dubious triumph of Charlotte to speak for itself as a protest against the narrow lot of women in Anglo-Irish society, which Moore's patronising rhetoric and wooden characters cannot rival.

The nationalist movement in the earlier part of the century did much to encourage Irish fiction writers who came from the new Catholic middle-class, often from small towns and rural communities. Their themes were those which defined the evolving sense of what it meant to be Irish: religion, nationalism and the land (as articulated by Daniel Corkery). George Moore, a Catholic though hardly middle-class, began the trend of the Irish short story in the mode of social realism with his collection, *The Untilled Field* (1903)). It is not surprising that Irish fiction in English should consolidate its career in this medium. For an emerging nation testing its fictional wings, the short story represented the most accessible medium of creative expression. From these humble origins, Irish men and women writers have made the short story their own. The precision and subtlety of many of our short stories often leave the more sprawling novel in the shade. In the words of Frank O'Connor, "More is less."

The first great writers of the Irish short story were probably Joyce, Sean O'Faolain and Frank O'Connor. They had the advantages of a university education and an opportunity to study their chosen form as treated by European writers (even Moore copied Turgenev's technique when writing *The Untilled Field*). All three travelled extensively, Joyce choosing to stay abroad. O'Connor and O'Faolain were actively involved in the rigours and revelations of the nationalist movement. They were modern urban men who had to earn their living in the public sphere, and they had plenty to say and protest about in the emerging middle-class society in Ireland.

The first Irish woman short story writer of note was, not surprisingly, a woman from the Big House, Elizabeth Bowen. The average Irish woman from the same background as Joyce or O'Connor was still struggling under the drawbacks of a poor education and a lack of encouragement to write from any source. In *A Portrait of the Artist as a Young Man* Stephen Dedalus saunters off to college after his mother has given him a bath. Later in *Ulysses* , when one of his unfortunate housebound sisters attempts to educate herself by scrimping on food and buying a secondhand book, all he can feel is pity and vague contempt. Bowen, on the other hand, had all the advantages of the Big House, without its confines. Unlike her Big House predecessors, she "got away" and experienced more of public life at many levels: travel, literary peers, marriage, and the Second World War. She is the least Irish of our list, however, because she spent most of her life in England. Unlike Joyce, who wrote of Dublin life in whatever corner of Europe he found himself, Bowen based only a handful of stories in Ireland, and only one novel.

No doubt her "escape" from the Big House explains her tendency to narrate her Irish stories in the perspective of an outsider. These narrators allow her a multiplicity of perspective on Irish Life. However, like Joyce's *Dubliners*, her most consistent theme is the individual who is caught up in a deadening social framework or a scheme of events which he or she cannot or will not escape. The prim narrator of her "Her Table Spread" is like Joyce's Gabriel Conroy in his ability to respond to the subtly expressed passions of the women at the dinner party he attends. Instead of awakening to the female protagonist, who, like Gretta Conroy is quivering with immanent feeling and desire, he thinks, like Gabriel, of his own inner dessication, his ultimate preference not to get his feet wet. Like Gretta, she must feed her lonely yearning with fantasies. In "Sunday Afternoon" Bowen juxtaposes two other frustrated characters: the returned soldier who is sickened by the strife he has experienced in London,and the young girl who dreams of London as an escape from what she sees to be burial alive in the insular, aging world of the Anglo-Irish Ascendancy.

Although Bowen's male characters are as convincing as her female ones, she tends to portray women as more obvious victims of this frustration. In "Summer Night", the woman who leaves her husband for an illicit though well concealed sexual rendezvous seems to metamorphose into a febrile animal as she

117

leaves her tame husband and puritanical mother-in-law far behind. Yet the following day she must return, while her spare-time lover relaxes back into the importance of his own status in the town. In both "A Love Story" and "Unwelcome Idea", women are the victims of the war. The former depicts two beached, paralysed women attempting to recover from the loss of a loved man in the war, their chaotic sorrow thrown into tragic relief by the inanities of two British couples who find themselves stranded at the same hotel. "Unwelcome Idea" is the conversation between two garrulous Dublin middle-class women on a bus, as their limited frame of reference grapples with the "unwelcome idea" of the war. Although the women's talk is very humorous in its guileless frivolity, it succeeds, like Edgeworth's Thady, in providing the perspective of those who witness change in a small and insular world. Finally, Bowen's portrayal of Miss Banderry in "A Day in the Dark" speaks for a type of repressed woman who crops up again and again in Irish fiction. The following could be a sketch of Charlotte: "She could be novelist's material, I daresay — indeed novels particularly the French and Irish ... are full of prototypes of her: oversized women insulated in little provincial towns."

Bowen's's only Irish-based novel *The Last September* — is set in the Ireland of the Troubles in the twenties. Yet here Bowen gives precedence to the inner conflicts of her heroine, to whose drama of maturation the public turmoil is a mere backdrop: "Trying enough it is to have to grow up, more so to grow up at a trying time." This is in contrast with the male protagonists of O'Connor and O'Faolain, whose struggle for identity is inevitably caught up with that of the nation itself. Men like O'Connor and O'Faolain had an active, self-defining role to play during this part of Irish history, so that their sense of the evolution of an identity would naturally be closer to that of their country's. Bowen shows how women are made the impotent victims of war, and how in many humiliating instances women are confined and repressed in public life. Like the deaf woman in "Summer Night", the only arena for a woman to find freedom and self-expression is in the inner depths of her psyche. Bowen, divided between two nations and excluded from the active struggles of either because of her sex, would naturally retreat into this private arena in order to show a female protagonist's self-realisation.

Like Bowen, Mary Lavin stands beside O'Connor and O'Faolain as one of the most adept and prolific at her craft. She did not start publishing until the mid 1940s. Like her male peers, she had the advantages of living abroad (she spent some of her childhood in America), and an impressive education. Like O'Connor and O'Faolain, she bases most of her stories in small town or rural Ireland. Going back to Corkery's triad of typically Irish concerns, by the '40s nationalism was no longer a burning issue, and Lavin, along with O'Connor and O'Faolain at that time, turns to the issues of religion and the land in Irish society. Like her female predecessors, however, she shows how these concerns get filtered into the personal lives of her characters – mainly women – in the limited realm of their domestic sphere. The short story is the ideal form for such glimpses into the private lives of her characters, who, though mere sketches, grow beyond their outlines to assume a three-dimensional quality. In this she is not unlike O'Connor and O'Faolain, both of whom are capable of using the short story as a means of depicting the deeply personal lives of certain characters, such as the child in O'Connors's "My Oedipus Complex".

Yet Lavin views short story writing as "looking closer into the human heart", while O'Connor describes his stories as a portrayal of "the Irish middle-class way of life." O'Faolain stresses the importance for "intellectual sophistication" in the Irish short story, and has been described as a writer who confronts the life he sees through ideas. O'Connor takes on the role of the modern-day seanachi, portraying his society through the depiction of characters within it. This is not unlike Joyce's aim in *Dubliners* , which he describes as "a chapter in the moral history of my race". O'Faolain's characters are used as representative types, which again serve to illustrate the nature of the society from which they emerge. "A Broken World" is a good example of this technique, where the stubborn inertia of

119

the farmer represents a whole section of Irish society, as do the priest and the detached "intellectual" narrator. Lavin, on the other hand, puts the inner life of the individual in the foreground of her work, with a consistent concern for mood, emotion and memory. Around this centre the layers of family and social networks are placed, often repressive, sometimes supportive, to the essential development of the psyche.

Lavin's characters are more often female, whose small public lives naturally throw their inner lives into large relief. We are rarely outside in a Lavin story: more often we are in the midst of some domestic scene, a farmhouse or a small town dwelling. When we are outside, the description of the landscape is often a vehicle to express the negativity of a character's mood as in the thoughts of Annie in "At Sallygap". It may be argued that Lavin's technique is merely one of the features of the modern realistic short story. For example, Joyce exemplifies the insularity of Dublin life by concentrating his description of the landscape on the buildings of the city. His characters move from one structure to the next, or hover like the "Two Gallants", around structures outside their social circle. Yet even this world is larger than Lavin's. It is the urban world of a capital city, while her arena is usually on a much more smaller scale, in a country town or farming community. The institutions depicted here, and frequented by the Dubliners, are often of a public nature, or, at least, not domestic. Dubliners, more often the men, have access to offices, pubs, hotels, bazaars, concert halls, political meeting rooms, even the King's Inns. Some of them travel to Europe for holidays. Also, in contrast to Lavin, Joyce uses the landscape of Dublin to express the mood of a whole society, while Lavin sketches in a landscape to reflect one, perhaps fleeting, mood experienced by one character in one specific situation.

Lavin is never partisan about apportioning blame for her tales of crippled marriages and family misunderstandings. Annie, in "At Sallygap" is a typical example of this. Frustrated at the few options open to her as a woman in her society, she marries Manny, hoping that he will liberate her narrow life. Manny's only fault is in marrying her out of pity rather than love. In their disillusionment the marriage becomes just another trap for which she now focuses her hatred on Manny, making his life as miserable as she feels her own to be. This sort of venting of distorted anger is reminiscent of Somerville and Ross's Charlotte, or of Little Chandler's wife in Joyce's "A Little Cloud". Like Manny, Little Chandler gives up his chance to escape the narrow confines of impoverished Irish society. Both choose marriage instead, to their cost. Their wives, deprived of such opportunities for escape, end up despising husbands who got the chance and didn't take it.

A critical study of Lavin terms her as a "quiet rebel". Like her predecessors, she uses her stories to protest against the weight of "absurd authorities" on the individual's freedom, especially women's. Her chief instrument of protest is, like Edgeworth, that of self-effacing irony. The main "absurd authority" for Lavin is the Irish Catholic Church, as it was in many of the stories of O'Connor and O'Faolain. As usual, however, Lavin tends to focus on the lives of individual women who are passive sufferers in the grip of this life-denying morality. In "Sunday brings Sunday" the priest can offer no guidance in his sermon to the sexually ignorant girl. This girl gave her body to her swain as passively as she imbibes the priest's euphemisms about the benefits of her prayer. We know that both swain and priest will be the first to shun her when the pregnancy makes itself visible.

"The Shrine" (1977) is a more recent story, but Lavin shows with characteristic irony that woman's role hasn't changed a great deal. In this story the Canon's self-aggrandising scheme is to exploit the presence in his village of what is said to be a holy shrine, where apparitions have appeared. His niece's fiance argues that the natural resources (valuable minerals) of the site should be utilised for the good of the village people, as a more practical source of income. The Canon has no scruples about using his "God-given" authority to deprive the young man of a job. Lavin ends the story with the Canon arranging this stratagem quite blatantly with another priest who has some "pull" in the matter. Their goodbye "God bless" is just another example among many of Lavin's irony. In the meantime the niece is caught between the two men, both of whom expect her passive loyalty. She will be defined by her allegiance as either the Canon's niece or the geologist's fiancée. If she stays with her uncle, she can expect a narrow, restricted life. The only alternative, that of her more likely loyalty to her fiancée, is to risk the possibility of being sent off to Australia, as a result of her uncle's scandal-mongering. She is not given any other option for defining her identity within the framework of Irish society as experienced by her in her native village.

The short story writers which we have examined, while often thematically aligned, tend to perpetuate the sex-based dichotomy of perspective which we have observed in their nineteenth century predecessors. Bowen and Lavin are more often "biographers" in Edgeworth's sense, where they focus on the submerged and private lives of individuals within a domestic sphere. O'Connor and Joyce take on Carleton's public role as the delineator and conscience of his people; while O'Faolain, like Moore, likes to use representative types to illustrate his vision of Irish society as a whole.

Alongside the realistic short story, the Irish novel was beginning to take shape. The most influential figure was Joyce, who led a general movement towards experimentalism with language, form and narrative technique with the publication of *Ulysses* (1922), and later, *Finnegan's Wake*. Other novelists who took the path away from realism were all men: James Stephens, Samuel Beckett, Francis Stuart and Flann O'Brien. Kate O'Brien was the first Irish woman novelist from the Catholic middle-class, and her work lacks the technical experimentalism which characterises that of her male contemporaries. Kate O'Brien's background is similar to that of Lavin and Bowen: she had the advantages of a wealthy family and a good education. She travelled and lived abroad at certain stages of her life. She also earned her own living by her writing. Of all the women writers mentioned in this brief survey, she has suffered most from lack of recognition. Her books were best sellers in the 1930s and 40s, but were out of print for many years, until recently, when Arlen House Women's Press and Virago Press began to reprint some of her novels. She is still ignored by most academics in studies of Irish fiction. In *The Irish Renaissance*, Richard Fallis gives her less than a sentence, sandwiched between two male contemporaries. Her lucid yet powerful portrayals of human feeling deserve more than this.

One factor which critics tend to highlight in the work of both Kate O'Brien and Lavin, is the autobiographical nature of their fiction. This is usually proffered as a limitation for which they should be forgiven. However, their contemporary male writers, for all their artifice, draw on the same source. Most of Joyce's male protagonists are discarded portraits of himself, and in *Ulysses* his younger and older selves seem to be split between Stephen and Bloom respectively. Francis Stuart's best known work is a fictionalised, parabolic account of his own experiences in *Black List, Section H*. We can find Flann O'Brien in *At-Swim-Two-Birds*, lurking behind the characters of Dermot Trellis, the inert dozer and novelist, and Mad Sweeney, the rebel poet who is both tragic and absurd. As usual, the difference between these male and female writers is not in their material, but in their presentation and perspective.

Kate O'Brien and Mary Lavin prefer the perspective of Edgeworth's "biographer": their narrative position is self-effacing and their perspective is intimate and personal. The male technical innovators, such as Joyce, deliberately take on a powerful role. Their use of artifice calls attention to their own omniscience within their fictional worlds. The reader must comply with the given terms of these narratives. And although Joyce is concerned with the private lives of his three main characters in *Ulysses,* the reader is constantly drawn into the more public, "historical" perspective of myth, philosophy, literary technique and thumbnail sketches of representative types. Flann O'Brien is never concerned with the personal lives of his characters. He uses them as a means of criticising and lampooning the public issues in Irish life which he saw as repressive or unnecessarily authoritative, such as the Gaelic movement in *The Poor Mouth*.

Irish male and female writers were clearly experiencing the same dichotomous psycho/social influences on their lives as the previous generations which we have examined. We see this different experience of emerging selfhood in the first Bildungsromans of twentieth century Irish literature, *A Portrait of the Artist as a Young man* (1914) and *Mary Lavelle* (1936) by Kate O'Brien.

Joyce provides us with the whole male Oedipal journey from Stephen's close relationship with his mother, to his eventual need to differentiate from her domestic and religious world in order to define his identity freely. We do not see Mary in childhood, but we can easily fill in the given outlines. As a daughter her experience of selfhood would not involve a differentiation from her mother, and the latter's socially defined sphere. She would not be encouraged to make the break from this familiar, private scene to enter the public realm which is the father's domain, and the son's inheritance. Both novels involve a journey away from home, but Stephen's concentrates on the process of differentiation which this involves, a shedding of old ties until he is alone and rootless. Mary's is all about her return to the familiar structures which dominate her close-knit community. Though she travels to Spain in a bid to "let her personality be" away from the cloying expectations of friends and family, she allows herself only a year for this imperceptible and vital process to occur. Afterwards she is in no doubt about returning to fulfil her expected role as wife and mother: "She knows her eventual place, and will be content to fill it."

Mary refrains from going far from the familiar even during her year away. Her job as governess is unassuming and domestic, not unlike her family-based experience of life at home. Her new friends are mostly governesses from Ireland like herself, so she never escapes a sense of the proximity of the judgemental eye of middle-class Irish society. Although she falls in love, and very passionately in a way Stephen could never allow, as it would involve too much self-abandonmen, she never allows herself to

124

consider the illicit romance as part of her real life. This would involve a break with the internal structure of her moral and religious beliefs, which she considers to be part of the framework of her own identity. Although she and Juanito are lovers for a night, she doesn't allow herself enough time to fully enjoy the sexual experience. She is hemmed-in by quasi-religious notions of sacrificing herself to the pain of defloration.

Mary leaves Spain, putting all thoughts of freedom and love behind her. Her journey of self-discovery shows that she can only know herself within the limited terms of Irish society. She anticipates the comfort which the familiar rituals of the church will offer her torn desires. This assurance of community, albeit one of sufferers, means more to her than a new beginning in a new country. In contrast, those structures to which she clings are anathema to Stephen, who feels he cannot express himself until he has flown free of all the familiar limitations imposed upon him by Irish life. In simple terms, Mary returns home to take on her mother's role, while Stephen leaves his mother's sphere to follow in the footsteps of his mythical father, the "artificer", Dedalus.

Thus, while both are "individualists", the terms within which they express themselves are different. Stephen's route to "self-definition" is public and defiant, Mary's route is private and ultimately acquiescent. She chooses to define herself within given structures and roles, and if she questions or defies their limitations, she prefers to remain undetected, forced against her better judgement to be a private exile within her own chosen community.

That Joyce entitles his Bildungsroman as simply "a portrait of the artist", reinforces the public perspective of the novel, whereby Stephen is not only himself, but also a representative of a whole caste. Joyce's deliberate choice of Dedalus as a name for his protagonist compounds this sense of a portrait which goes beyond the specific and personal to that which is mythic and timeless. Kate O'Brien's title – simply the name of her protagonist – indicates that this is the biography of one individual's dawning self-awareness. O'Brien is of Edgeworth's camp – what history disdains because it is private and unvoiced, she reclaims: "Her future is her treasure, small but proportioned to her, as history and mountains are not." O'Brien never changes the narrative in order to give Mary a voice of her own, thus indicating that Mary cannot expect to claim this public recreation of self which Joyce gives Stephen at the end of *A Portrait*. Mary's destiny is to allow society to create the yardstick by which she will measure her public self, and her passive position within the narrative of the novel reflects this. Her realm of self-expression is internal and thus withdrawn from the public eye.

This psycho/social paradigm which we have been exploring can help to further illuminate the differences between male and female narrative techniques. The male writer, rejecting existing, familiar structures in an effort to consolidate his own artistic identity, ends up creating his own structural system in its place.

The Irish female writer seems content to write within existing forms and structures, rather than breaking with the familiar and setting up her own alternatives. She doesn't see herself as the toppler and re-inventor of the world through the machinations of her craft. This has not been the prerogative of Irish women on any public level, after all. Just as the Irish woman's experience of identity (as seen in *Mary Lavelle*) has been that of the individual who works towards a vision of selfhood within the given limits of society, so the Irish woman writer tends to work inside established conventions of form and narrative, highlighting instead her subject's private journey towards self-definition.

Yet, just as Mary Lavelle achieves certain private anarchies within the overarching structure of her public role, so many Irish women writers achieve subtle protests within the limits of their texts. We tend to think of Joyce as the writer whose work suffered the most from the Irish censors, yet Kate O'Brien's novels were also banned in her day. She often depicts scenes of illicit love, such as adultery, and *Mary Lavelle* contains an avowal of sexual passion from a lesbian. The difference between them is that Joyce's description of his characters' sexual experiences is uncompromising and explicit, and as such, represents his public gesture of defiance against Irish sexual taboos. Kate O'Brien is subtle and suggestive in sexual matters, indicating her hesitation to take an authorial stand of defiance. The usual fate of her quietly anarchic protagonists is that the public arena of restrictive morality and prescriptive expectations interferes and punishes, as in *That Lady* (1946), where Ana da Mendoza is imprisoned by Philip II because of her sexual peccadilloes. O'Brien's defiance is thus tempered, like that of her protagonists, with the understanding that there are certain limits beyond which a woman cannot go. Joyce betrays no such hesitation or resignation in *Ulysses,* where his character's sexual gratification is shared openly with the reader and is seen to be one of the real areas of liberation for those who are otherwise lonely or confused. The novel ends with Molly Bloom's orgasmic "yes" to the limitless world of sensuality and pleasure.

James Joyce and Kate O'Brien are an incongruous pair – the former the giant of male Irish writers, the latter one of the least recognised of Irish women writers. Yet people once laughed at the idea of comparing Shakespeare with Jane Austen. They don't any longer. At their best, both O'Brien and Joyce manage to blend a sense of private and public worlds, as in *That Lady* and *Ulysses* respectively. Ana's personal drama is balanced against the public arena of politics and the inevitable unfolding of history. Bloom is both a private and a mythic wanderer. Ana is both one obscure Spanish princess, and every woman who must exist in the forgotten niches of historical annals. In this fashion, both novels combine the perspective of the "biographer" and the "historian": the scaffolding of myth and history is melted by a spotlight on that which is personal, local and unsung.

Yet Joyce's private world is most insistently that which exists within his own creative imagination. This is shown by his ultimate artistic endeavour, *Finnegans Wake*, which is, for the reader, akin to entering Joyce's own cerebral lacunae. O'Brien never draws attention to her authorial role in such a public way, and if our entrance into Ana Mendoza's inner world is also an introduction to O'Brien's, we are never forced into an awareness of this. While Joyce became more public as the creator of his fictive worlds, O'Brien became more private, and many of her later works are not novels, but biography and autobiography, such as her monograph on the life of Teresa of Avila – (1951), and her autobiography, *Presentation Parlour* (1963). The upshot is that Joyce's readers are increasingly unable to follow this artificer into his own mosaic of myth, philosophy and language, which is accessible only to those who take the time to understand Joyce himself as thinker and linguist.

O'Brien's preference for biographies in Edgeworth's mode of the"plain unvarnished tale", despite their focus on the private underbelly of "history", pose no such problem for the reader. As a woman writer, O'Brien is prepared to work within the constraints of the world as she finds it, rather than recreating her own version, so that her scenario is readily identifiable as that which we all experience as part of our daily lives.

In the last twenty-five years Ireland has produced some fine writers of fiction. Thanks to the increasing change in the socially-perceived role of women, there are now more published women writers than ever before. While, in the previous generation, Kate O'Brien was outnumbered by about half a dozen to one, today the numbers are more equal. Thinking of current women writers, a dozen names spring to mind, ranging from well known, established figures such as Edna O'Brien and Jennifer Johnston, to newcomers such as Evelyn Conlon and Dorothy Nelson. Other names include Val Mulkerns, Kate Cruise O'Brien, Mary Leland and Maeve Kelly.

This most recent era of Irish fiction-writing has seen a lot of changes in Irish society, not only the gradual shift in attitudes towards women's rights, but other trends such as the urbanisation of the Irish population, the increasingly cosmopolitan nature of Irish society, the decline of the influence of the Catholic Church, the upsurge of renewed violence in the North, and the increase in emigration. Our fiction writers continue to chronicle the selves in progress who develop within this changing landscape. Old themes die hard, just as Irish society is still haunted by issues from the past: our writers continue to remind us of religious intolerance and sexual repression which refuse to exit gracefully from Irish life. The current breakdown of a sense of fixed community has effected the perspective of the Irish writer, so that now both male and female writers tend to focus on the experience of one individual in a shifting scenario. This narrowed focus is also the result of a more insistent questioning of socially accepted roles for men and women in Ireland today, and the intense struggles within the individual psyche which this engenders.

Edna O'Brien and John McGahern are the first two significant writers to emerge in this most recent era of Irish fiction. They both broke new ground with the publication of *The Country Girls* (1960) and *The Dark* (1956) respectively, wherein Irish sexual taboos are publicly defied. The protagonists of *Night* (1972) and *The Leavetaking* (1974) show how the self-in-process has changed for men and women since Mary Lavelle and Stephen Dedalus, and how in some ways, it has remained the same. Mary Hooligan in Edna O'Brien's *Night*, as her anarchic name suggests, has broken all the ties which Mary Lavelle could not: she has left Ireland for good, she has spurned the roles of wife, mother, daughter, and she refuses to conform to any orthodox expectations of women in general. A self-made outcast, she lives on the edges of other peoples' lives, camping in their houses, experimenting with sex, and indulging in strange whims. Yet for all her bravado she has not found "the one true love" and she is essentially unhappy in her self-imposed exile. Cocking a snook at society has not achieved any recognition or sense of agency: "I am in authority here but it's negligible." Her voice comes out of the vacuum of her renunciation, out of the darkness of an empty house which she does not own: "Oh Connemara hills, where will I go, where will I not go now? Fucking nowhere." In order to define herself she returns to the broken ties with the past, piecing herself together out of remembered relationships, finding herself again as daughter and mother. Thus even in the height of her sexual experimentation, she gains a sense of meaning chiefly from playing the maternal role. "She kissed me ... I wanted to put diapers on her ... and turn her into a little child again, give her back to herself." Her derivation of comfort and identity-affirmation from the sense of return to the often restrictive ties of the past suggests a modern-day Mary Lavelle, highlighting the dilemma of the woman who decides to make the tempting break with home for the sake of the sexual freedom which Mary Lavelle sacrifices.

Patrick Moran, the protagonist of McGahern's *The Leavetaking*, leaves the cloying pieties of Irish life like Mary Hooligan, for the sake of sexual freedom and the space wherein to find himself. Unlike Stephen Dedalus, the preservation of his love relationship is what sends Moran away. Public roles such as those of teacher or academic hold little importance for him, unlike the self-definition of Stephen in the public role of artist. Nevertheless, there are certain basic similarities between Patrick and Stephen, such as their view of their departure from home as a final differentiation from the realm and expectations of mother, who is closely allied in their minds with the limitations of the Catholic Church. Patrick's renunciation is calculated and publicly defiant, in the manner of his Joycean predecessor. He deliberately waits to be sacked from his teaching job at the Christian Brothers school after it is discovered that his marriage has not been sanctioned by the Church. He then makes a stand in front of the head priest, defending the essential rightness of his position. He knows what the verdict will be, yet it is important for him to make a public gesture of defiance. This enables him to leave, like Stephen, on a tide of what appears to be his own making. This is unlike Mary Hooligan, who rushes off to London in the fear that she might be pregnant, a private escape from the scrutiny of the public moralists of her community.

This attitude is reflected in their different narrative styles. Patrick's voice is, like the tone of Stephen's diary at the end of *A Portrait*, that of a man who has made his own decision to leave and offers a public testimonial on the eve of his departure. Although Patrick is not a self-proclaimed artist, he is, like Stephen, a "priest of the imagination", wherein the world of memory and experience is forged anew: "I embellish them with what I know." Thus his own story involves the telling of the stories of his loved ones in his own words, with a ritualistic, elegiac attention to the merest detail of a peripheral character's appearance and life story. Even his own, most intimate and abandoned acts of love are rendered in this same ritualistic and seamless prose. He never appears to lose control: even in his lover's arms he is still the presiding priest in what he sees as the "only communion left to us." This is quite different from Mary Hooligan's rambling memories and associative, spontaneous-seeming thoughts. Her descriptions of intimate physical acts include down-to-earth references to the messier details of the bodily functions which are beyond anyone's control: "Threads were hanging from me, the threads that were erstwhile his, in loops, suspended." Her language is at times crude, at times clichéd, abrupt, lyrical, imagistic, immediate. Unlike McGahern's, there is no obtrusive sense of a presiding pattern. Mary's self-revelation is thus idiosyncratic and individual first, and we see the wider world within which she moves only as a backdrop to her emotion-centred memories. Patrick's self-portrait is elusive due to his awareness of self as a medium for the enlargement of biography to social comment. This represents an après-Stephen Dedalus tendency to set himself up as the conscience of his race; as a new and different authority to those which are driving him from his native land. Mary Hooligan's aim is the less public process of piecing herself together within the nocturnal reverie of her thoughts, and the personal comment which this involves.

This difference between their protagonists can be extended to explain the divergent perspectives of the authors. Like Hooligan's audacious behaviour, O'Brien frequently uses the confessional voice to narrate stories which have the powerful, repetitive themes of autobiography. Like Hooligan, O'Brien has moved away from her native community in the west of Ireland to the laissez-faire, cosmopolitan world of London. Yet, just as Hooligan's richly evoked past contrasts with the shifting, indistinct landscape of her present, so it is O'Brien's stories of her native community and girlhood which define her as a

131

writer.

Without a sense of these constraints of small town Irish society, her work loses the full impact of its sexual daring and emotional intensity, just as Mary Hooligan's bold bid for selfhood loses its impact unless we have a clear portrait of the structure from which she has emerged.

Frank Tuohy has said of Edna O'Brien: "the world of Nora Barnacle had to wait for the fiction of Edna O'Brien." O'Brien, like Mary Lavin, focuses on the unvoiced lives of Irish women in Irish society, highlighting the forgotten feminine perspective. Her work lacks Lavin's self-effacement, so that while portraying passive figures in restricted settings, her own authorial voice protests, either overtly ("I thought that ours indeed was a land of shame, a land of murder, and a land of strange, throttled, sacrificial women.") or through her use of irreverently honest language and images. McGahern, on the other hand, places himself in the role of the Joyce of *Dubliners* and *A Portrait*, in that he proffers a vision of "the conscience of my race" in place of a personal biography in *The Leavetaking*. This explains his overt echoes of early Joycean motifs, whereby he conveys his stance in the traditional role of the Irish male writer. His oeuvre, unlike the repetitive biographies of O'Brien, follows the public trends in Irish society, so that recent stories in *High Ground* introduce contemporary issues such as the urban anasethetic of TV. Edna O'Brien has been criticised for the comparative similiarity of her theme and perspective from fiction to fiction, in the same way as Kate O'Brien and Mary Lavin. Yet this recurrent pattern strengthens our sense of the deadlock of Irish society, wherein women still struggle for autonomy, for differentiation from the fate of their mothers, while finding the rootless option of sexual freedom abroad lacking in depth or fulfilment. It is odd that McGahern has not been brought to task for his obvious rehashing of Joyce, if critics are so jaded with variations on a theme.

Molly Keane and John Banville, two other well-known Irish fiction writers today, exhibit a similar divergence in perspective in their novels *Good Behaviour* (1980), and *Birchwood* respectively. These novels are the successors of previous generations of portraits of life in the Big House. Keane's is the biography of her protagonist, Aroon St. Charles, whose development has been accomplished within the four walls of her family home, and within the cardboard codes of "good behaviour" exemplified by her mother, and aspired to by the rest of her dwindling class. She tells her story only after the death of her mother, as though suddenly liberated from the latter's inhuman standards: "Tears are such rotten behaviour, but a disgraceful warmth and ease followed them for me." Yet Aroon, now in her late fifties, finds it too late to achieve her own vision of selfhood. Like her exuberant breasts which she was forced to bind in her youth, it's too late for release from long tutelage to maternally inherited codes. Thus she constantly judges herself according to her mother's impossible yardstick of seamless manners, satisfied only when she can take over her mother's role in the end as fastidious regulator of the domestic scene. The option of marriage, which she had been brought up to expect as an inevitable part of her life, is shelved due to lack of socially approved swains. Instead of becoming a wife, she takes the next most socially acceptable option of the dutiful daughter. It is in this role which she chooses to define herself in the course of her story, motivated not by a need to articulate her own, separate identity, because that she has never possessed, but by a need to understand the reason for her family's unhappiness.

The irony of the novel lies in Aroon's lack of awareness that it is the very life–denying "good behaviour" which she tries so desperately to espouse that is responsible for the paralysis of her own life, and of her class in general. She refuses to have an affair, which would satisfy her body's clamouring appetites, simply because the amorous bank manager is not of her class. Her naivete highlights the absurdity and tragedy of this incestuous entropy, just as Edgeworth's Thady, in his blind allegiance to the undeserving Rackrents, succeeds in further accentuating their folly. Like Edgeworth and Mary Lavin, Keane uses humour as an ironic subtext which undermines the posturing of authority.

However Keane is less self-effacing in this protest against the deathly structures which suffocate her heroine. Like Somerville and Ross, she is capable of poking fun at her own protagonist for submitting to these codes, but Keane's humour is positively black in comparison with the lighter touches of her predecessors. Like Edna O'Brien, her anarchy is thus more evident, more insistent. A potent mixture of pathos and absurdity, it sticks in the reader's throat like an indigestible ball of laughter and outrage, ending in a grimace, as in Aroon's pathetic gratitude when her brother's effete friend pays her some cursory attention: "I was so happy ... 'Pig-wig' he called me ... to this living moment I experience a shudder of bliss."

In *Birchwood* the protagonist's perspective of his life in the Big House is different from Aroon's. His name, Gabriel Godkin – little God – recalls Stephen Dedalus's view of the artist as creator of his world. Gabriel thus calls attention to his own role as inventor of the story he portrays, and his own role therein: "I invent, necessarily." Unlike the local and personal view of life in the Big House which filters through Aroon's biography, Gabriel exists within a compilation of the characteristic features of the Big House over several generations and historical eras, including the Great Famine, tenant problems, and rebellious insurgents who attack his house and kill his family. In his case, private biography is subsumed in a view of social history, as in *The Leavetaking* and certain other texts by male Irish writers, including George Moore, another Big House writer. Like Gabriel, Banville himself draws attention to his authorial role of inventor of his text by his deliberate references and allusions to philosophical ideas and the literature of other male writers. Just as Gabriel's portrait of Big House life becomes illustrative of the wider framework of its history as a whole, so Banville's text opens out into the wider framework of abstract theories and ideas on the nature of memory and the meaning of life. His public perspective contrasts with Keane's focus on the unvoiced niches of such a history. We are back to Edgeworth's perceived discrepancy between the biographer and the historian. Aroon's memory is like "cast iron", where the events of her life have been engraved by the hands of others and remain like carved signatures on the bark of a stunted tree. Banville's protagonist is caught up with his own world of broken mirrors and artifice, fearful of the impotence, which Aroon accepts, if he ceases to actively invent.

Banville's allusive style is reminiscent of Joyce in its exclusivity, postulating a familiarity with a charmed circle of other male texts. The novel loses its deeper significance if the reader fails to pick up Banville's plethora of hints and references. Seamus Deane has praised *Birchwood* as "the only modern Big House novel that addresses wider questions about fiction, its nature and status, its methods and its philosophy which we associate with Borges, Nabokov, Barth and others, and which belongs to the Joyce, Flann O'Brien, Beckett experimental tradition." Keane's novel, in its insistence on human biography rather than the largely male history of ideas, is thus implied as somehow lacking in significance in comparison. Yet Keane, as a woman writer, would hardly choose to let the impact of her own work rest on the framework of such a public and male-dominated inheritance, within which she could not be expected to define herself. Her work benefits from the lack of inaccessible narcissism which Banville's relationship with this rather overwhelming tradition involves. Her voice is fresh and individual, her only inheritance the human-centred biography of Edgeworth, which unlike the rigidities of abstract theories, expands to accommodate the self which it portrays. The fact that *Good Behaviour* was shortlisted for the Booker prize, and continues to be widely sold and read, while *Birchwood* is the fodder of philosphically-minded critics, speaks for their appeal, and certainly does not suggest the inferiority of Keane's text.

Two figures who have more in common are the well-known Northern Irish writers, Jennifer Johnston and Bernard McLaverty. Their novels are often located within the context of the sectarian strife in their part of the world. Whatever the locale however, both writers tend to portray a similar situation, wherein two social outcasts from opposing backgrounds form a mutually supportive relationship based on shared visions of harmony, tolerance and love. Thus Cal (an unemployed Catholic youth) and Marcella (the half-Italian Catholic widow of a Protestant police officer) find trust and intimacy in the midst of sectarian violence in McLaverty's *Cal*. Kathleen (a Protestant from the Republic) and Joe (a Catholic schoolboy from a Derry ghetto) discuss poetry and eat sticky buns while bullets whistle down the street in Johnston's *Shadows on our Skin*. Both writers show how such outcasts are eventually punished by those who uphold the unwritten social codes of bigotry and suspicion. Thus in both *The Captains and the Kings* (Johnston) and *Lamb* (McLaverty), the innocent friendship between a boy and an older man is branded as perverse by the self-appointed public moralists of the community, and the two are hounded to death (literally). The intimacy and delicacy of the alternative, imaginative worlds created by these protagonists is sacrificed, as the "lamb" of McLaverty's title suggests, on the altar of Irish society's changeless prejudices and binary divisions.

McLaverty's male protagonists are more aware of the threat of the outside world, because they are more involved, in spite of themselves, in its machinations. Cal reluctantly does driving jobs for the IRA and "the brother" in *Lamb* cannot escape the institutionalised Catholic in himself, despite his adventures in London with his young charge. McLaverty thus shows how it is harder for adult males to withdraw from the public world within which they have been taught to define themselves. The half-hearted connection which remains, however, allows them to expect and understand a social punishment which they recognise as inevitable. The children and women who are the protagonists in Johnston's novels are more innocent and passive victims of public machinations which are out of their control and of which they are often scarcely aware. Theirs is more a calculated withdrawal into a private arena of self-definition, while McLaverty's heroes make more public, and thus more obviously punishable, gestures of defiance. Thus Diarmid and Mr. Prendergast in Johnston's *The Captains and the Kings* meet quietly in Mr. Prendergast's old mansion to invent their own

136

lost world of forgotten heroes and noble battles, while Diarmid is supposed to be at school, or looking for a sensible job. McLaverty's Christian brother, on the other hand, simply leaves the reform school one night with his young friend in *Lamb*. Johnston's protagonists, caught up in their inner modes of escape, suffer more when these private worlds are intruded upon; the bubble bursts with all the horror and violence of the unexpected: "Each shattering unveils the eye. ...I mourn the needless dead" (*The Railway Station Man*). Like Helen, protagonist of the latter, they are left with an indelible sense of their own impotence and vulnerability. Reminiscent of Kate O'Brien's Ana da Mendoza, Helen is left with the feeling that she can only be autonomous within the undetected privacy of her own thoughts: "The recollections that I keep in my head are part of my private being."

McLaverty and Johnston are unusual in their basic similarity of perspective. Johnston's peripheral adult males, such as Joe's older brother in *Shadows on our Skin*, or Damian in *The Railway Station Man*, are similar to Cal, half "in" the dubious activities of the IRA and half searching for love and security. Marcella in *Cal* is like a Johnston heroine in the manner of Kathleen (*Shadows*) or Helen (*Railway*), when her privately nonconformist idyll with her young lover is rudely broken by the intrusive and punitive denizens of the public world of sectarian strife. The focus of both writers is on the biography of the personal lives of their characters, so that social is sacrificed for the sake of psychological realism. They have both been accused of misrepresenting the public body of the IRA. (Nevertheless, despite the fact that Johnston is the more prolific writer, it is McLaverty's two novels which have made the most public impact.

Mary Beckett and Julia O'Faolain, two more recent women writers of note, also depict the individual as victim within the larger, more powerful frame of political turmoil. Like Johnston and McLaverty, Beckett is largely a Northern writer, and most of the stories of *A Belfast Woman* are based in her native Belfast. If anything, her characters are less privileged than those of her contemporaries; while Johnston's heroines are usually from the upper middle class, and can afford to get beyond the millstones of family duties, Beckett's women are lower middle class Catholics who are enmeshed in the selfless tasks of wife and mother. the protagonist of "The Master and The Bomb" tells us: "I'm a woman. I'm supposed to be passive. I've got three small children. I'm expecting another." The fact that she never even introduces herself by name, or shifts the locus of the story beyond her kitchen, exhibits her lack of a sense of public identity, and her domestically-based self-definition as mother rather than individual. Mary, the protagonist of the title story, is similarly selfless: "I'd be a nuisance to them if I got sick." Her protest against political violence is not on her own behalf – she reacts with complete lack of self-pity when she is threatened with being burnt out – but for the sake of others in her community who have no public voice: "It's not right to put the blame on poor powerless people. The most of us never did anything but stay quiet and put up with things the way they were." Beckett shows us the torn world of Belfast from the inside out, from the domestic and personal accounts of the lives of her overlooked heroines. Unlike, Johnston, who allows her protagonists to escape from social demands before a final unexpected punishment, Beckett's women live in a given world of suffering, but their capacity to endure their trials gives them a strength and convinction which Johnston's heroines do not possess. Also, while Johnston's denouements involve a sudden disaster in the lives of her characters over which they have no control, Beckett hinges her stories on small and unexpected acts of defiance perpetrated by her characters within the limits of their domestic roles. Thus the heroine of "The Excursion", after a day of frustration and impotent yearning caused by her selfish husband, allows herself the momentary revenge of shoving him towards the fire when he comes home drunk.

Julia O'Faolain's protagonist in *No Country for Young Men* (1980), Grainne O'Malley, though a Dubliner from a wealthy and politically powerful family, is similarly circumscribed. She is caught up in her socially defined role as wife, mother, family member, and "supporting actress" in playing out the old nationalist causes. Like Mary Lavelle, she takes a short trip away from these restrictions, yet soon comes running back to the familiarity of the housewife's role: "The skipped meal left her feeling that the family structure had collapsed. Meals were the pivot of a housewife's function." When she allows James, the attractive American to fulfil her fantasies of the knight/satyr/lover, she achieves a sense of liberation within these constraints. Under the nose of Owen Roe, her powerful politician cousin and former lover, she discovers with James the delights of sexual satisfaction. This allows her to feel, like Kate O'Brien's Ana da Mendoza, that her private self-definition can co-exist with the accepted limits of her public duties. Yet Owen Roe, like Philip II in *That Lady*, has the power to obliterate even this small and intimate transgression of public codes: his plans dominate, limit and finally terminate Grainne's bid for self-discovery. James is killed by Owen Roe's pawn, confusing patriotic verve with the "protection" of the Irish woman's sexuality (summed up by his verbal inability to distinguish between "country" and "cunt"). This brings us back to the work of Johnston and McLaverty, where those who try to define themselves in the nonconformist intimacy of sexual trust are punished (women) or even killed (men) by the public cause-mongers of society.

O'Faolain does not give Grainne her own voice in the novel, and this heightens our sense of her position in a structure over which she has no sense of control. This passivity in her heroine is in contrast with O'Faolain's own subtle, though hardly self-effacing presence as author within her own text. She heightens the theme of the repetitive nature of Irish myth and history, whereby women's private worlds are subsumed in the fruitless and destructive power-struggles of public life. She does this by manipulating historical events in the novel into implausible coincidence, whereby Grainne's aunt was similarly caught between a politician and an American swain, and finally deprived of escape due to the former's elimination of the latter. O'Faolain also suggests the mythic dimension, whereby Grainne's legendary namesake was also caught between her sweet lover and the vengeance of Fionn. O'Faolain uses these public frames to serve the purpose of biography, however, and she is careful to let her characters notice the mythic parallel, rather than calling attention in a more obvious way to her own artifice.

Two recent novels, *Very Like a Whale* (1986) by Val Mulkerns, and *The Ikon Maker* (1976) by Desmond Hogan show how old themes are given a new twist. Mulkerns looks at many of the changing roles for women in contemporary Ireland through the eyes of a young male who is himself working out new modes of existence. Hogan's perspective is that of a middle-aged woman who learns to re-evaluate her own life decisions through her view of her son's refusal to conform to social expectations. Mulkerns' Ben, rather than in the initial stages of the young man's Oedipal journey of differentiation, is back home after his four year stint of self-exploration in the flexible social climate of Holland and Germany. He is quite resentful that the familiar world of his youth has now caught up with the urban trends he experienced abroad: the loss of religious faith, sexual laissez-faire, the breakdown of communities, the advent of serious crime and drug addiction. He is especially unsettled by the break up of his parents, which he somehow sees as responsible for the larger fragmentation of the life he knew as a child. Mulkerns thus highlights the dilemma of the young man who thought he was defining himself in opposition to his mother's familiar sphere, only to discover that she is rejecting the same set patterns in the search for her own identity. Ben is also rattled by the changes he finds in his ex-girlfriend, whom he expected to find similarly unchanged. He scoffs at his sister's "yuppie" existence, while secretly rather impressed by her abilities to balance a more successful career with motherhood. He eventually sets about finding his own place in this changing social scene, realising that the modernisation of Irish life allows women as many good or ill-advised options for self-definition as are available to him. He can be inspired by their choices, finding himself in the same role as the social worker, Anita, when he takes a teaching job in the

140

inner city. Mulkerns ends the novel with an ironic reversal of the ending of *A Portrait*. In the latter, May Dedalus lays out her son's clothes for his journey into a new life. In *Very Like a Whale*, it is Ben who stays at home to usher his mother, another aspiring artist, into a voyage of self-discovery as he chooses her clothes for her trip to Venice. Hogan's protagonist, Susan, is also an update of May Dedalus, in that she follows her son's Oedipal journey across to England, attempting to find new visions to live by there. Yet the chief source of her self-definition is in her maternal love for her son. This is the mainstay which buoys her during her mini-odyssey through urban life in England: it is a quest for her son's identity in place of her own, as she searches through the choices and people he has sampled and discarded. She is crushed by his decision to cut himself off from her in a very decisive manner, by moving to Yugoslavia with his male lover. Her tender and simple process of understanding his development, which has helped to illuminate her own, is thus rudely truncated. In the vacuum her new vision of self, as liberated by his, shrivels, and she retires to the backwater of rural Irish life to become "another local tragedy". Her fate echoes that of Mary Lavelle and Grainne O'Malley, but is intensified by her age and isolated, insular community. She and her son are thus polarised into extreme attitudes of resignation and defiance, unlike the mother/son relationship of Mulkerns, which is allowed the breathing-space of general urban change and readjustment.

Hogan's is a biography of Susan that is both delicate and intimate, caught up in the internal workings of her psyche, concentrating on her memory and limited experience of life through which we glimpse patches of the social history of her time. This unusually feminine perspective is belied, however, by Hogan's own, very evident presence within his text, whereby his concern with avoidance of cliché becomes as significant to the work as the biography of his character. This drives him, to the extremes of "vegetables hung in the air like infants", and reminds us of Banville's self-conscious relationship with the language of his text. Hogan thus defines himself as author in the public and defiant fashion chosen by the young man in the novel. This works as a contrast to the more passive, tentative attitude of his female protagonist. Mulkerns as author is self-effacing, and we do not see a contrast between her narrative technique and the perceptions of Ben, simply because it is him as the successor of Joyce and the other experimentalists. His parodies of Irish life and his penchant for myth and symbolism in *A Curious Street* confirm his inheritance.

Both Susan and Ben must break out of their solipsistic expectations into the cold light of reality: Susan to discover that her son's route to identity must involve the ultimate deprivation of her own; Ben to see that Dublin is no longer the cosy, fixed sphere of given roles and structures which he has imagined. Yet Mulkerns offers Ben alternatives, while Susan is seen to have no comeback. This is partially to do with age and sex, and mainly to do with Ben's position as a member of Dublin's privileged upper middle class, within a wealthy and influential family. Recent fiction such as *Different Kinds of Love* (1987) by Leland Bardwell, *My Head is Opening* (1987) by Evelyn Conlon and *The Woman's Daughter* (1987) by Dermot Bolger portray the fate of the Dubliner who is not employed, well housed or mobile. These isolated, disempowered individuals, mainly women, contribute to their own marginalisation by failing to find what they need in the society which is offered to them, and retreating into further anonymity. Bardwell's "Dead Elm" and Bolger's novel both portray the voluntary exile of a mother and her mentally disturbed daughter, while Conlon's "The Day She Lost the Last of Her Friends" is about a single mother who also, partly through her own sense of her unacceptability, and through her awareness of social disapproval, ends up in isolation. Some find a consolation in their sense of connection and networking with other, similarly circumscribed women. This solidarity is evident between the mothers in Conlon's "Park going Days". In Bardwell's "The Hairdresser", the women band together to form protective oases in an urban wasteland. These are bleak landscapes, where men are largely absent, or at least fly-by-night escapees. In Bolger's novel the immured woman conceived her daughter in an incestuous coupling with her brother, before he, too, disappeared. It is impossible for these women to attain a sense of agency or identity, in spite of Bardwell's protagonist in "Euston", who whispers Neitzsche's lines to herself: "Whenever order is disturbed, whenever disorder rises, I create myself anew". One of the few protagonists in Bardwell's stories has her own voice for half of the tale, when she is seen to piece together the passively suffered atrocities of childhood in an attempt to find herself. This is done from the undetected depths of insanity however, where, like Bowen's deaf woman in "A Summer Night", she can attain a state of imperviousness to the outside world and its expectations (*The Dove of Peace*). Most of these women, however, see themselves according to the limitations of a woman's socially defined role, and though from a very different background, the crippling effect of this self-restriction reminds us of Keane's Aroon St Charles.

The male protagonist in Bolger's novel is similarly marginalised and disempowered by a society which no longer respects his druidic role which is akin to that of the old seanachai, or chronicler of his community. The community has been fragmented and alienated by the urban blight of unemployment, poverty and emigration. His role is an anachronism, and he is forced to let his stories run through his own imagination, for lack of an audience. The fact that the woman's voice appears to speak for itself for the major portion of the book, and that Johnny only appears as the medium for her tale at the end, highlights his sense of his own lack of significance as teller of the tale. Unlike Stephen Dedalus, he goes reluctantly to his inherited fate, and he finds no public recognition for his role. His lack of self-importance and/or narcissism is in contrast with other male protagonists which we have examined, such as Banville's Gabriel Godkin. Nevertheless, this does not alter the fact that he, as much as the woman and her daughter, adheres to the traditional route for the male sense of self, which is public and actively involved with social history, while their's is passively domestic, reliant on his rendition of their story to give them life. This sense of the polarity of male roles is highlighted by the fact that the druidic inheritance is handed down from father to surrogate son in an exclusively Oedipal ritual every generation. Rendering the woman's story becomes for him the vehicle for affirming his own identity as local storyteller, so that he is dependent upon a sense of her passivity in order to actively define himself. This perceived deadlock between the sexes which is also as much part of the stories of Conlon, Bardwell, and other writers such as Mary Beckett, is in contrast to the more daring and suggestive vision of Edna O'Brien in *Night* and Val Mulkerns in *Very Like a Whale*.

Deirdre Madden is probably our youngest and most exciting Irish writer. At twenty-seven she has just published two accomplished novels with Faber & Faber: *Hidden Symptoms* and *The Birds of the Innocent Wood*. Both novels are primarily concerned with the private lives of female protagonists. *Hidden Symptoms* recalls Johnston and McLaverty in that it focuses on the punishing effect of a sectarian murder upon the inner life of the bereaved protagonist, Theresa. The title of the novel highlights Madden's concern with the "little peripheral pains" of a central tragedy – the privately experienced pain which follows a public atrocity. This focus on personal biography links Madden with her litreary foremothers.

If Theresa's murdered twin brother represents the capacity for joy, then she is the surviving representative of suffering (they agree that life consists of both). Theresa finds no alleviation for her solitary mourning, while her two friends, Kathy and Robert, move further away from her by discovering routes back to joy and security through their respective family reunions. Theresa clearly sees redemption in the solidity of family warmth which has been denied her; in the shape of a newborn baby in her arms.

She is thus unlike the domestically suffocated protagonists of Beckett, Conlon and Bardwell. Neither does she seek fulfilment in sexual liberation, in the manner of Grainne O'Malley or Mary Hooligan. Like Val Mulkern's Ben, Theresa represents the new generation of university-educated, sharp-witted and uncompromising young men and women, who, having found themselves amid the chaos and violence of the new Irish society, look wistfully back at a secure family unit, now lost. Their essential confidence is echoed in Madden's own third person description. Their uncompromising quality is also upheld by the end of the novel, which unlike those of Johnstson or Beckett, offers no obvious denouement or resolution, but the reality of Theresa's unchanged, unceasing despair: "Could there be anything more wearisome, she wondered, than to stand alone, alone, alone before a mirror?"

Apart from the obvious purpose of examining the significant contribution of women writers to Irish fiction, this brief survey highlights certain trends in the tradition, most significantly the thematic alignment of male and female writers, contrasted with their divergence of narrative perspective. Maria Edgeworth's definition of the biographer and the historian pinpoints the self-effacing female focus on the private world of one quietly evolving self, and the male's more public concern with his own role as social commentator and interest in abstract frames of reference. Women writers such as Edgeworth and Somerville and Ross dominate the earlier part of the tradition, followed by a middle period where the male experimentalists shone brighter than their female peers, of whom there were very few. The contemporary scene has achieved a more homogenous balance of male and female writers who are increasing in number all the time. Recent fiction also exhibits a narrowing of their divergent perspectives. Male writers are focusing more on the inner life of one protagonist, and authors such as McLaverty don't pose as the "conscience" of their "race", while Bolger shows a male character whose Dedalian role is complicated by new shifts in Irish society. Women are taking more public authorial positions within their texts. The increased use of the confessional voice by writers such as Edna O'Brien and Jennifer Johnston allows the female author a more immediate and insistent mask for her own voice, while simultaneously appearing to achieve a fuller revelation of the evolving self of her protagonist. The sexual explicitness of Edna O'Brien and Julia O'Faolain, the small defiances of Mary Beckett's protagonists, the black humour of Molly Keane and the diversity of roles open to women in Mulkerns'*Very Like a Whale* represent a new element of open defiance towards the unwritten constraints of Irish society in the work of our women writers. This mirrors the changing position of women in Ireland, whereby they are slowly coming to see themselves as less impotent in the public sphere than their overlooked, domestically swallowed mothers.

Nevertheless, women's long, unspoken self-marginalisation in accordance with social repression has taken its toll on our female writers. Many potential women writers never blossomed in this arid environment. Edgeworth allowed her own considerable talents to be overshadowed by her father's influence. Most Irish women writers have enjoyed less public recognition for their achievements, often simply due to their absence of the more public, self-confident and defiant behaviour of their male peers such as Joyce. Thus Desmond Hogan enjoys more publicity than the equally talented and cosmopolitan Julia O'Faolain. By capitulating to the current fad for "marginalised minorities", women writers will not redeem themselves from this lack of deserved acclaim. Like the watered down translation of Peig Sayers' autobiography, women writers' natural talent has been disempowered by their translation of it into acceptable codes. A new adherence to abstract and binary theories of feminism will ultimately give rise to a new conformity to limiting expectations.

The Irish woman writer is hovering on the brink of realising that she can detach herself enough from the tyranny of social or literary conventions in order to create her own fictive worlds. Some women writers have already started to do this, in countries where the cause of women's rights is a little further along the road, such as Doris Lessing (England) and Margaret Atwood (Canada). In the meantime, the growing acclaim for the novels of Black American women writers wherein women also struggle for self-definition in a repressive society heralds a new critical appreciation of the kind of biographies which are the trademark of our own women writers.

Nuala Ni Dhomhnaill provides us with an inspiringly outspoken definition of the Irish Woman writer's perspective as a fitting conclusion to this short survey: "I don't believe in 'passion' in big capital letters, but I do believe that you should be able at some level to say 'I love. I want. I am. I shit.' The 'I' is important, there are all sorts of techniques but the personal input and the personal talent are ultimately what counts ... the 15 years to the end of the millenium is ours. By 'ours' I mean the female voice, the feminine voice, whether it is men or women who have it."

ART FOR THE PEOPLE ?

Anthony Cronin

With one exception, these essays were originally *Viewpoint* columns in the *Irish Times*. Many of the pieces which I wrote for that newspaper about art as a social phenomenon or public policy towards the arts have been outdated by events; for instance it is now public policy to support the individual creative artist and we have Aosdana; so there did not seem much point in reprinting pieces calling for such support. One piece here, "The Muse in Captivity", is, I think, a bit out of date also. Eng. Lit. is not what it was; but I thought it was interesting that its decline was forecast and also that there was enough truth in the attack on the still influential mode of criticism then dominant to let the piece stand. The essays now reprinted are, in fact, more about attitudes than about policy; and there does still seem to me to be a good deal of relevance in them all. Only in one have I made major changes.

Anthony Cronin,
Dublin,
May 1988.

SOCIETY AND THE GOOD CITIZEN

Contrary to widespread opinion, art is not in the ordinary sense "a civilising influence." Knowledge and understanding or, indeed receptivity to works of art and the finer manifestations of the human spirit does not necessarily make people better citizens. People who are highly receptive to works of art are often dirty, lazy, dishonest, untrustworthy, cruel and even violent by disposition.

People who create works of art are often these things too, only more so. Many people who are extremely responsive to works of art are also inclined to political or revolutionary violence, for romantic or other reasons. Some works of art (not usually, however, the greatest) have undoubtedly the effect of making people more warlike.

Some societies (not all) which have produced works of great art with the profusion and naturalness of a meadow producing buttercups have been cruel and violent to a degree, and so also have been their rulers. On the other hand, it should be said that adolescents who have been properly exposed to works of art and who prove responsive to them seldom turn out to be grannie bashers. The reason probably is that most grannie bashing is the result of acute and very horrible forms of boredom and frustration, while people who are truly interested in or excited by works of art are seldom bored or, in that sense, frustrated. Art brings its own frustrations, but a feeling of complete aimlessness is not one of them. Analogously, it might be said that societies which are receptive to great works of art or have the capacity to produce them are not commonly guilty of the more inane and pointless kinds of societal cruelty: they are cruel either for utility or for gratification.

For the above reasons, however, it is a mistake to look upon art or art education as a branch of civics or ethics. Art does not

149

necessarily make people gentler, or more co-operative, or more amenable to reason. It does not either, to echo a current confusion of thought, make them "more Christian." What it may do, in part, is to confer enormously important and significant kinds of self-knowledge on them, which can have the effect of saving them a great deal of inchoate and inanimate thrashing about, even if they are otherwise neurotic; and it may, therefore, where human motive, impulse and desire at least are concerned, make them more aware and almost certainly more compassionate.

A loving acquaintance with, and feeling for, the immediacy of the works of art of the past also deepens, or perhaps even creates, a sense of history; indeed it might be said that anybody who has not got such an acquaintance has not much sense of history. For this reason, if for no other, most, though not all, politicians have little entitlement to talk about history, and the people who make it seldom understand it. Some contemporary works of art whose creators have been aware of just how seriously our links with man's historic and pre-historic past are threatened have set out deliberately to maintain them, the artist as it were dredging up the past from within himself and from such sources and resources, imaginative or otherwise, as were available to him. Mr. David Jones's "The Anathemata" is such a work, as are many of the paintings and sculptures of Picasso, and "Finnegans Wake."

The experience of art is in itself, however, a deep and rich one, endlessly rewarding and endlessly capable of extension and development. Moreover, since it comes through the faculties, it develops them and therefore deepens and enriches almost all other experiences, visual, auditory, tangible and psychological. That is why people who are responsive to works of art are thought of in non-artistic communities as being "too sensitive"; and why indeed they sometimes are so. Since the experiencing of works of art is an enrichment, however, and since it enriches other experiences as well, to deprive people of the opportunity of responding to such works is to deprive them of a form of wealth in a very literal sense.

The word "deprived" is, of course, often used nowadays as a piece of special pleading; people are commonly said to have been deprived of things which in truth they or their equivalents in other societies never had. The experience of works of art, however, was a common daily one in all societies other than ours since our kind of man first walked this earth, and in the perfectly plain ordinary and literal sense, our society deprives people of it and is unique in doing so. It does this by physically destroying and removing works of art which were part of people's daily experience, works of architecture being perhaps the most obvious example. It does it by substituting mass-produced articles for artifacts which were works of art, and which were in common daily use.

It does it above all by substituting mere mass entertainment for the experience and enjoyment of works of art and encouraging what might be called an art expectation. Ordinary folk once listened nightly to the re-tellings of the Ossianic tales; now they are offered nightly television serials.

This form of deprivation was initially accidental and a product of the Industrial Revolution. A myriad of interests in the media and elsewhere are now vested in its continuance, and of course it will have ever graver and more impoverishing effects as the art-less generations succeed each other and become each other's instructors. Since it is a societal matter, however, only society can rectify the account and give back what it has taken away. It does, let it be said, make attempts to do this at the moment by dissemination and instruction, by providing people with some sort of access to works of art or reproductions of them either on a commercial or public service basis and by instructing them through the same channels in the proper response to what is offered.

It is possible, however, that no amount of exposure to works of art or literature after a certain age will increase the initial receptivity, and that age may well be around 16 or so. Most "art education" where adults are concerned is therefore doomed to failure. Further, there is no such thing as a proper response to a work of art. Any response, provided it contains an element of pleasure, is a correct response and most attempts to tell people what they should feel or see or look for only produce anxiety and stultify whatever response there might otherwise have been. They may produce an illusion of receptivity: indeed the lectured may be able to go away and lecture others, publicly or privately, but that means nothing. Human beings are sedulous by disposition, like their forefathers the apes; and indeed it is very probable that Pavlov could have induced his dogs to respond, or give an appearance of response, to works of art.

(1976)

ART AND DEMOCRACY

Modern democracies are peculiar in that they seemingly attach some importance to art without knowing precisely why. The religious autocracies of the past brought art into existence for a variety of reasons other than the mere love of proportion, order and beauty. Self-aggrandisement bulked high among them; but self-aggrandisement is specifically forbidden to a modern democracy, or at least to its elected rulers.

Before the triumph of modern, liberal ideas also, the rulers of Europe, lay and clerical, had a view about the purpose of existence; and hence almost all European architecture, an astonishing amount of its painting and sculpture, much of its dramatic and poetic literature. Hence a general agreement that art was a "good thing", either to call into existence or to make people aware of it. Art hopefully confirmed the view about the purpose of existence which the rulers held; it proferred ideal questions which were believed to be salutary.

But modern democracies are also forbidden to have views about the purpose of existence: that sort of thing is for autocrats and dictators. True, our own Constitution does put us all under the protection of the Most Holy Trinity, but in the best liberal circles our Constitution is an embarrassment. The modern liberal believes that the state should have no opinion on the question of why we are here and what for. Even instinctive or inherited attitudes (such as patriotism) which beg the question make the modern liberal uneasy.

But of course even we have theories about why art is desirable and why it should be disseminated to the multitude. A fashionable one of a few years ago was a variant on the old "devil finds work for idle hands to do theme". At its most pretentious, as in the correspondence columns of *The Irish Times*, this was headed "Creative Leisure" and "The Leisure

153

Society". If certain people were kept occupied appreciating art or even creating it, there would be less mugging and burglarious entry. People of a non-mugging rank and station might even be able to occupy the years of redundancy in ways more rewarding than their education or their outlook had previously fitted them for.

The present writer finds this theory repugnant. There might indeed be less vandalism, rape and robbery if the unemployed were as wholeheartedly concerned with art as, say, dear Clive and Virginia were; but the likelihood of their being so would be considerably improved if their surroundings and circumstances were more comparable. Art does positively serve, in Ezra Pound's phrase, as "nutrition of impulse", a life impulse, whereas many of the aimless and destructive things that people get up to in our society come from the very dregs of the death-wish; but it is far from being as good an opiate as television and spectator sports are; and the fact of their minds being on higher things will not, thank heavens, prevent people from wanting ordinary – or even extraordinary – human satisfactions. And there is something extremely distasteful about the idea of art being rushed as a last resort into that particular gap.

Another theory that seemed to suit democracy was the "every man his own artist" idea. The creation of works of art was, if you don't mind, a privilege which certain people enjoyed. On common or garden egalitarian grounds other people ought to be enabled to get in on the act. The result was a sort of baby out with the bath water effect which was probably the reverse of what was intended.

Art is, let's face it, a bit of a mystery. It is engaged in, for not fully explainable or justifiable reason. The creation of a work of art, which is, like it or not, the attempt to attain perfection is, in a world which acknowledges only commercial and utilitarian motives, an exercise so gratuitous as to be daft. It distorts its creators lives and imposes burdens on them so intolerable that they frequently result in breakdown and madness. It is a categorical imperative which has to be obeyed for the most part not knowing why or even how.

To make it into a mere pastime or social distraction or even therapy is therefore to take the very things that make it important out of it, the mystery, the terror, the placatory and, yes, sacrificial elements.

Which is not to say that as many people ought not to have as much experience of creativity as possible, or that people do not need creativity in their lives. In the old days people got that out of the work they did in the ordinary way for survival, or comfort, or reputation. They got it from craft-work, from agriculture, from building, from certain forms of societal organisation. In previous eras with less complex technologies they even got it from manufacture, from spinning, weaving and other activities.

To enable people to get some sort of creative satisfaction out of life is also a societal problem of great urgency, but again the burden should not be put entirely on the arts. Doubtless a good deal of creative satisfaction is to be obtained from a community theatrical production, say, or even from engaging in forms of writing which do not consume the living person in their flame. But to pre-suppose a society in which all questions of work satisfaction, seeing the end-product-of-one's-labours satisfaction were to be loaded on to art is to pre-suppose a monstrosity.

But an equal monstrosity, and one with which we are all too familiar, is a society in which most people have no experience of the ordering, annealling, compassionating and re-vivifying power of art at all. It may be that our society no longer places obstacles in the way of peoples' access to art of the sort with which previous generations were familiar: class barriers, literacy barriers etc., or at least if it does, it does it in a more subtle way than was the case forty years ago. It simply has little power to generate art of such a sort and on a scale that people become familiar with in the ordinary course of their lives. Its commercial agencies are more powerful than any other and day and night they encourage a passive entertainment expectation which is in fact deleterious to people's powers of response. Only the fact that some of what passes for entertainment contrives (as it has always done) to be art as well alleviates the barbarising effect.

155

And it is mostly negative reasons that force a democracy to treat art as important, to become both patron and impresario. In the days of Clive and Virginia there was a large rentier class living comfortably on what were laughingly described as modest private incomes. Even when the present writer first went to London in the 1950s the number of people with what was called "private money" was legion (there were a few of them in these parts too). It was this class which had taken over from the aristocracy the role of patron; indeed with true bourgeois economy it supplied artists, patron and audience all at once.

But then a change came over the world. Inflation and monopoly capitalism together destroyed the cultured class which the industrial revolution had created. There was as much money as ever in the world, but it was in fewer hands and it had to be more brutal and active to survive. Capitalism in other words began to eat its own rentier children. This left the state as the only possible patron for the artist; and it also left the state as the only agency which could pretend to any sort of interest in the survival of the civilisation which its citizens were supposed to have inherited. True, of late the large corporations which have succeeded the individualist manufacturing and rentier class have decided to become art patrons and disseminators as well. They began by commissioning art for their office buildings and it is largely due to their influence that we owe the era of bland statement-free abstraction from which painting has just emerged; but largely for negative reasons, the state remains the primary agency and the primary patron.

But even if the reasons are largely negative, the results may be positive. As long as there are works of art and people to contemplate them, art will do its re-vivifying, re-ordering and life enhancing work. As long as there are artists what they create will insist that the present order of things is not the ideal nor the only order of things, and that whether they consider themselves progressives or reactionaries, radicals or conservatives. But a more positive democracy would nevertheless produce more positive results. A democracy which contrived to have a sense of collective purpose might produce a great art which reflected that purpose, just as previous eras produced theirs; and if as a result of that collective purpose and collective effort a society came into being which was truly a leisure society for all, then art might properly supplant the old job satisfactions and survival satisfactions with a good conscience. Indeed it would be about the only thing that could.

(1988)

THE ROAD FROM RYDAL MOUNT

In 1880, or just over a hundred years ago, Matthew Arnold wrote a preface to *The English Poets*, an otherwise forgotten anthology in several volumes, edited by one T.H. Ward. Subsequently reprinted as "The Study of Poetry" in the posthumous *Essays In Criticism*; enunciating, as it did the doctrine of "high seriousness", and containing inter alia, the famous statement that "Dryden and Pope are classics of our prose", Arnold's essay exercised for a long time an apparently enormous influence over whoever was supposed to be concerned with poetry in the English-speaking world.

Indeed it may be doubted whether any single piece by any critic whatever was so often quoted as Arnold's, at least until the rise of T.S.Eliot and the coming into existence of the critical movement associated with the name of I.A.Richards. Then, with the rediscovery of the Metaphysicals and the re-establishment of Dryden and Pope, the doctrine of "high poetical seriousness" or "high poetical quality" began to sag; and sometime between the two wars, possibly with the publication of W.H.Auden's original *Oxford Book of Light Verse* it was, if not actually blown to bits, irretrievably holed below the water-line.

Yet Arnold's essay was a landmark. It is still reprinted; still willy-nilly discussed in all surveys of English criticism whatever; still quoted; and, one therefore presumes, still read. Which makes it even more extraordinary that neither the remarkable prophecy with which it begins, nor the still more remarkable failure of that prophecy to achieve any sort of fulfilment in the world of today, are ever adverted to.

Arnold began by quoting something he himself had written the year before, in the preface to yet another compilation called *The Hundred Greatest Men*: "The future of poetry is immense, because in poetry where it is worthy of its highest destinies our race, as time goes on, will find an ever surer and surer stay". And he now continued:

"We should conceive of poetry worthily, and more highly than it has been the custom to conceive of it. We should conceive of it as capable of higher uses, and called to higher destinies, than those which in general men have assigned to hitherto. More and more mankind will discover that we have to turn to poetry to interpret life for us, to console us, to sustain us. Without poetry our science will appear incomplete; and most of what passes for religion and philosophy will be replaced by poetry. Science, I say, will appear incomplete without it. For finely and truly does Wordsworth call poetry "the impassioned expression which is in the countenance of all science"; and what is countenance without its expression? Again, Wordsworth finely and truly calls poetry "the breath and finer spirit of all knowledge": our religion, parading evidences such as those on which the popular mind relies now; our philosophy, pluming itself on its reasonings about causation and finite and infinite being; what are they but the shadows and dreams and false shows of knowledge? The day will come when we shall wonder at ourselves for having trusted to them, for having taken them seriously; and the more we perceive their hollowness, the more we shall prize "the breath and finer spirit of knowledge" offered us by poetry".

Now in reading these extraordinary words and reflecting on what has actually come to pass, it is essential to remember that the author was neither a visionary nor a crackpot, nor even the sort of poet who mentally compensates for his outcast lot by making exorbitant claims for the value of his vocation. Matthew Arnold was a level-headed man; and more than any other comparable English poet of the nineteenth century he was immersed in the duties and obligations of what we may well call ordinary life.

At the time of writing he had been Inspector of Schools for longer than was good for him; and, if nothing else, he might have been expected to know what was happening in England on the educational level. But there was much else. He had sat on Royal Commissions and written Government Reports. He had travelled the length and breadth of England and met local dignitaries of all descriptions. When he attacked the English upper and middle-classes he did so as a representative figure; one who, as John Gross says, was "deeply committed to the values of his own class, that of the university educated gentleman." When he erred as a writer, he erred on the side of reason, not on the side of rapture or Dionysiac frenzy. Yet if we knew nothing else about him, than the words quoted, our respect for his judgement at least would be extremely low.

It is true that philosophy has continued to take hard knocks ever since; and that it may be doubted whether it nowadays exists at all as a study or a discipline or whatever it is supposed to be. It is also true that religion has continued to make a fool out of itself by the sort of liberalisation and modernisation which gave Arnold such amusement when he encountered it in the work of Bishop Colenso.

But to maintain that mankind in general, or even the educated upper middle-classes of Arnold's native England have turned to poetry instead, or that people anywhere in the English-speaking world look to it in large numbers to interpret life for them, to console them or sustain them, would be idiotic. And in spite of all the many agencies and factors which might have been expected to (which indeed were supposed to) work that particular oracle in the intervening century, the probability is that proportionately fewer people do so look to or turn to poetry now than did in Arnold's own day.

As every poet knows, the truth is that only poets, would be poets, critics, pedants, and prisoners in the various strata of the educational process read the stuff at all; and in the course of a lifetime you are lucky to meet one or two people belonging to none of these categories for whom poetry is a major factor in existence or who may be said to live by it in the rather melancholy sense that poets do.

Yet within a few years after Arnold had delivered his prophecy, the production of poetry readers in the most thorough fashion and on the very largest scale was, under

160

pressure from Mr Churton Collins and others, inaugurated in the universities; and before very long the process of expounding and explaining poetry was extended to include contemporaries as well as the dead. That this, had Arnold known anything about it, could have been expected to contribute to the "immense future" he foolishly foresaw for poetry might have been a fair assumption. Yet the fact is that immersion in the chilly waters of the academic process, though it makes pedants and writers, does not seem to make readers and enthusiasts (to use no stronger words) of people in the ordinary sense at all.

In the fashion of homeopathic medicine, the immersion seems rather to cure the fever than increase it; and – to alter the metaphor – there seems to be some unexplained leakage in the pipe line whereby the steam heat generated in the pressure chambers of the examination system escapes before reaching ordinary life. So far from persuading the hundreds of thousands of graduates they indubitably turn out that poetry was "capable of higher uses and called to higher destines" than those which in general men had assigned to it hitherto, the academics have failed to make even habitual readers of it of those who fall into their clutches. No sight is more melancholy than the half shelf full of books in the home of the erstwhile English student. But though the negative and homeopathically curative aspects of the academic treatment may be important enough, the factors which have made Arnold's prophecy look foolish are many and extend far beyond the confines of academia.

II

There is a sense in which, in all but the rectitude of his private life, Matthew Arnold can be regarded as the first representative of the genus Bloomsbury. Lytton Strachey may have made fun of his father, headmaster of Rugby, and sneered at his friend, the poet Arthur Hugh Clough, but over and over again Arnold's attitudes seem to prefigure those of the circle which included J.M. Keynes, the Woolfs and E.M. Forster, as well as Strachey himself.

There is the career as a public servant and the partial, establishment-directed involvement in public affairs, which are both at odds with an apparent aestheticism. There is the insistence in his poetry that if the gap between people as individuals could be closed all would be well. ("Only connect..."). There is the class-orientation – he speaks always to the middle classes – combined with a denunciation of the class to which you speak: it was Arnold, not Bloomsbury, which established the word Philistine in the language as meaning those members of the middle-classes who were lacking in culture or over-given to mere money-making. And above all there is the repeated assurance that the truly cultured member of the middle classes is *ipso facto* a member of a missionary group.

In E.M. Forster's novel *Howard's End* the Schlegel sisters open up a whole new life for the young clerk by bringing him to symphony concerts and exhibitions of paintings. In Arnold's prose there is an ultimate certainty that if the circle of middle-class readers who can distinguish the good from the mediocre is increased the illuminations they derive from art and poetry will sooner or later become the prerogative of the lower orders too.

Well, we know now it wasn't to be so. Arnold, like the members of the Bloomsbury group, had a very high notion of what it was to be a person of taste and culture; and in his view, as in theirs, the increase in the number of such persons would go hand in hand with a great deal less insistence on material and practical pursuits. In other words, though they didn't emphasise this, it would mean that somebody else took care of or had already taken care of, the material and practical pursuits for you. You would be, like most of the members of the Bloomsbury group, like the heroines of Forster's novel, a member of the second or third generation of moneyed middle-class people; and product of puritan forbears that you were, you would show both the wastrel aristocrats, who had different ideas, and the working classes, who had none, what the proper use of leisure ought to be.

Arnold's power of social analysis did not enable him to discuss how the working classes were to acquire sufficient leisure to acquire any culture in the first place; but then neither did he foresee, any more than J. M. Keynes, who was in a better position to do so, that the proportion of middle-class people who would be freed from money worries by the accumulation of capital would sooner or later begin to contract rather than expand. He did not foresee that with the advent of inflation and takeovers capitalism would begin, in the fifth and sixth decades of the twentieth century, to eat its own rentier children.

When that day came of course whatever reality resided in the dream of a middle-class elite who would introduce young clerks to the delights of symphony concerts would altogether vanish; and Arnold's prophecy of the "immense" future that lay in store for poetry, based as it was on an unwarranted assumption about the creation and expansion of cultured elites would begin to look silly.

But sneer at it though we may, there was another assumption behind it which would begin to vanish as well. And it may be this latter vanishing which explains why none of the agencies of apparent culture-propagation, including the universities have produced, either in the matter of mere numbers (although there are millions of English graduates) or in that of the intensity of their response (although intensive criticism flourishes as never before) anything like the audience which he foresaw.

In the course of a lifetime apparently divided between the claims of poetry and that of public duty (and the distinction is itself significant) Matthew Arnold delivered many lectures and became the author of many essays, tracts and treatises. The puritan conscience he had inherited from the presiding spirit of Rugby School impelled him doggedly forward not only through the composition of "Culture and Anarchy" or "Literature and Dogma", but through that of "Higher Schools and Universities in Germany", "Middle Class Education and the State", "Reports of Elementary Schools 1852-1882", "St. Paul and Protestantism" and much else that is now forgotten.

He concerned himself, as a responsible citizen should, with all the great questions of the day, both general, as in the case of religion and science, and immediate, as in the case of Irish and

Italian nationalism. (He was, incidentally, the brother-in-law of "Buckshot" Forster and made more than one private visit to Dublin). At first sight he seems like the complete citizen which every government says it aims to produce, one who believes that cultural interests go hand in hand with social ones, and are no more – if no less – important. But in fact he was nothing of the kind.

Matthew Arnold belonged to the generation of poetically inclined young Englishmen who had absorbed from the romantics, but above all from Wordsworth, a conception of the dignity and importance of poetry which they carried with them to the grave. In his own acceptance of personal and social duty – his decision to be merely a part-time or Sunday poet – he presages the long decline of commitment which eventually resulted in Mr. Philip Larkin's advice to a 20th century generation that a part-time poet was all anybody ought to be. But Arnold, like others, had made the pilgrimage to Rydal Mount, where, "stunned by oratory", and sometimes charged for their tea, they had "gathered from a fine old eye the living flame"; and the result is that when he speaks of poetry, its consequences and its position in the scheme of things, he speaks in an entirely different tone from that which he brings to the discussion of any other subject.

It is true that Wordsworth's claims for poetry were, in fact, more measured and more reasonable than Arnold's; that Wordsworth did not suffer from the perhaps Byronic illusion that poets are different in kind from other men, and that Eliot put a cold finger on a significant difference in their attitudes when he said "For Wordsworth and for Shelley poetry was a vehicle for one kind of philosophy or another, but the philosophy was something to be believed in. For Arnold the best poetry supersedes religion and philosophy." It may be that Arnold over-compensated for his own guilt feelings in his claims for poetry; and that his attitudes towards it, as well as those of all the later representatives of middle-class England, would have been better for absorbing something of Wordsworth's noble distinction, made in the "Essay Supplementary to the Preface of

1815", between the Public, which he despised, and the People, in whom he reposed his hope.

Yet Wordsworth who believed to the end that poetry and scientific discovery should go hand in hand, was still under no illusion that art in general and poetry in particular were merely good things, like public hygiene, or the spread of debating societies or geographical knowledge. Poetry to him, was "the first and last of all knowledge" and "as immortal as the heart of man". It was poetry which informed, illuminated and humanised everything else. It was poetry which touched the springs of human existence and altered man's conception of life by the touching.

But the belief that art in general and poetry in particular are merely good things like other good things which can be approved by people of a liberal, humane and progressive disposition is one which is built in to the teaching of "English" as a discipline among other disciplines in the liberal arts departments of the universities of the Western world and a belief to which all government agencies and arts councils whatsoever are particularly prone.

That, as Malraux put it, man is an image-making animal, compelled in the prison of his days to make images of himself which deny his nothingness and inform his being, is a fact of supreme importance and a mystery which touches on the mystery of life itself. To treat poetry as a mere concomitant of the public weal is to deny this; but our era has chosen for the most part to treat it so; and the public for whom the boon was intended has reacted, quite rightly, by treating the poetry with contempt.

(1978)

TOUCH OF THE POET

An informal survey conducted by a contributor to *The Times Literary Supplement*, Mick Imlah, recently revealed that out of a random sample of one hundred people in a London suburb, not one had purchased a book of poems in the previous year.

This is hardly sensational and neither the information that out of the hundred people questioned, only five claimed to read poetry "at all regularly". (Four out of these five, incidentally, were still at school). It is another figure of Mr Imlah's which is really startling.

Out of the same hundred people, of whom none buy poetry and only one past school leaving age ever reads it, "no fewer than thirteen claimed to have written something they would describe as poetry more than once in the past year".

In other words, a considerable number of people habitually write poetry who feel no necessity or desire to read the stuff. They may or may not have read their meed of it in the long ago; but anyhow they go on blithely writing it, regardless of what Messrs Heaney, Larkin, Hill or Hughes may be up to. And if you project, as Mr Imlah does, these figures nationally, you get a total of seven million people in Britain who write poetry on a scale and with a facility that many published and practising poets might envy.

Hardly anyone ever takes the extreme, dangerous and expensive course of going into a bookshop and buying a book of poems. On the other hand, supposing Mr Imlah's figure to have no class or regional variations, about half a million people in Britain do claim to read poetry, a figure somewhat lessened in its impact by the fact that four hundred thousand of them are schoolchildren. But seven million people write it.

Mr Imlah describes this as an "appalling statistic". Perhaps he ought to be reminded that numerous arts administrators, egalitarians, sociologists, social crusaders, educatonalists and psycho-therapists have been beavering away for some time now to bring about the day when every man, woman and child would be his or her own poet, and if it comes to that, playwright, actor, musician, cameraperson and painter too. To suggest that they were on the wrong tack has been elitist heresy.

To say that one of the primary concerns of arts policy should be to look after the talented in our midst has been to convict oneself of some sort of cultural snobbery; to advance any argument or express any doubts about encouraging people in the mass to do their own thing when their own thing is necessarily inferior or second-rate has been to leave oneself open to the charge of being anti-democratic.

But the truth is, of course, that the things people do for themselves will be ugly, boring and depressing even to themselves unless their experience of contemporary art is intense and habitual. Nor is the role of reader or spectator or "art-lover' in any way an ignoble or, in the ordinary sense, a passive one. Far from it. To be open, to be receptive, to admire a work of art is an active as well as an enlarging experience. Which brings us back to Mr Imlah's findings.

Every poet, in the English-speaking part of the world anyway, has long known that the audience for poetry is now composed solely of poets, would-be poets, critics, pedants and prisoners in the various strata of the educational process. In the course of a lifetime you are lucky to meet half a dozen people who belong to none of these categories, but who read poetry habitually and for the sake of whatever satisfactions and illuminations it may provide.

Everybody else has an ulterior motive. The most enthusiastic person after a poetry reading will sooner or later make the shy confession: the hand will go to the top pocket and the first typescript will be produced. The next in line will want to know your opinion of somebody who is on a course. Whatever they may feel compelled to say about your own work, most of those who write poetry will be found not to read it. Almost all of those who "study" it will be found only to read what some

167

pedagogue or committee of pedagogues has ordained they should.

Why? After all, Byron's "Manfred" sold one hundred thousand copies on the day of publication. Old men in country rectories once read Tennyson with the avidity which latter-day clerics bring to John Le Carre. Whitman and Edward Carpenter were read and quoted in working men's clubs.

Housman as well as Ella Wheeler Wilcox was once on sale in the gifts department of Harrods, and when Messrs Holder and Stoughton did a deal which enabled them to bring out a selected Kipling in a popular series in the 1920s, they were held to have brought off a publishing coup.

The reasons commonly put forward for the shrinking in size and enthusiasm of the poetry audience – supposing it is admitted to have shrunk – are the rise of the mass-media and the wilful obscurities of the poets themselves, with T.S.Eliot held to be the arch offender and encourager of half a century of inaccessible hermeneutics. Why the omnipresence of newspapers, films, and television should have affected poetry but not the novel remains unexplained: as do the reasons why the obscurities of W.H. Auden should alienate a 20th century audience when those of Browning, or indeed Shakespeare, did not do likewise to the Victorians and Elizabethans.

Of course nobody mentions cultural deprivation, or, if they do, it is with reference to the past. Cultural deprivation is something we are all moving out of. It belongs to the bad old days, not to the advancing present with its multifarious agencies of concern.

We have raised the school leaving age and brought about more or less free secondary education for all. We have turned out arts graduates, including English graduates, by the hundred thousand, and tens of thousands have learned how to answer a knotty answer or two about Wallace Steven's use of primary symbols or Yeat's theories of the mask. Those whose job it is to educate are of course oblivious of the distinction between knowledge and enjoyment. Many of those whose anxiety is the social advancement of ordinary humanity see nothing wrong

168

with a situation in which thirteen people claim to write poetry for every five who claim to read it, even though four of the latter are still at school.

But there is something wrong, something which goes to the very roots of our culture and our attitude to what art has to offer. The enjoyment of poetry is a primary human activity, the writing of it only a secondary one. The first contributes to the full development of the human being. The other may even narrow him.

Of course most of those who claimed to write poetry in Mr Imlah's survey were after what is called self-expression, with little knowledge of the rigours, discipline, and sacrifice which go into the expression of anything at all. But to restore the capacity to enjoy and admire is not to encourage passivity or a feeling of inferiority. It would, in fact be part of the restoration of full cultural activity to those who are now in truth condemned to merely being informed or humoured.

(1984)

THE MUSE IN CAPTIVITY

The real division in contemporary poetry is not between left and right, formalists and anti-formalists, realists and romantics or any old stuff like that. It is between academics and the rest; and if we regard it as a war which in many of its aspects it is – it is a war in which the academics now control all the passes, all the means of communication, all the heavy weaponry, as well as all the foreign embassies and all the gold reserves.

If those of my readers who are aware of names of poets will proceed to think hard for a moment they will, I am convinced, find it almost totally impossible to come upon the name of a reputable American poet who is not also an academic in good standing with the management and with his union. And what is true of America is nearly as true of Great Britain; and true, only more so, of Ireland. The names you appear to have taken to your bosoms, dear readers, the names you dwell on at those dire moments of the day or night when the necessity for discussing poetry rushes upon you like a thunderclap or a worry, are for the most part (for the very, very most part) the names of ladies and gentlemen who have been trained in the mysteries of literature in one of the academies set up for the purpose of such and other training round about the two islands and who have acquired sheepskins or other parchments therein enabling them to instruct others in their turn.

There were in America, it is true, the Beats of a few years ago, a collection of rather stagey outsiders who proclaimed themselves in revolt against Academia and all its standards. They got themselves a good deal of publicity in the doing of it – through the most talented of those who might be thought members of the school, Mr. Edward Field, got, needless to say, the least publicity.

There were also the Liverpudlians in England. Both these

groups succeeded merely in confusing the issue almost beyond recall by virtue of the fact that they proclaimed that the struggle was against academic formalism rather than against academia – as if every poet who did not write like a broken-down Walt Whitman and who had ever written a sonnet was the enemy. Under this ridiculous banner they naturally succeeded in enrolling only a few incompetents and large numbers of the culturally deprived, including some who actually could not read, and therefore had to imbibe their poetry orally in the pubs. Then the academic sneer and the academic freeze, weapons long matured and perfected in secret against helpless aspirants to the sheepskin, were deployed in public to such good effect that Messrs Corso and Ferlinghetti vanished from the scene.

Of course the position across the Atlantic is complicated to some extent by the fact that the US is and long has been – given that it operates under the profit motive – a civilised country; and one moreover in which those who support academia ask value for their and their children's time and money. For this reason the academies cannot be run as entirely closed shops, or as emporia which offer no attestations whatever as to the standards of their wares. So there grew up the custom of calling in the living representatives of a great country's literature, and putting them on show in the literature departments of universities, thereby proving that the whole thing was, to some extent anyway, for real. Thus every poet who earns his living or part of it in and around the purlieus of universities in the United States is not a parchment-holder. Nor is every parchment-holder, contrary to what you and I might sometimes be tempted to believe, a scholiast and nothing more. Mr. Richard Wilbur, is I believe, a very distinguished parchment-holder indeed, and a member of the Society of Fellows of Harvard, whatever that may be; but he is also a great poet, and it is now my pleasure to salute him as such, across the gulfs that separate us.

But the real division is not – or at least not entirely – between parchment holders and others. Nor is it, though the grapes be sometimes sour, between job holders and others. The division is between those who have so subjected themselves to the process

171

as to be incapable of responding to poetry in any other way than the process dictates and those whose response is a natural, if complex and aware response in the sphere of criticism. In the matter of creation, it is between those who are constantly aware of the demands of the process in the hours of composition and those who are not. The process likes metaphor, analogy, symbol, reference, complexities of all kinds. Given metaphor, analogy, symbol, reference, complexities of all kinds, it is happy and cares not whether the spark was ever there, or whether the poem was written out of true impulse or because the time had come to write.

The process likes to be able to go back over the thing and reveal the deliberations and calculations, like a film put into reverse to show growth. It thrives on elaborate metaphor construction which can be explained and it seems to think that once it has explained the elaborate likeness and the anagogical meaning thereby suggested, admiration must of necessity follow. (The truth of course is otherwise: a stupefying boredom may well be the result.) The process likes to trace the connection and is tireless in its surprise and wonder at mere automation. Thus, should Ossis feature in the poem, the process emits yelps of admiration when Knossis is piled on top of it. The process is never happy unless the lily is gilded. The process is overcome with delight when the poet decides to number the streaks of the tulip. The process demands analogy, convolution and mere automatic extension. The process's criticism is for the most part unreadable. What is appalling is how many unreadable poems have come into existence as a result of its demands, and how they now choke the wells.

Of course much bad poetry has always been written as a result of the demands of readers and the formulae of critics. One of the differences between the present situation and any previous one though, is that the poem of elaborate metaphorical convolution and extension is easier to fake than eighteenth century social poetry, say, was. Its effect is also, I find, somewhat more chilling: certainly more chilling than the nature whimsey of the Georgians or the social protest, often warm-hearted and open to

172

ridicule, of the English thirties. In a previous age you modelled yourself on a great poet, Pope or Auden or some other, and that perhaps took some doing. Now you model yourself, so to speak, on a method, and it is a method whose basics, born of alleged learning, can be learned.

Another difference is that those who take to the writing of such poems or the explication of them do not do so in the old weak or villainous way of minor poetasters or critics merely influenced by passing fashion. They are themselves the products of a terrible brainwashing which began at a formative age, whose basis was presumed fact, and whose primary trick was the apparent proving of a point. The critics among them are determined to impose their view on the entire corpus of poetry in English, past and present. Here is one of them, Michael Allen, on a familiar poem by Patrick Kavanagh (I know not whether Mr. Allen be a true sheepskin-holder or mere camp-follower, and of course it is no matter):

Words like "black" and "north", the depressive sound of the mundane placenames, Shancoduff, Glassdrummond, the inveterately rural and provincial ring of Armagh almost allow us to take up the vernacular perjoratative implication of "Eternally." The stanza hinges on that word, which finally retains its traditional (religious and artistic) force in association with the perpetually arrested vision of whiteness artistically heightened by a "north light", the chapel backed up by the ancient religious capital of Ireland. Somewhere behind the poem the knowledge that Armagh was once the "metropolis", the bishop's seat, is balanced against the fascination with the wicked city which ruined Lot's wife. And the concern with provincialism conditions the impeded development of openendedness of the poem. Against the mainly euphoric literary cliches of the speaker of the second verse ("They are my Alps and I have climbed the Matterhorn") is set the dour realism of the (mobile) cattle drovers.

The most important difference of all, though, is that at a moment in history when the natural audience for poetry (wherever it came from, and it came from different classes and sections in different ages) has vanished and only the manufactured audience remains, they control its manufacture

173

and its views. While the original mentors controlled things behind the closed doors of universities to which not every one went, it was no matter. But then, in the post-war era, at the precise moment when, as a reaction to war-time rhetoric and sentimentality, the natural audience for poetry had shrunk to almost nothing, every young person of the middle class and many, in England at least, of the working class began to go to university.

Those who were mildly fond of books rather than slide-rules began to take English. Critics and poets according to the new model began to swarm; and as they swarmed they emerged from academia and began to take over the columns devoted to poetry in the weeklies and monthlies. Why wouldn't they, indeed since they now composed the readership of these columns? The critics, the poets and the audience were now the products of one methodology, and it was increasingly everywhere, even in journals which officially flew other flags. The result has been, as a glance at any contemporary anthology will show, disastrous, alike for criticism and for poetry.

Of course, there was an economic basis for all this; and it is in the collapse of that economic basis that the seeds of hope are, however fearfully, to be found. There was or appeared to be, a natural connection between sheepskins and jobs. Teaching English was, or appeared to be, the natural occupation for those who were fond of books or who had felt the first stirrings of an impulse to write poetry before they went to universities and put their sensibilities at risk. But there is no longer any automatic connection between sheepskins and jobs; and, whatever your attitude to the process, nobody appears to want English teachers any more.

The number of drop-outs is accordingly increasing, and so is the number who just don't bother. These are not, however the flighty drop-outs of the sixties; rather products of that wonderful harsh law which says there is nothing in this world like having your options closed. Among them are the poets and the possible audience for poetry, assembling now, hither and yon, in small enclaves outside the gates. They are disorganised perhaps, uncertain of direction, but raising again that banner which proclaims obedience to no law but the sterner laws of the calling. Academia beware.

(1977)

DEPRIVED AT BIRTH

The word "deprivation" has ceased to be fashionable, and that is no loss. It implied a norm and naturally, it was a middle-class norm. People were deprived of the suburban house, the car or two in the garage and the opportunity to pass numberless examinations that the middle-class young rejoiced in.

Above all, of course, the latter. You might be seriously "underprivileged" in certain other ways. You might lack manners, morals, milk and mother-love. But if you had the schooling, the environment and the encouragement to swot for interminable series of examinations during the best years of your life, all would be well.

There was a fixed, perhaps divinely ordained, causative connection between the exam and the job. If you passed the exam, you got the job. If you got the job, you became middle-class. The rubbish that Professor John Kelly was in the habit of talking about the "equal opportunity" society was proved profound wisdom. Even such restlessly concerned people as Sister Stanislaus and dear Doctor Garret could sleep sound in their beds at night. Things were looking up.

What was not so often remarked on, though, even by people as immersed in the educational process as Professor Kelly, is that the examination itself is a positive act of deprivation.

To begin at the wrong end of things, it deprives many otherwise excellent teachers of the chance to display their real talents. A teacher gifted with such positive assets as imagination, sympathy and concern for the feelings of others is seldom allowed to display them. A teacher who has the marvellous ability to discern a real vocation in an obtuse-seeming individual can be guilty of dereliction of duty.

One possessed of real joy in imparting knowledge for its own sake can be a liability to the school he or she works for, and is,

176

in fact, often, treated as such.

But from the pupil's point of view the list of deprivations is practically endless. The first thing the young victim is robbed of is peace of mind, an asset that may never afterwards be recaptured, even in a long and honourable lifetime. Then there is the joy of satisfying intellectual curiosity at whim, something that has to be discouraged with sarcasm and obloquy by all who are concerned for the little ninny's advancement in after-life and, who knows, perhaps ultimate securing of the doctoral dignity or even a professorship. There is the contemplative disposition, a characteristic that should be a priceless asset to the race as well as the individual and is, it may be remarked, the only source of true religion or knowledge of identity with nature.

And there are the nearly allied capacities to day-dream and to moon, an evolutionary requisition which we discourage at our collective peril. More important, perhaps, there is a very positive diminishment of the number of subjects that can plausibly be regarded as proper to the school system at all. If you include them, you have to straitjacket them in horrible ways.

If you put Wordsworth, for example, on the curriculum, the next thing you have is somebody's opinion of Wordsworth's merits, probably Professor Augustine Martin's and this becomes the real subject of examination.

You can conceivably teach and examine at the same time in the realm of science, mathematics, languages and history, even. You cannot conceivably teach and examine at the same time in the realm of aesthetic appreciation. If you try, you drive everything out of the window.

The reason is not that art is something divorced from or elevated above ordinary life. It is that it is a matter of feeling. Whereas these other things are matters of fact. The experience of a work of art is a funny feeling inside. And you cannot examine people, least of all adolescents, on their feelings. You can examine them on Professor Augustine Martin's feelings, but not on their own, which are almost certainly different, and probably just as good.

177

This is what short-circuits much of the debate at present going on in concerned circles about the current revision of the curriculum. Quite a number of people want it revised, in favour of art, and so indeed it should be. But while the examination system lasts you cannot revise it in favour of art, without damaging what you seek to encourage.

You can revise it in favour of more drawing or painting or more essay writing. You can cheat, and revise it in favour of "art history", instead of "art appreciation", but when you try to do the latter, you kill off the feelings, which are all you have to got to go on, at source. If they had succeeded in expressing them, you could conceivably examine adolescents in the feelings of such philosophers of aesthetics as Croce or Santayanna or Lessing; that is, you could teach them to parrot emotions they do not have, as you already do in the case of Professor Martin's responses to Wordsworth, but since all of these gentlemen (lacking Professor Martin's techniques for formalisation) largely failed to get their feelings across, it seems only logical to assume that adolescents will fail likewise.

And in any case, how do you assess their feelings, supposing they do succeed in giving them verbal form?

And so not the least of the deprivations caused by the examination system is that, while it lasts, most forms of art appreciation can have no real place in the schools, and poetry (for example) only a perverted place, probably damaging to the sensibility and counter-productive of the effect intended – though, since nobody seems to know what that is, nobody can be sure.

Art in the schools should of course be like art anywhere else, a matter of the wind blowing where it listeth: plenty of opportunity to practise and, beyond that, the miracle of introduction to something magical by a teacher who can convey enthusiasm without anxiety for a rehearsed response.

The examination system effectively kills that. It is not the only thing that it kills, and it may not even matter as much as some of the others, but it kills it all the same. Of course whether the curriculum authorities know it or not, the examination system is probably doomed. Its economic *raison d'etre*, the certainty of a job, has gone as has its political one, the gloss it gave to guff about equal opportunity. And not many things in our society — except of course some forms of art — survive such losses.

(1985)

ART FOR THE PEOPLE ?

Not long ago I saw Mr Tom Paulin on television. Since I had never seen him before, in the flesh, the spirit or the image, I was interested. He was discussing a recent anthology, published by Messrs Faber and Faber, called *Hard Lines*. (For those who do not know anything at all about him, Mr Paulin is a poet, what in some quarters is called "a northern poet").

Hard Lines is an anthology of poems by young British people, most of them unemployed, many from what are known as depressed areas, which means areas that have been more or less abandoned to dereliction by the present British government. When "Hard Lines" first appeared, it made a bit of news, partly because there was an angle, which is what media people like: partly because Messrs Faber are notoriously good at the hype. It is now in process of being forgotten, but no matter. There will be other such reminders of where we are at culturally, and the reactions to this one remain interesting.

Appearing with Mr Paulin was Mr A.N.Wilson, an extreme conservative, a novelist, the biographer of Hilaire Belloc and author of the sort of book about "Why I Am a Catholic" which was popular in the 1920's, when Chesterton was a lad, but which one had wrongly assumed had vanished from the world.

Mr Wilson, being a conservative, said the poems in *Hard Lines* were terrible, that if this was proletarian culture, he wanted none of it. The pieces in the book were badly written doggerel, of no interest as poetry. They should never have been published.

Mr Paulin, being on the left, defended the publication hotly. More, he advanced claims for its contents which suggested that he had derived a great deal of pleasure and illumination (or whatever one derives from poetry) from them. A number of the pieces included, he said, were far more interesting as poetry than much that got into print through the normal cultural conduits of the society in which he lived.

Mr Wilson, unfortunately, was right. Nearly all the pieces (there are two exceptions) in *Hard Lines* are painful and embarrassing. Whether free or formal, they are simply badly written. But worse still, their authors see their own situation, like many popular song-writers, through the cliches which have come down to them from literature, "real" literature if you like, but a literature which had its own false poeticians and catch-all-catch-nothing locutions.

It is these which, by the operations of some sort of awful historical and cultural irony, have been transmitted to them, or which their own class culture has seized on. The result is that they do not really see their own situation at all, though they may of course experience it, and acutely and painfully too. And so one of the questions is, why did Mr Paulin advance such claims for them?

Some time in the 1960s the left generally became aware that Marx and Engels had said that culture was a class matter. Most of the world's art, most of the world's literature, had come into being as a result of the cultural needs of the governing classes of previous eras. Contemporary art, contemporary literature, were to a large extent expressions of cultural dominance also. Some of it was overt justification of class hegemonies or their imperialist extensions. Much of it, consciously or otherwise, expressed an "us and them" attitude.

There was surprisingly little justification of all this, nor much detailed examination of how much or how little class attitudes or assumptions permeated or affected the work of say, Virginia Woolf or William Faulkner or Henry James, or Wordsworth or Shakespeare.

But the truth that it undoubtedly contains gained hold in certain quarters and from there it was only a short step to "junk of the ages" and "do it yourself" attitudes. Oppressed groupings, not least among them women, began to attack what they saw as the high elite culture of the societies in which they lived, and to claim that they had a right to oppose it with an art which was an expression of their own situation, or even, heaven help us, of objective reality. In pursurance of this right they demanded from arts councils, subsidising bodies and the publishing apparatus a recognition of special category status.

The arguments thus begun, over-lapping and entwining (often maddeningly) as they did with other discussions about art as a collective or individual expression, art as individual solace and illuminant or art as instrument of social change, are with us still. They are the bane of many arts councils and policy-formulating bodies' lives. They have even been the commercial salvation of some publishing houses.

Therefore some propositions.

The art of the dispossessed is seldom great, precisely because it is the art of the dispossessed. Since cultural deprivation usually accompanies other kinds of deprivation, it shows in the product.

Artists are special people in their sensitivities and innate or acquired powers of expression at least, though they may not be anything to write home about humanly or morally.

All great art is liberating in some of its effects, even though it may be indifferent to these effects, or even authoritarian in intent.

Good art is concerned with de-limiting the area of choice and the area of necessity, which is something every good Marxist should know about. Much propagandist art is bad precisely because it blurs these limits, though some propagandist art, or radical art is good because it brilliantly overturns previous, societally-loaded assumptions about them.

Those who believe in the people must surely consider them worthy of the best. If the people are to have a kingdom it must be worth coming into.

It is an insult to the members of any grouping to treat them as children, whose efforts must be over-praised to ensure that they continue to make them. (It is probably an insult to children too).

The cultural starvation of large numbers of people is a tragedy for the artist who is thus forced into an even more corrupting relationship with the literate elements in society, but the remedy is not to change the mode of communication, it is to change the society.

And so back to Mr Paulin, who, as I understand him, does wish to change the society he lives in.

It seemed to me that in praising the stuff under discussion he was failing to identify and attack the effects of cultural deprivation. Of course, as has been said here before, to use a world like "deprivation" is almost to accept a bourgeois-academic norm. The effects of what is culturally wrong with our society are even more clearly to be seen in the products of the high, or elite or academic culture, in the pages of the literary weeklies and monthlies and the books issued in the ordinary way by approved publishing houses than they are in the pages of *Hard Lines*.

(1986)

THE GREAT TURN OFF

All summer the art galleries of Europe have buzzed with the sound of lecturers explaining works of pictorial art to anxious bemused audiences. As I write the process of explaining works of literary and visual art to anxious, bemused students is about to begin again in our universities.

It is all a waste of time. Nothing that can be explained about a work of art enriches or deepens its impact on anybody. The scientific basis of *pointillisme* may be interesting in itself as a piece of curious information, and relevant to Seurat's biography, but it contributes nothing to the impact of "La Baignade" or "Les Poseuses." Yeats's belief in the effect of the phases of the moon on human affairs, supposing it can be explained, which I doubt — it isn't as simple as it sounds — may be interesting as an illustration of how far the credulity of a great man can stretch, but it contributes nothing to the impact of "Ego Dominus Tuus.'

And the same applies to the endless discussions about the technique employed, whether in terms of physical constituents or aesthetic disposition. There is absolutely nothing to be gained by pointing things out.

"Notice", the lecturer says, "the triangular element in the composition, the placing of the tree in the left foreground to balance the figure on the right." But the work has already either made its impact on the senses, the central nervous system and the psyche, or it hasn't.

If it hasn't, none of this is any good. You can not recreate the effect on the central nervous system retrospectively and by rational explanation. Probably the design element has nothing to do with it anyway. If it had, great works of art could be produced by the score, simply by obeying certain rules.

"The dragging consonants of the last line slow the poem

down, producing a sensation of effort." says the professor. And so everybody looks again. Those upon whose psyche the poem has already made an impact feel nothing extra. Those whose psyches have remained untouched feel nothing at all.

And, if explanation is useless, so, almost equally, is information, the second stand-by of those who are employed to talk an effect into existence. Discussion of schools, movements, influences, dates may gratify our need for categorisation. Knowledge of these things may even give some sort of pleasure, as all knowledge does. We may be glad to have a domain of knowledge, even if we cannot call it our own. But such knowledge will not add one whit to our delight in the work itself, supposing we have felt any, nor produce delight if we have not.

We may admit minor exceptions. "Jane Avril at the Entrance of the Moulin Rouge" is the title of a Toulouse Lautrec on the Courtald Institute in London. The figure is that of an anxious, respectable woman, conventionally garbed for the winter street in gloves and cheap fur. It adds something to the impact of the picture to know that Jane Avril was a dancer, and that she performed at the Moulin Rouge, a not very respectable place. But anybody who had the slightest acquaintance with the work of Toulouse Lautrec would know this, or could be trusted to pick it up from the simplest of books about him. To make it matter for a lecture is spoon-feeding.

And other information additional to what may be contained in the work is of more dubious value. "My nerves are bad tonight, stay with me, stay with me" is a famous line from "The Wasteland." A recent biography of Eliot relates it, once again, to his personal circumstances. There may be those who feel the impact of the poem increased. Eliot himself would have denied that this could be so. And explicators are, in any case, seldom content with such direct simplicities, the necessities of their calling insisting that they should gild the lily of fact with further analysis and comment. But a vast system of explication has now grown up around works of art.

In most cases it is uncertain whether an attempt is being made to tell people what they should feel and why, or to tell them what the thing means and how the explicator knows this. If the object is delight, or what is now called in the universities art appreciation, it is doomed because no amount of explanation, whether of technique or presumed intention will produce the desired result. If the object is to add further depths to an already existing response, we are up against the doubtful proposition that works of art have any meaning outside themselves or, if so, that this meaning can be conveyed by other methods than those employed in the work itself.

Either way the effect is almost certainly opposite to the intended. The interposition between people and art of guides and interpreters, who claim more knowledge and sensitivity than they have themselves, destroys their confidence and receptivity.

It encourages them to believe that there are arcane mysteries which they are, at present, too ignorant to comprehend, arcane satisfactions which they are, at present anyway, too blind to receive.

But the relationship of people to art should be a joyous one first and foremost. And it should seem personal. It does not matter that the work will produce the same effect on a million individuals; in each case it should seem like a personal visitation and a personal joy. Of course, the second effect is the impulse to share, but it is an impulse to share delight, not knowledge, and all good criticism has something in it of the adolescent's attempt to share this original delight.

What is appalling is that the widespread destruction of response now going on should take place in the name of education, that is, of democracy. The results, in nine cases out of ten, are fear, incomprehension, boredom and resentment, even though the bored and the uncomprenhending may pass examinations, and the tenth case is only saved because he or she refused to be brow-beaten or intimidated and continues to confront the work of art with a natural camaraderie towards it and its creator. We live in a sort of desert of non-appreciation of poetry and probably painting, precisely because peoples' ordinary responses to art are being destroyed wholesale by elitist bores who pretend to extraordinary knowledge and sensitivity.

What democracy should be doing, of course, is spreading the good news, the best means of all being the dissemination of the works themselves, whether through reproduction or otherwise, without any apparatus of intimidation.

If anything further is required it should be left to those whose principal qualifications would be good prose, eloquence, the spirit of adventure and missionary zeal. To attempt to recruit along those lines of course would be to strike at the very basis of our high qualification, which is to say elitist, society.

(1984)

16 ON 16

FRANCIS STUART
(b: 1902)

I was a dreamy, uncouth fourteen year old on holiday from an English public school when the Easter 1916 Rising gave me a promise that everything I feared and hated was not going to go unchallenged forever. I knew and cared nothing for politics and came on both my father's and mother's side from a strictly Ulster Protestant tradition. My delight at the news, which was being deplored all round me, although I could not have analysed it at the time, was because it showed that authority could be flouted on a large and public scale. Till then the only reassurance I had came from accounts I read avidly in the papers of criminal activities.

It did not occur to me to ask if the rebels' cause was a right or just one. I was ready to leave the righteousness to Authority, one of whose unpleasant characteristics was to lay sole claim to it.

I was not the only enthusiast on my return to Rugby School. My closest friend, a Polish Jew called Biernacki, greeted it with the same kind of relief and hope, as might someone at the first sign of recovery at a patient's bedside. Another, who at least mentioned it (weeks had elapsed and what seemed more historic events were happening in France) was a boy named Tooth whose father had a famous gallery in London. He seemed pleased and his comment was something like "Good show!" Although only sixteen, he was in the Upper Sixth, youngest boy in the highest form, and as such rated a fag to tidy up and run errands for him. At the time this fell to my lot and, against all likelihood and school tradition, he discussed the military aspects of the rebellion with me and was, I think, somewhat disappointed at my lack of knowledge.

188

Indeed, the First World War, in which several of the boys in my house had brothers, and in which, before I left, boys I had known as seniors had been killed, did not concern me emotionally. I saw it as a clash between two dominant authorities, and whatever the outcome, it would presumably mean a more powerful and righteous Authority than before.

As though the Easter Rising had set off a chain reaction, which had been my secret hope, it was followed soon by the Russian Revolution which I judged as an even more damaging blow to the Establishment (a word I had not heard and possibly had not been coined) because of the outrage with which it was greeted by our Housemaster and the matron of the school sanatorium where I had gone for a change of scene. In those days I could conjure up symptoms of illness that kept me there for weeks at a time.

Then, three or four years later still, by when I had left my school days behind, came the Irish civil war. This I saw not so much in terms of nationalism, in which I had scant interest, but as a rejection of the new authority set up after the Treaty. A figure like Arthur Griffith embodied for me all that was most self-satisfied and distasteful in authoritarianism.

Now too, as previously, there were few a others who shared what turned out my misconceptions. We made up our minds that we were fighting to make Ireland a place fit for poets to live in, unharassed by jacks-in-office and mediocrities with ballot boxes or missals. I thought, and had from the first, of myself as a "poet", if a poete maudit, had I known the French definition.

Much later, and after several further false hopes and misinterpretations of world events, I was left with very little to pride myself on in the way of prophetic instinct. But once at least I still believe my instinctive response was a true one. Looking back, I can see that besides the challenge to the Status Quo, it was the sacrificial nature of their acts that made the leaders of the Easter Rising figures of such stature, people of one's race whose memory redeems at least some of the shame that race has brought on itself since.

If "the poet" of fourteen had not read the word of The 1916 Proclamation, his passage into maturity would have been that much more uncertain and uneasy.

MERVYN WALL
(b: 1906)

If I were asked what personal information I have about the 1916 Insurrection, I would reply as follows:

In the summer of 1915 when I was six, two boys of a family who lived opposite us on Palmerston Road, invited my elder brothers and myself to accompany them to St. Enda's where they were pupils, to recover a pair of football boots inadvertently left there when the school had closed for the summer holidays. Some distance beyond the gates of Loreto Abbey a man came towards us kicking a football along the road. "That's the Headmaster", said the elder of our friends, and they drew themselves up and walked more sedately. Pearse stopped to speak affably to them. We went on and were received at the halldoor by Willie Pearse who smilingly shook hands with each one of us. While he went searching for the football boots, we admired a small lead soldier in German uniform on the table of the reception room.

Nine months later my sister and I were playing in our backgarden when an elder brother came down the path to tell us that there was a rebellion in town and that Jacob's biscuit factory and Stephen's Green had been seized by the Volunteers. A tiny tin pistol which I had bought for a couple of pence, was impounded by my father in case some soldier saw me with it in my hand through the curtains and, mistaking the situation, fired at me in self-defence. I much resented its loss, but my father promised it back when the fighting was over. That afternoon my two brothers aged eleven and fourteen crept out of the house and into town "to see the rebellion". Getting as far as St.Stephen's Green, they peered through the railings until a uniformed Volunteer thrust his head through the bushes and stared back at them. They turned and ran.

Later in the week Army lorries disgorged scores of British tommies in Palmerston Road. A soldier was placed at the gate of every front garden. Our servants, very excited, said each

190

house was expected to give its particular soldier a cup of tea. They hastened to do so. I think this may have been in the course of a search of Joseph McDonagh's house. Joseph, a brother of Thomas McDonagh, certainly lived near us in later years. On Easter Thursday we were allowed out on to the front steps to stare at a great fire in the city. "It's Jacob's", my father said. It wasn't; it was O'Connell Street.

Years later a woman whom we employed on a daily basis to help my wife with the housework, told her that she, when a girl of sixteen, when going to work on Easter Monday, passed along St.Stephen's Green. She saw a column of British soldiers led by an officer emerging round the corner from Harcourt Street, and saw "that slut Markievicz walk right out into the middle of the road and shoot that lovely young officer dead. I seen it, Ma'am, with my own two eyes."

In 1922 when I was fourteen studying music and painting in Bonn in Germany, I was befriended by John Ryan, a Jesuit cleric who kindly undertook to give me lessons in Irish and English. Dr. Ryan became in later years Professor of Ancient Irish History in U.C.D. The Civil War was raging, and we spoke a great deal about Irish politics. He told me that in Catholic theology three conditions were necessary to justify armed rebellion against established government. There must be tyrannical oppression at the time, general agreement by the population of the need for rebellion, and there must be a reasonable hope of success. He said that none of these conditions was present in 1916, and that therefore the Insurrection could not be morally justified.

He introduced me to Myles Dillon, a fellow student of his in Bonn University, and repeated to me Myles Dillon's conviction that the 1916 Rising had been a disaster for Ireland. In this Myles was no doubt repeating the views of his father John Dillon and of the Irish Parliamentary Party. Great Britain, he said, had promised Home Rule after the War. This would have brought about a united Ireland under one government, and independence in the course of time. But the 1916 Rising had fastened partition on to the country, and divided North and South beyond all hope of unity.

PEARSE HUTCHINSON
(b: 1927)

At the foot of the altar in a church in Italy, I saw, just after Easter 1988, four tall vases filled with Easter lilies. I couldn't help thinking that was more than I'd seen in the streets of Dublin in the whole of Easter Week.

When I was growing up, and for a long time after that, the whole city was ablaze, every Easter, with those lilies. Elegant bits of oval paper, pinned to lapels. Intense green, deep orange, pure white. The coat without one was the exception.

It made the city more beautiful, it made the people more beautiful. A lovelier emblem can seldom have been invented. We wore it in honour of the brave people who went out in 1916 to fight for the freedom of Ireland. To risk their lives for that hope.

They believed that Ireland has as much right to independence as England (or Italy, or Brittany, or Catalonia). A simple belief — though now, apparently too difficult to grasp for some of "the best brains in the country" (as Fine Gael used to advertise themselves).

My father was born in Seville Place, the son of a carpenter. When he was five, the family was flooded out, my grandfather couldn't find work here. He found a job in Glasgow, where my father grew up. He became a printer, rising in due course to the dizzy height of managing director of a firm called Millar's (I asked Hugh MacDiarmid about it once, he remembered the firm well). My father was treasurer of Sinn Fein in Glasgow. During the War of Independence he was offered the choice of resigning the job or resigning from Sinn Fein — and all other pro-Irish activities. He refused to do either, was sacked, deported, interned in Frongoch, imprisoned in Mountjoy.

My mother's parents — one from near Convoy, one from near Moville — met, both aged 16, sitting on butter-boxes in the steerage of the Derry boat; both going to Glasgow, one to be a messenger-boy, the other "into service". He prospered ("a well-doin' mon"), they married. My mother was born in the

Cowcaddens ("worse than the Gorbals") before prosperity struck. She met my father in Sinn Fein.

She was a friend of Constance Markievicz, whom she always talked about as "Madam". One Sunday the two of them were collecting for Sinn Fein outside a largely Irish church in Glasgow. Mass over, the pious poured out, and put the two heretics to flight – incited thereto by the Irish-born West Briton in the pulpit. (The West Britons, the wealthy in spirit, we have always with us). Running for their lives, Constance and Cathleen Sara were hauled onto the back-platform of a tram by a big Highland conductress, who pushed them inside, urged the driver to get going, and fended off the loyalist harpies.

Cathleen and Harry took the losing side in the Civil War. So, like many another, he couldn't get work in his native city. They went back to Scotland, she went back to teaching, and kept lodgers. I was born there in 1927. When de Valera got into power in 1932, she wrote to him asking him to get my father a job in Dublin, so they could bring up their only son in "holy Catholic Ireland". Considering their sacrifices for the cause, he complied: with a job in the Labour Exchange for two pounds a week (was that good even then?). In the Forties, Harry was rewarded with a better job, in the Stationery Office, at twelve pounds a week. My mother kept lodgers, and sometimes worked on the Sweep.

Growing up, these were among the household names: Madam' Markievicz, Madam' Despard, the Honourable Albinia Broderick, Senator Margaret Pearse (who got me into St. Enda's, the last to be enrolled before it closed), Mrs. Pearse, Father Dominic, Father Albert. Those were on Mammy's lips (are there any Mammies left or are they all Mummies now? : West Britain Abu). The names Daddy kept harking back to were: Keir Hardie, Willie Gallacher, Voroshilov, Herbert Spencer, Connolly, Larkin.

Since the setting-up of the state there has been no greater tragedy than this: the sundering of separatist and socialist.

Dan Breen said on TV, not long before he died: "We got our freedom too late. We should have got it in '98."

He also said, in the same interview: "They talk about a God of mercy. No God of mercy could allow the pain I'm suffering now." He was dying of cancer.

I was forced to learn Irish at school (the Gaelic League via the Easter Rising). I was also forced to study other subjects. I liked languages, so I didn't get biffed for Irish, or English or Latin. I did get six on either hand, not with a leather but with, much worse, the leg of a chair, for not being able to sing in tune. It didn't make me hate music.

At 15, I discovered sex; at 17, booze. I rather liked both. My mother, a passionate thwarted woman, claimed to disapprove of both. This led to constant wrangles.

Brought up to be both a Republican and a Catholic, I opted out, fairly early on, of Holy Rome. (The great saint from Bergamo came too late for me). Opting out of Irish Catholic Puritanism, I, for a few years in my twenties, identified Irish Nationalism with it – a stupid and simplistic mistake (not unlike the simplified, and from the mammonite viewpoint highly convenient, version of "revisionist" history peddled at us for too long now by politicos and media-pundits).

We live in an age of euphemism, lies, misnomers: "Northern Ireland", "The Province", "Europe", "the special relationship", "the Gulf". There was even a radio lecture-series called "The Long Relationship" (frequently acrimonious). When did you last hear a "respectable" Irish politician risk the word Imperialism?

Anthony Coughlan said on the radio in 1987 that the 1916 Rising and the Proclamation "were the title-deeds of this state". I believe he was right – as were Gerry Adams and John Stalker when they spoke, in their different ways, of "unfinished business". Are Irish "liberals" against all imperialism except English? Against no murders except the I.R.A's?

The Proclamation spoke of "welfare". How many of those multi-national money-lenders, none of whom will ever die on a trolley, know what the word means?

Who stopped us wearing a beautiful emblem? Was it really the Stickies and the Pinnies? Or bourgeois shoneens?

I want to wear an Easter Lily in honour of Pearse and Connolly and all their comrades; of my father and mother and all the other sacrifices; of all the suffering generations – Black and Basque and Irish.

Perhaps when we're all "neat and clean and civilized", and misruled incurably from Brussels, room may be found in a glass-case for an Easter Lily captioned: "captured off Rockall from the last of the terrorists."

It's a lonely thing to wear a beautiful thing wronged.

ANTHONY CRONIN
(b: 1928)

When I was a victim of the educational process, 1916 seemed very remote. The new State was in full swing and the events that led to it had been so sentimentalised as to make them seem to belong to a different world. Pearse in particular had been turned into an utterly unreal and boring figure, a mother-lover who was without human frailties and, consequently, without human virtues. His writings might have corrected this impression, but they were available only in embossed editions which some people kept in glass-fronted bookcases.

However, Irish history has a way of returning on itself and 1916 seems on the whole less remote now than it did then. Hostile interpreters, anxious to prove that Pearse was a homosexual failure, so deeply in debt that rebellion was his only recourse, have done Pearse a great service; and so have paperback editions of his writings. He turns out to be a deeply interesting person who stood for a lot of unpopular things. He was for women when very few people were for them; and for children when nobody at all was. And he wrote two, admittedly rather Whitmanesque, poems which are immortal.

Of course, he has to be understood historically. All over Europe poets were in love with the idea of blood sacrifice and looked on armed conflict as a cleansing bath in which the sins of humanity would be washed away, including their own sins and complexities, whatever they were.

One supposes that 1916 was in some sense necessary. It was certainly inevitable, given that "once in every generation" etc. and that the British ruling class, having its own form of death wish, had embarked on a suicidal war. The years of nationalist and Catholic triumphalism that followed left us a craven people; but at least we were craven before our own gods.

JOHN MONTAGUE
(b: 1929)

LIVING FOR IRELAND

I disavowed 1916 in 1966, with "Patriotic Suite". Three people
helped me to that political and literary decision. Sean O Riada,
first; we were very close in the Sixties and his "Mise Eire"
arrangement I found overwhelming. But I was also suspicious of
its effect, and drafted my sequence as an answer, an antidote to
the aisling of nationalism, which I defined as "The Lure", leading
the artist astray like a marshlight. My contrast between the ideal
Ireland and the reality was dedicated to the composer, and while
no acknowledgement came from the depths of Coolea, I
gathered he was pleased, instead of being nettled, as he might
well have been by its criticism of his ethos. As far as I know, it is
the only poem dedicated to him, during his lifetime.

The second is also dead, my Tyrone lawyer brother, Turlough
Montague, who brought me to a meeting to decide a nationalist
candidate for the forthcoming elections. Feelers had been sent out
to the lads, in the hope of having an agreed name, in this Holy
Year of Irish nationalism. Unexpectedly, my freckled brother rose
to speak and I noticed that his courtroom manner was gone: he
was trembling. He said, very slowly, that while he was from a
strong Republican background, and proud of his ancestry, it was
time, perhaps, for a change in emphasis. We should forget, surely,
about all such old divisions, and strike a new note, by
campaigning in the name of Social Justice, like the people in
Dungannon. If we could break from the stranglehold of the past,
then perhaps we might ask some local Protestants of good will to
join us: they lived in Tyrone and Fermanagh as well.

There was a cold silence in the room before the senior
statesman present rose to speak, if he had ever mentally sat down.
In measured but angry tones, he informed us that he had never
expected to hear the like, that my brother was a disgrace to the
dead generations, that in this year above all, he was speaking like

197

a traitor to the ideals of 1916, a self-confessed traitor. It caused him great personal pain to hear someone of our name speak like a renegade: he hoped it was a temporary lapse. My brother took his chastisement without comment, but in the tearoom afterwards we were shunned, in a heavy, embarrassed way, although one of the Charltons of Irvinestown found it a moving speech, and said so to Turlough, and then turning to me: "You always manage to turn up when there's something buzzing: you must be proud of your brother." Remembering the phrase in the Proclamation about cherishing all the children of the nation equally, I certainly was; the brave sanity of his plea was prophetic, as well. In a few years the storm clouds would gather over Ulster as such a non-sectarian vision, or banner was raised by the marching young.

The third element in my disillusion was the response of a previously friendly editor to my text. The editor of *Studies* had broken tradition by publishing some of my early work, like "Meditations in Time of Peace" or "The Sheltered Edge", my milder response to the great Yeats meditations. He had also published Kinsella, on my insistence, and I cherished the link because, while it was a Jesuit journal, a priest editor had published the young Yeats. A Special Issue was being prepared, and while he was puzzled by "Patriotic Suite" he set it up and then, like Maunsel and Roberts on a much more important occasion, refused to print it. Meanwhile the Department of Education was offering a prize for poems on 1916, and I was determined to embarrass them with my piece. But the Reverend Editor would not return the manuscript; although he now declared that it was "putrid".

No magazine publication, no prize money, no public scandal, no new platform for our frozen semi-province in the North: all the poem had done so far was to lose my editorial link with the most serious Catholic journal in the country. Liam Miller, my bearded publishing pal, designed it as a pamphlet, linking a section of "The Rough Field" for the first time with the Derrick illustrations. Tom Kinsella in Carbondale was amused by the parody of Reidy's Band as savage woodkernes on the cover and provoked enough by the contents to produce "Nightwalker" as his, much less playful response.

One can speculate that 1916 should not have happened, but it did, and we cannot ignore it; the meaning of the adjective "terrible beauty" in the Yeats refrain has trembled all the way from "awe" to "awful". Nevertheless, it gave dignity to aspects of Irish life that one does not find in Wales, or worse, Scotland, where one can smell the defeat. Small matters, indeed, but I am glad to sport an IRL plate, glad to see my country's representatives in London, or Bruxelles. But we should live, not die for Ireland; the necrology of the hungerstrike, the blast of the timed explosive device is the opposite, a thwarted impulse turned cancerous. Living for Ireland is a complex process: at my brother's funeral: the Chief Justice of Northern Ireland arrived with an army escort, the Country Inspectors of Tyrone and Fermanagh with an R.U.C. one – the graveyard was, as they say, ringed with steel. My father may have been whirling in his grave, a few yards away, but my Victorian J.P. grandfather would have approved, the member of our family my dear brother liked least.

ULICK O'CONNOR
(b: 1929)

So many arguments today about the state of Ireland are based on the premise that the 1916 Rebellion should not have taken place: that Home Rule was on the Statute Books like the Welsh Disestablishment Bill, and that the latter had after all come into effect after the Great War.

The fact is 1916 did take place, and we have to see how it has affected us since for better or worse.

The benign face of liberal England was the one more or less accepted here, by the comfortable classes before 1914. They were the new breed who were waiting to assume the duties of the leader class in a Home Rule Ireland.

The executions after the Rebellion shocked so many, not because of their brutality (Connolly, as Monk Gibbon said, "afforded the amenity of a chair so that he could be shot sitting up") but because they disclosed an aspect of English rule which had become blurred in the wake of Gladstone, Balfour and Asquith's conciliatory approach to the Irish problem. Now people saw England in its traditional relationship with those she governed – the ruler with the lash ready for the lesser breeds if they dared growl.

By the time the prisoners were released in 1917, because of the internment and executions, a substantial section of the population had become aware of the elements underlying English rule here.

This made it possible to conduct the first urban guerrilla war in Europe against an occupying force and to back it up with flying columns in the rural areas. Without the "water for the fish to swim in" which was created by the 1916 Rebellion, the Anglo-Irish war of 1919-21 could not have taken place. In this period the forces underlying the Government of a country which ruled a quarter of the globe showed themselves in their true light. Murder, torture, and civilian massacres by Crown forces created an image that England could not sustain if she was to continue the masquerade of a great power which had recently won a world war against the forces of Evil. The Irish formula of guerrilla and rural warfare was used elsewhere as colonial administrations broke up in Algeria, Malaya, Kenya and Cyprus after the indigenous race had adapted the Irish blueprint for self-government.

The majority of the first Dail, both Treaty and anti-Treaty, when they debated the Treaty in 1922, did not see Northern Ireland as a problem; two counties were due to come in under the Boundary Commission and the remaining four were not seen as a viable entity. No one saw then that once the revolution is over the bargaining positions change. We had got what we did by force and when we renounced it no matter how admirable the reasons for doing so were, without it we were stuck where we had stopped – with twenty six counties.

There is no point in blaming now those who made the decisions then. It was a first try. The Statute of Westminster which was the charter for a Twenty-Six County Republic, changed the face of the Commonwealth, and de Valera's remarkable manoeuvres over the ports and the new Constitution were notable achievements.

But gradually as we accustomed ourselves to self-government, the twenty-six counties lost touch with what the Rebellion had done for the country. The prospect of the Common Market and the Second Economic Programme turned a frugal backward society, into a spendthrift backward society with social ambitions beyond its status. The 1916 Rising was of course played down. The rebel image didn't suit a new class, absorbed with status-seeking. The universities disgorged large quantities of them, and many because of the increased salaries available, headed for the media and found a home there. The writings of Pearse and Connolly remained unread, and as a result were easily presented by academics in an unfavourable light. Yet the intellectual testaments of both leaders had much to say to contemporary Ireland if they were properly debated. Pearse's writing on education for instance is a challenge to both the laity and Church. He had run a lay school without clergy where painting and drama were taught like history and maths. He believed in the cultivation of the individual personality in his pupils. Connolly's socialism and his writing on the control of the forces

201

of production should have been eagerly debated in a post-revolutionary society. But he was shanghied by an alleged socialist movement, many of whose most recent leaders have lost credence because having moved in on the party crying havoc to the privileged classes, they quickly acquired ministerial posts, collected their pensions and went back to their expensive residences secure from revolutions and cutbacks.

Naturally the new class growing up with their eyes fixed on the comfortable options of a consumer society were not anxious to get involved with the Northern Ireland problem. An easy optimism prevailed that once our economy improved down here the North would quickly join us. Cardinal Dalton devised an all-Ireland solution based on rejoining the Commonwealth. There was a feeling that Britain, who had fought a recent war against barbarism would somehow deliver here. Remember how James Callaghan was hailed when he greeted the people of Derry with a loud-hailer. It seemed that the granting of civil rights to all sections of the community was inevitable in Northern Ireland.

We underestimated the ferret-like grip of a colonial power. The thirteen dead at Derry and the subsequent cover-up by Lord Widgery should have prepared us for the time when a former Master of the Rolls would Uriah Heap-like wash his hands of justice, as Lord Denning did when he declared that in cases such as the Birmingham Six it was better that they should stay in jail, even if they were innocent, than that the English system of justice should be undermined by an admission of error. Stalker, Birmingham Six, Private Thain, McAnasbie, have shown the naked face of Imperialism as the executions in 1916 and the atrocities of the Black and Tans in the 1920s did. Thus at its most basic the legacy of 1916 is that it exposed the real nature of colonial rule here which the colonised themselves are often the last to recognise, until someone wakes them up to it. It showed us how England really feels about Ireland – and if we forget that we're living in a fool's paradise.

JAMES SIMMONS
(b: 1933)

The Rising of 1916 was not an event celebrated in my Derry childhood. The only public ceremony I remember was Remembrance Sunday, the wreathes of poppies, the Last Post played on a bugle, that sad harsh sound, and the sonorous recitation: "They shall not grow old as we who are left grow old. Age shall not weary them nor the years condemn. At the going down of the sun (and in the morning) we will remember them." Both world wars were part of my life. My father served in the Royal Navy, two of my uncles were in the army and one was shell-shocked at the Somme. There were khaki uniforms in a cedar chest at my grandmother's house, Elagh Hall, and old copies of *The Illustrated London News* of that time, which we browsed through on wet afternoons. None of my relations that I knew of were active in the Orange Order or the Unionist party; but my mother told us how she cried when the Union Jack was lowered from the barracks in Donegal in the Twenties, unable to imagine the locals producing an adequate army, unable to conceive that it might not matter. If Irishmen wanted to fight Hitler they would join the British army. The Second World War was very much in our minds when I was a young schoolboy, not only the news and the movies, but Derry was the port for convoy escort vessels. English and American sailors were an exciting presence in the city and many of them visited our house and came down to relax with us on holidays in Inishowen.

The notion of Ireland being, for a few years, in the vanguard as the first colony to achieve independence from The British Empire came much later. At school we learnt the history of England and of the Empire. It was only in my last years there that I found sophisticated friends who were exploring modern literature and history. The Spanish Civil War began to impinge, notions about Socialism through Auden and MacNeice and Koestler. We heard of The Depression and The New Deal and

The Health Service. MacNeice and our own observations made us patronising about political life in Ireland. We heard of gerrymandering and learnt that Stormont was a rubber stamp for English legislation. We presumed our local leaders were ignorant, puritan, possibly corrupt and not interested in the arts. Slowly we began to understand why.

Learning at that age is so haphazard. Along with a lot of rubbish I was probably responding to Rupert Brooke and James Joyce at the same time. Joyce's anti-clericalism and anti-puritanism were inspiring, but his religious guilt incomprehensible. I had precociously discerned that there was a radical compassionate figure alive in those confused New Testaments whether historical or fictional and his cheeky pacifist egalitarianism has been my spiritual centre ever since, an ideal by which to judge Churches, Empires and Ideologies. More particularly it gradually became apparent that the history of the English in Ireland was one of cruel exploitation to which one's first reaction must be, "Brits Out"; that Northern Ireland had no business to exist. However the evidence for this opinion came slowly, and with it came the confusing evidence that free Irishmen had produced a state even worse than Northern Ireland, where books and plays were banned, where there was no Health Service and where the Catholic Church had inordinate power to inhibit freedom and progress. It was in all the good writers: Joyce, O'Connor, O'Faolain, McGahern, Kavanagh. By the time I came to think of Ireland as a place to live rather than to get out of, the positive thing seemed to be that Northern Ireland should discover socialism, rather than that it should join with the even more backward South. By the time I knew something of the history of Ireland I knew that the Irish people had tried and failed. They had produced a few good writers, but were not in any vanguard.

The 1916 Rising therefore stands as a sad mistake in hindsight. If it had not taken place Irish independence might have come to seem irrelevant as it is now, or it might have taken place peacefully and democratically. The Rising led to the guerrilla campaign and all the hideous techniques of terrorism and repression, followed by a Civil War, followed by what O'Connor calls "the patriots taking their profits". We had made tremendous political progress during the 19th Century and serious political parties might have developed. So might the Trade Union movement. The Rising is the legacy of Patrick Pearse who knew as little about Christ as he knew about Cuchulain, reducing both to his own image. His hideous mixture of sentimentality and blood sacrifice informs the Provisional I.R.A., that took over when the Officials were inspired to lay down their arms, and is now trying to claim responsibility for The Civil Rights Movement it so bitterly betrayed, after so much had been won by peaceful protest. Long live The Workers Party!

Of course the Protestant/Loyalist community has little to be proud of: the brutal backlash at Burntollet, the ousting of reasonable compromisers like O'Neill and Faulkner and the various civil administrators like Tom King who only want to tie us in to a workable way of life; but, ironically enough, it makes more sense to celebrate The Battle of The Boyne or The Siege of Derry, which are historic landmarks in establishing The Reformation.

ALAN TITLEY
(b: 1947)

THE BRASS TACKS OF THE SITUATION

The pub "fatriots" of today and the last twenty not so odd years
have been fed on a diet which has included at the top of the
menu such new favourites as "Willie McBride" and "The Band
played Waltzing Matilda." Alas, poor hourlickers, you knew
them well.

The more sober among them realised full well, in good sooth,
that these were ditties that were generally against the madness of
war like most of us are against headaches and earthquakes and the
doings of the devil, if you remember him. Not as many will care
to remember the particular lunacy of World War 1, when a lot of
incredibly stupid people, fought an incredibly stupid war, and
died incredibly useless deaths, on the urgings of the lunatic
centre, in the cause of absolutely nothing.

Just for the sake of a few figures it is worth remembering that in
1916, the year we are writing about, in the battle of the Somme,
the dumbfool Germans lost more than 500,000 men while the
cretinous Allies threw 600,000 lowbrows to their fruitcake death,
give or take a few thousand mutilated and dismembered finagling
dingalings in the cause of statistical accuracy, no doubt. Even
today, throughout the uncivilised world, small groups of the
remains of that most criminal carnage come together at ugly
monuments and in unashamed churches to commemorate the
savagery and the barbarity. Even the most bottle-scarred General
windbag of those terrible times could hardly now say what they
were fighting for, although, no doubt, it was something, or other,
or whatever, wethinks.

Maybe, of course, they were fighting for Syphilisation, or was it
National Security, or The Common Good, or Our Way of Life,
or The Ould Sod, or Demockracy, or Crispianity, or Uncle
Tom's Cobblers because as we know most governments, most
places, will, when they see fit, fight any war, breach any

agreement, ban any books, (including this one), cry any wolf, sink any ship, pollute any environment, fudge any report, bribe any functionary, honour any cad, bug any headquarters, steal any documents, invent any lie, intern any dissident, gag any newspaper, juggle any figures, build any bomb, justify any horror, rewrite any history, prosecute any printer, burgle any bank, assassinate any opponent, split any hair, degrade any suspect, crooken any straight, appoint any hack, arm any spaceman, cook any goose, suffer any embarrassment, float any kite, postulate any bogeyman, crucify any prophet and roast any sacred cow if they think they can get away with it in the maintenance and the pursuit of power and gory.

Into this madness of madness the Irish revolutionaries threw their popguns. They were swiftly crushed by Maxwell's silver hammer, proving once again that violence gets you everywhere, especially if it is bigger, bloodier, and more brutal. My pocket calculator tells me that the 1916 Easter Rebellion was at least two thousand five hundred times less fatally bloody than the battle of the Somme, not to mention the rest of that year, and yet we are being prevailed upon to deplore the violence of the IRB (although most of the casualties were caused by the British), out of all context of time, place, and circumstances. As somebody whose conscience boggles before removing a daddy-long-legs from a bedroom, I crave a sense of proportion. Violence is not the issue with regard to the Easter Rising; most people support violence to the tune of billions and billions and billions of units of currency every year, they only quibble as to which violence they support, and lo and behold, it is always their own.

Our own 1916 has given us a creation story as good as any we were ever likely to get and has shown us men and women more worthy of respect as revolutionaries, poets, social philosophers, and educationalists than all the other loony tools of the running bow-wows of boorjoie adhocracy of then or now. They have given us The Good of Knowledge of Ourselves, and what else is there?

Their relevance for today is not so much in what they did – as that is done – but in their imaginative strike. Now that our lords and masters are urging us to join NATO or a European Defence

Union against the windmills of imaginative enemies, their example may show us that the stab in the back can often deflate the madness of the great. Just as my grandparents had nothing against the Austrians or the Turks in 1916 I don't have any quarrel with the Rumanians or the Estonians in 1988. If they land on Dollymount Beach I may go to greet them with my axe but until then I will hold my piece.

Pearse and Connolly and the boys tell me that it is better to light your own birthday candle than curse the eternal darkness that another World War would bring.

PHILIP CASEY
(b: 1950)

Some years ago I worked with a man, then in his sixties, who told me about the great day in 1922 when the British Civil Service marched in single file out of Dublin Castle. Dressed in Civil Servant attire of bowler hat, pinstripe suit, briefcase and brolly, they were immediately replaced by the Irish Civil Service, who marched into Dublin castle dressed in Civil Service attire of bowler hat, pinstripe suit, briefcase and brolly. Apocryphal tale or not, it sums up for this writer the meaning of Irish Independence. Less neatly but more tangibly, so does a walk from Stephen's Green through Grafton and O'Connell streets in Dublin, counting the meagre number of Irish-owned businesses.

In 1966 I was on the flat of my back in hospital, so I missed the 1916 Jubilee celebrations. The outside Ireland intruded in only two ways which I recall: I heard the boom which spelt doom for Nelson on his pillar, and the TV was switched on for Hugh Leonard's documentary drama on the Easter Rising. At sixteen, it was a stirring mixture of fire and unblemished nobility, and that was enough.

Recently and for the first time, I visited Kilmainham Gaol. There, the drama contracts to lonely, human proportions: the chapel where Plunkett married on the night prior to his execution; the haunted stillness of the yard where Connolly, in agony with his gangrenous foot, was shot.

It was very moving, but I have long come to regard 1916 as an act of monumental foolishness, however undeniably heroic and noble. I believe their putative military descendants to be even more foolish. Ostensibly struggling to unite the island, they have before their eyes the evidence of what lies before them should they succeed.

The Republic doesn't and wouldn't want them, just as it didn't and doesn't want the hundreds of thousands of its own citizens who have been forced out since the foundation of the state, including many who fought for its independence. Less than 25

209

years after 1916, hordes of young Irish were forced to brave World War 2 in Britain and beyond, while their government, elected by their betters, stood blithely by, contravening the spirit if not the letter of Article 45 of the Constitution. It didn't give a damn. It still doesn't, to the point of facilitating its citizens in their exodus (all those green cards!). If alive today, John Stuart Mill, who estimated that Ireland could support 15 million people, would be mightily puzzled by government ministers pronouncing on the lack of room in a free Republic.

I am proud to be Irish, but that pride derives from a cultural source. I believe Pearse and Connolly gave their lives for a political freedom which is of little benefit to the mass of the Irish people, its workings confined to meaningless arguments about non-issues and the clash of a few dominant personalities. Economic freedom has been tenuous and largely mythical. If it were otherwise, we would not be faced with the shame of mass migration and the subsistence of a constant third of those who stay behind. Even the Church has been lately appalled.

Noel Brown demonstrated that it could have been otherwise, but of those who have held power, he is one of the few to have had the imagination or will to do so. It should have been otherwise, all through the mortal coils of those who are now pensioners, but despite the pious rhetoric, the Easter Rebellion remains a pathetic waste of life.

NUALA Ní DHOMHNAILL
(b: 1952)

THE BLACK BOX

Back in school in 1966, during the "ri-ra" leading up to the 1916 Commemoration we were all asked to write an essay on one of the leaders of the rebellion (never revolution, mind) much to the disgust of our history teacher, who prognosticated a dire end to all the frenzy and drum-thumping. A lone voice amid a wave of enthusiasts she was drowned down, and I was subsequently to find myself on stage in the Boarders Concert hall, reading out my prize-winning essay to "maithe agus móruaisle luimní". As I gabbled through my text in acute embarrassment, valiantly trying to keep my regulation beige kneesocks, the elastics gone as usual, from falling about my feet, I realised that about the man who was purportedly the subject of my essay, Sean Mac Diarmada, I knew actually nothing. Oh the facts, gleaned from "Inniu" and various books and articles borrowed from the library, the facts were there right enough but what he really was like, what he felt, what had moved him, this had entirely eluded me. He was a dark horse. Like my grandfather.

Of course the substitution of one dark horse for another was entirely unconscious and it is only now, in hindsight, that I can trace a possible connection. All I knew about my grandfather, Padraig O Domhnaill, (Graindea) was that like most of the bright young men of his time he was somehow involved in that fracas. A Native Irish speaker from Clogane, in Co. Kerry, a spoilt priest or an escapee from the Irish College in Paris, whatever slant you want to put on it, he was known to have been seen in full Volunteer uniform drilling young men on the streets of Cork. An intelligence officer for the Volunteers and later a Sinn Fein Judge, he became so disgusted at what he saw happening around him during the Civil War that he resigned from all Movement activities and took no active part in politics ever again. About his previous activities not one word was ever spoken to any of his

211

four sons. He shut up entirely on the subject, like the proverbial clam. He led a prosaic enough life as a Timire Gaeilge and later as a school-inspector for the next thirty years. Quiet-spoken and gentle, only the odd weekend bout of drinking gave any inclination of the turmoil within. On this detail even, the reports are contradictory. If you ask my father what he was like he has only praise for him as marvellous. An uncle is not so sure. "A cranky old so-and-so" I heard him call him. After years of mystification I now think they are both right. A non-smoker, he died of lung-cancer at the age of 62, when I was less than a year old. There are members of the family who surmise that it was the inarticulated and conflicting loyalties of the two different oaths he had taken, one as an I.R.B. man for a Republic and later, following Michael Collins, for the Treaty, that had destroyed his health. Hard to say. Undoubtedly inner stress had a large part to play in it.

I was the only one of his grandchildren he ever saw. When my parents, both doctors in England, brought me home to Cork that first summer, he used to tiptoe down at night to check on me in my carrycot, muttering that these young people nowadays shouldn't have children at all, they didn't know what to do with them, imagine it, going out and leaving a child asleep in a room alone. One wonders what he whispered to me on those nocturnal prowls. He left me a whole library of children's books in Irish, which I knew no better than to scribble all over. I still remember the woodcuts with which they were illustrated; An Giolla Deacair, Bodach an Chóta Lachna, who it seems, got his head knocked off him and put on again, only the wrong way around. There seemed to be a lot of blackberries everywhere and one horrific picture had a clawlike hand coming down the chimney to steal small children. My father and most of his brothers having opted for the modern world of medicine, I must have felt obliged to shoulder the heavy but unspoken burden for Irish in the family, otherwise why have I devoted my life to mastering something that is not only unfashionable and unprofitable but downright difficult into the bargain. I wonder what else my grandfather bequeathed me.

For he was typical of the bright young men of his day, an

activist, an idealist. Reading again Sean O'Faolain's autobiography, *Vive Moi* I seem to get an inkling of what they were up to. They were creating a new legend, a new myth. They were engaged in the job that every artist does, hypothesising life, imagining themselves in it, new Adams in a new Eden. A clean slate, a tabula rasa. Not only in Ireland was this happening but right across Europe and around the world. It was somehow part of the spirit of the age. Natasha Mandelstam in her two memoirs, *Hope against Hope* and *Hope Abandoned* describes in great detail how her own generation of young Russians were engaged in the great experiment. Again it is Natasha Mandelstam who best paints a picture of what happened to those light, and blithe, idealists. Ruthlessly, in the sense of without faltering her gaze, she chronicles the horrific realities that overcame the Great Ideal, until a whole generation is drowned in ever darker and darker events. A Natasha Mandalstam is surely what is most sorely lacking in Ireland in regard to 1916. Pearse, MacDonagh, Connolly, Mac Diarmada, Plunkett and the rest, all young men cut down in their prime, have become crystalized in an eternal frieze, like stone carvings of the Sumerian Gods. They look down on all the subsequent developments of this country with the laser gaze of the immortals. Their sacrifice is the ultimate criterion to which we must rise or fall, they who never had to face the challenge of the reality of going on living, and becoming old.

By my generation the relationship with 1916 has become pathological, if not down-right psychotic. The symptoms are as plain as day. Complete denial or an acting out so stuck in its rigid appellation of the dead gods that it is nothing but re-enactment of the last twitch of rigor mortis. It is a situation curiously analagous to that of the children of people who were involved in the Nazi Holocaust, either as victims or perpetrators. (Sinn Fein judge, intelligence officer, do those words mean what I think, not what I dread them to mean?). An all-pervading sense of guilt remains, for what we cannot rightly tell. When we probe at all the reality of what it all meant, silence descends, before us like a portcullis, or we are given a snow-job of shibboleths and inanities, a sure sign of an underlying neruosis.

Because 1916 happened, whether we like it or not, and try as we will it will not go away, only sink deeper into the unconscious, personal and collective, and with its inherent energy act as magnet to all kinds of numinous forces. I still dream of a slightly built, dark officer, in full Volunteer uniform only by now he has the full murderous arsenal of modern armaments at his trigger-finger. He is on top of the roof of an imposing-looking building, directly in front of a main thoroughfare. He has started to spray the street, and me in it, with a hail of machine-gun fire, when out of the corner of my eye I see coming over the brow of a hill, a veritable Children's Crusade of young people, "Plúr na bhfear is na mban óg", with my son to the fore, and instictively I know that all my positive impulses, all my hopes and aspirations are imaged in these young people. I know that the only chance I have to prevent their destruction in the hail of machine-gun fire, is to drag myself and my wounded companions to a triangular or pyramid-shaped tower to the left which has a door in it, and to somehow leave off a warning flare. I awake in a fever, the dream still detonating inside me and lines of poetry still sticking to my hair;

Is ceaig dinamít
 ar chosa mé,
ná taidhl liom
nó pleascfad.
Tá bosca dubh
istigh im' lár
inar dhun mo mhuintir
gach a tharla.............

This black box is like the one in the crashed aeroplane, which will purportedly make sense of the wreckage. If I could only find it and open it I might have at least the consolation of knowing.

One of the many things locked up in that black box is "Eirí Amach na Cásca 1916." We must sift carefully through the wrecked "plane" of their idealism to find what was the particular time-bomb that came aboard with the luggage. Was it the murderously potent image of the sacrifice of the Son to the anger of archaic fathers, fleshed out with Christian overtones;- "Eli, Eli

214

Lamas sabachtani?" Or was it the overt death-wish that rises up from this passage by Patrick Pearse, printed in "An Macaomh" in 1910:

"Sometimes rabbits come out and gambol under the trees in the evening; and they are happy, in the foolish way of rabbits, till one of the river rats wants his supper. So day and night there is red murder in the greenwood and in the world. It is murder and death that make possible the terrible thing we call physical life. Life springs from death, life lives on death."

Until we find that particular time-bomb, and address it, it holds us all in thrall. Denied consciously it is all the more powerful unconsciously. Táimíd faoi gheasa aige; whether we know it or not, we are under its enchantment, and cannot come out and build a new myth to live by, not one which calls for the constant sacrifice of young men, and now, with Máiréid Farrell, of young women as well, but one which is rooted in the earthy concerns of living on this island, which is large enough and rich enough for all of us to inherit.

THOMAS MCCARTHY
(b: 1954)

"I teasingly reminded my 10 year old daughter that having been born in Co. Kilkenny she could have an Irish passport someday, if she wanted. "Never," she declared instantly. "I don't want everybody to think I'm a terrorist." Max Hastings, *Daily Telegraph* 22 August 1988

"I have been told the time is up, and I will therefore say that I am in no way despondent about the future of our country. I believe our sun is but risen, when others are setting. That is the attitude we should adopt about our affairs." Eamon de Valera, Dail Eireann, 17 July 1958

Poets are obsessive creatures constantly looking at facts through poem-coloured glasses, therefore they make bad politicians and even worse historians. Even Yeats, our national poet and master-witness, has created an unreliable body of history. Take the poem "Easter 1916", for example. At the Yeats Summer School in 1986 the poet Tom Paulin said that the feelings described by Yeats in his poem "were alive and well and living in the Democratic Unionist Party." But Conor Cruise O'Brien said "It is now part of the I.R.A. and I have heard Republican sympathisers say it in and out of the Dail." (*Irish Times*, 23-8-86). Yet it is the very ambiguity of poetry that makes it important: a poem constantly reaches for the other side of the argument, for complete humanity. Where political interests are concerned writers should always make sure that they are either parasitic or treasonable. To transcend politics is everything – Connolly's *Labour in Irish History* and Erskine Childers' *Riddle of the Sands* will survive all changes in political perspective.

Therefore when I think of the Easter Rising I do not think of it in terms of my imagination and the creation of poems; rather I think of it constantly vis-a-vis Dail Eireann and my Irish citizenship. The Rising was that momentous event which released the distinctiveness of my people and brought us true citizenship. It is comparable to the American Declaration of Independence. The I.R.A. of 1916 was the Army of the Dail as

216

Washington's Continental Army was the Army of the new Congress. There is no reason why people should confuse the current Provos with the first Irish Army of the Dail. No revisionist historian will usurp my sense of belonging to, and my pride in, that first full expression of distinctively Irish power. Once de Valera entered the Dail in the late Twenties the victory of Sinn Fein was complete: over five years before that event, de Valera had warned Liam Lynch that the Irregulars would have to choose political action. The Provo campaign of the present day, the near-genocidal war against poor Protestants in Fermanagh and Tyrone, breaks my heart. They have forgotten the words of Connolly "Ireland, as distinct from her people, is nothing to me." Coming from a Fianna Fail background I know the intimate details of the bigotry and repression of the old Stormont regime, I know the Ulster Catholic yearning for Irish Unity. Ulster Catholics are our Quebecoise and need the legitimate protection of the Dail. But even as early as the Treaty Negotiations the Republicans told Lloyd George that Irish Unity could not be created by force – because to use violence against Ulster Protestants would be to repeat the mistake that Britain had made with Irish Nationalism.

If poetry teaches us anything it is that peace is the right condition and proper destiny of all Irishmen, and peace we will have eventually when politicians are left with no other option. The making of poems teaches me that every conflict contains the seed of its own resolution. Only the conservative are pessimistic. Revisionist historians like to blame our Nationalist victory of 1916 for the current terrorism in Ulster; that is rubbish. Since the foundation of our State the Irish people have been passionately loyal to its institutions. But we must be generous in our politics, inclusive and slow to use the word "terrorist". Words can often leave people out in the cold. The success of our Irish state proves that we can be as obsessive and pig-headed as we like in literature. But politics is something else. As Sean Lemass wrote in An Poblacht in 1926 "We must forget all the petty conceits and formulae which bedeck us, like rouge on the face of a corpse."

FERDIA Mac ANNA
(b: 1955)

I was eleven when I met Padraig Pearse. He was tall, skinny and slightly confused. He wore a flabby green uniform, two gun-belts and a wide-rimmed khaki hat that made him look like an Irish Pancho Villa.

This Pearse didn't come across as the kind of guy who could lead the Irish Nation to freedom. He didn't look as though he'd be much use to the Mexicans either.

But when the spotlights came on, and the imitation Padraig Pearse strolled out into the centre of Croke Park, he inspired just as much turmoil and bloodshed in the name of Mother Ireland as did the original. The difference was that these heroics were part of "Aiseiri", the special Gloirreim Celebrations of 1966. It was only make-believe.

A bunch from my school were chosen as extras for the crowd scenes. Most were picked because they acted in the school plays. Others because they lived near Croke Park. I got the gig because my father was directing the pageant.

After an hour of rehearsals, some of us were singled out for more important tasks. I was promoted to letter-carrier. My job was to walk on at the end holding up a massive plastic letter E. This formed the final letter of the word Eire, the visual centrepiece of the closing celebrations of the birth of the new republic spawned by the Rising.

It was a massive production. The entire Irish army seemed to have been divided up as Insurrectionists, British army and civilians. The civilians got the worst of it. Every time there was a riot scene the soldiers charged the crowd and chased them out of the stadium. For some reason, the audience always cheered whenever the civilians got it.

Some of the soldiers used the battle scenes to settle a few old scores. People said there were more casualties in the dressing-rooms after each show than during the whole of 1916.

It should have been a humdinger. There was action, spectacle, colour, excitement and schmaltz – everything you could possibly ask for in a decent epic.

But the four-night run coincided with the worst storm to hit Dublin for decades. Speeches were distorted. Actors were blown off their feet. Props ended up in the stands.

One night a gust of wind totally demolished a British armoured car. It was hard for an army to maintain credibility when its heavy artillery was floating somewhere over Hill 16.

On the third night, the wind snapped off the bottom half of my letter. From the stands, it appeared that the glorious, heroic Blood Sacrifice of 1916 had culminated in the birth of the republic of "EIRF". Diehard nationalists must have been mortified.

RTE also chose that week to show "Insurrection", their rival big-budget account of the 1916 Rising. Modern technology now brought Padraig Pearse into the living rooms of the people of Ireland. Croke Park in the middle of the hurricane season was no competition.

Because of the freak weather, "Aiseiri; Gloirreim Na Cásca" drew poor crowds for the first two nights. Insurrectionists sometimes outnumbered the audience by three to one.

But the show received a lot of acclaim and finished its run to full houses. The production was deemed an artistic triumph, which meant that it lost a packet.

As far as we were concerned, the only important thing was that the letter-carriers be paid. We made representations to management. There were some frank discussions.

At one stage there was talk of a strike: there would be no new nation at the end of the show, we warned, unless financial terms were agreed.

Eventually, we we were instructed to wait until the last night. Each letter-carrier would then receive a special surprise, we were told.

On the final night everyone was handed a brown envelope with a newly-minted limited-edition souvenir ten-shilling piece inside. One side of the silver coin showed Pearse's profile, the other featured an illustration of An Cliamh Solas (The Sword of Light). It wasn't exactly what we had in mind.

But the real surprise was that we couldn't spend it. The coin would be extremely important many years from now, people told us. We'd appreciate it when we were grown up. We would show it to our grandchildren. "Bolix to my grandchildren", one boy said, "I want to go and buy things."

None of the adults would listen. The way they looked at it, we had been paid for our labour with coins of inestimable historical and social significance. We were told that Pearse himself would have approved. That was the start of my disillusionment with Pearse.

The final night's party was the scene of much intense coin-dealing. Some of the letter-carriers sold their Pearse coins to disgruntled adults at half-price and went off to buy cokes and sweets. A half-cut sergeant bought one for a pound. It was the bargain of the century he boasted; his grandchildren would know where he had been during Easter 66.

But I held onto mine. I felt guilty because of all the school lectures I remembered about the suffering and sacrifice of the martyrs of 1916.

Afterwards, my mother informed me that we were related to Sean Mac Diarmada, one of the original signatories of the 1916 Proclamation. Now, it would be blasphemous to spend the ten-bob bit. The coin was more than a souvenir, it was a symbol of nationhood.

For weeks, I kept the coin in a small plastic pouch in a matchbox in my pocket, as you would a pet mouse.

At school, I showed it to my friends. Some were impressed. A few were jealous. All laughed when they found out I wasn't allowed to spend it.

Being related to Sean Mac Diarmada was no big deal either, I found. One of the guys in my class boasted that his mother was a daughter of James Connolly and his father a brother-in-law of Pearse himself. Mac Diarmada was smallfry, he said.

That lunchtime, I fought my classmate until both of us were bleeding. The feud continued each break for a week. Finally a christian brother put a halt to it. Then the brother beat us black and blue for fighting in the yard.

Gradually, the power of the special coin waned. Pearse just didn't seem that important anymore. Most kids I knew were far more interested in the next Manchester United game, or the latest from The Beatles, or who had the biggest collection of 64-page comics. Nobody seemed to give two hoots about the 1916 Rising.

Besides, we reckoned that anyone the christian brothers liked must be a wimp.

One day, I walked into the shop around the corner from the school and swapped my 1916 special souvenir Padraig Pearse coin for ten 64-page comics, that week's editions of the Victor and the Valiant, a box of aero chocolate bars and a plastic German paratrooper's helmet.

For years afterwards, I felt like a traitor.

Note: "Aiseiri; Gloirreim na Cásca" ran for four nights at Croke Park during the Easter celebrations of 1966. Frank Grimes played the part of the young Padraig Pearse. Ray MacAnally played Pearse the Revolutionary Leader. The production cost over seventy two thousand pounds. The special commemorative ten-shilling coin is still available from certain coin-shops and dealers.

ANNE HAVERTY
(b: 1956)

A woman used to come out from town to our village on Saturday afternoons to teach the children Irish dancing. My father was very keen for us to attend. He probably had fond imaginings of an array of gold and silver medals on the sideboard won by his daughters in Feis Ceoils up and down the country. But my sisters and I were hopeless Irish dancers. The classes were held in the schoolhouse, a place we deeply resented having to go to on a Saturday, and we were made bored and abject by watching the star pupils progress to the hornpipe while we remained at the three-hand reel. Our special shoes with silver buckles on the front were little consolation. We would have much preferred it if a skating-rink had appeared in the village or someone to teach ballet, which were the cultural activities we read about in our beloved English comics.

That I experienced no sense of shame at my lack of enthusiasm for this expression of national identity, I feel I owe to the men and women of 1916. It was they who liberated us from nationalism with all its psychological and intellectual limitations. My boredom with Irish dancing, my preference for reading English instead of Irish was not a betrayal. There was no longer any side to betray. An earlier generation would have considered such preferences a form of shoneenism. The word shoneen no longer existed.

1916 made us Irish, lifting from our shoulders the burden of self-definition, of constant self-assertion. We are the achieved people, unlikely though we may seem. Of course we are not as they would have liked us to be. We don't speak Irish or dance at the crossroads and we have embraced foreign cultures and foreign things and foreign money with open arms. Being people of their time, what they wanted for us was conditioned by their experience, not ours.

But we do now possess freedom, which was what they fought

222

for. And if we interpret this as the freedom to be Irish in whatever way we want, and reject what they might have wanted, this is what freedom is. They made it possible for us to be everyday citizens of the world rather than inferior citizens of an empire. They walked us out of the obscurity of the celtic twilight into the light of common day which, if clean and true, is also banal and, being Irish, gloomy. They gave us reality. It is not the reality they wanted nor the one we might imagine, most of us, but they were the travellers, starry-eyed and hopeful, and we are the ones who have arrived. It is the common experience of the generations.

The men and women of 1916 were no doubt, often tedious in their fanaticism and their earnestness and their single-mindedness. But they liberated us from the tedium, anxieties and the absurdities of aspiring nationalism.

FINTAN O'TOOLE
(b: 1958)

1916: THE FAILURE OF FAILURE

For quite a while, I confused the Seven Leaders with the Magnificent Seven. In the same school hall where we recited I See His Blood Upon the Rose and The Mother, where we waved tricolours in thanksgiving for the fiftieth anniversary of the Easter Rising, the Brothers, for some reason, gave us a showing of The Magnificent Seven. We crunched our crisps in time to the gunfire and, when the good guys fell in the dust, brushed away incipient tears with toffee-apple fingers. The number seven, the nineteenth century rifles, the barricades, the cowboy hats that the rebels wore, above all the quiet, dark leader, pure and brave, willing to sacrifice himself for the humble, cowering peasants, all contributed to the intermingling of images. Yul Pearse and Patrick Brynner became one.

There were, however, two disquieting elements in the parallel. One was that in the movie, one of the seven made a speech to a little boy, telling him that heroism was not the preserve of gunmen, that courage was manifest more in the daily struggle to survive and raise children than it was in showy violence. That disturbed me. And the other was that The Magnificent Seven won. Theirs, at the end was the equivocal failure of success, not the triumph of failure. Not for them the casuistry of Pearse at his court martial: "We seem to have lost. We have not lost. To refuse to fight would have been to lose; to fight is to win. We have kept faith with the past, and handed on a tradition to the future." But when the school football team went to Croke Park to play in a final and lost, we knew that to lose is to lose. There is no glory in defeat, only bitterness.

And yet, Pearse's claim to have kept faith with the past had, in that year of 1966, its own truth. The images of 1916 were renewed and refashioned for a new generation just at the time when they had finally lost all reality. 1966 was the year when the last Taoiseach of the revolutionary generation, Sean Lemass, retired. It was the year when the living embodiment of 1916, Eamon de Valera, came dangerously close to the humiliation of defeat in the presidential election. It was, above all, the year of Cornelscourt Shopping Centre, of Ballymun Flats, of Brendan Bowyer and the Royal Showband, of the Bishop and the Nightie, of a 15 per cent increase in the number of Irish people taking continental holidays. It was the year the census showed the number of young people in Ireland to have risen by a shocking 25 per cent. It was the year when 1916 needed to be divorced from all reality and turned into a movie, a movie that would run forever in the minds of a new generation in a new country and keep them loyal to the past.

And, in truth, the notion that failures would miraculously transform themselves into triumphs was one that we were more than ready for. Our parents had been fed on failures – the failure to provide work, the failure to find freedom, the failure to cherish the children of the nation. Now all of this was to be transformed into success, just as the failure of 1916 had somehow stirred the reawakening of the people and brought us to our historic destiny. Now the proclamation of the republic of prosperity had been read, the flag of poverty lowered at sunset. The phoenix of defeat was rising and we were not to know then that it would soon return to dust and ashes. We were not to know either, because we were not told, that 1916 had relatively little to do with the upsurge that led to the foundation of the state. We were not to know that it was a mass democratic campaign against involvement in a brutal war, the anti-conscription campaign of 1917, rather than the 1916 executions, the refusal to die rather than the glory of death, which was decisive in causing change. Protests, demonstrations, mass movements, above all successful mass movements, were not the sort of thing to be encouraged or held up as examples. Heroic defeat was less dangerous than successful organization.

1916 inured us to failure, befuddled us so that we don't know the difference between an inept tragedy of errors and a solid achievement. It has given us a theatrical masochism, content with suffering so long as the gestures and symbols of defiance are right.

Itself an acceptance of failure, an attempt to make failure glorious and memorable, rather than a serious assault on success, 1916 was turned, in 1966, into an image which would convince us that our losses and defeats would be rewarded in the heaven of economic expansion. And again, in the eighties, we are told that suffering is good for us, that the more losses we can absorb now, the more will be our reward in the future.

In his poem *The Mother,* Patrick Pearse identifies his mother with the Blessed Virgin, himself, by implication, with Christ. At his moment of defeat he transforms himself into a god, holding up his wounds like the stigmata of a crucified Christ, turning Jim Larkin's shout of anger "You'll crucify Christ in this town no longer" into a self-pitying apotheosis of defeat. It is a shrine we have prayed at for too long. If Pearse is Christ, give us Barabbas.

MICHAEL O'LOUGHLIN
(b: 1958)

It is, I believe, almost impossible for any one of my generation to think about 1916 as an actual event in History, discrete and autonomous. The way in which 1916 had been presented to us was an important process in our understanding of the nature of our society, and of ourselves. For my generation, the events of Easter 1966 were crucial, so much so that I think it is almost possible to speak of a generation of '66.

People from that generation tend to share a number of characteristics. An almost total alienation from the state, a cynicism with regard to the national institutions and political life which is analogous to the situation in a country like Poland; an unspoken assumption, that everything emanating from official sources is a total lie. 1916 has been the vehicle, if not the cause of this. In 1966 I was 8 years old, and I remember vaguely the hullabaloo that surrounded it. My strongest memory is of the TV drama, Insurrection. To what extent I absorbed the myth of 1916 and the Irish republic I don't know. But it certainly made an impression.

However, by 1969-70 the North had begun. In my school, and in other schools, and on the media, republican emotions, if not republican principles, were openly encouraged. Nowadays, when I talk to people of my own age group, we sometimes wonder if we are not suffering from some kind of collective hallucination. Can it really be true that in school we were handed out bulletins detailing the atrocities committed by British soldiers in Belfast? Did we really get a half day from school the day Stormont finally fell?

What was coming from Northern Ireland was republicanism with a vengeance. The South's political lies were finally catching up with it. One of these, was that 1916 was the culmination of the 700 year struggle for an "Irish Republic". This lie, comfortably shared by Fianna Fail and the Provos, eventually became too embarrassing. In an act of astonishing political opportunism, 1916 was revised. By 1976, and the 60th celebrations, a different tune was being played. For people of my generation, who were and are, in an important sense, neither republican nor non-republican, this was a lesson they would never forget. To see history so swiftly re-written was to realise that what was called history was in fact a facade behind which politicians manoeuvred for power. It was not that Fianna Fail was republican which offended, it was the fact they were only pretending to be. This lesson was to be seen elsewhere, in for example, the official promotion of the Irish language, while in reality the government was doing its best to destroy it, by neglecting to build an economic infrastructure in the Gaeltacht areas. The new school of Irish historians played their part in exposing all this, and their books, rather than any novels or poetry, are the essential texts of those years. This I suppose was a necessary phase.

But now that 1966 and '76 have cancelled each other out, and generations are growing up who have no other experience of Irish history than the revisionist one, it may be possible to reassess. Like others who were brought up to believe that history is debunking, I am beginning to realise that there may well be something in all that bunk, that maybe countries do need to have a pantheon before they abandon them. But that is another story. As for the 1916 leaders as poets: much has been written about the curious intertextual quality of 1916: poets living out their poems, binding their lives to their poems in a Mephistophelean pact, then popping up in the texts by other poets or rather, poet. But we can see from numerous examples in other cultures, this experiencing of one's country in textual terms is really only possible when that country does not yet exist. For those born after 1922, the poetry has to be found in the semi-state body. Besides, I have been much too conditioned to seeing their work as a pretext to view this with any kind of detatchment.

KATIE DONOVAN
(b: 1962)

THE DYING HERO AND THE GODDESS

When I think of 1916 it is the poets and visionaries who spring instantly to mind. The most obvious of these devotees of myth and abstract causes is Padraig Pearse. His mystic convictions took their root in the figures of Christ and Cuchulainn, whom he saw as heroes dying in a gesture of self-sacrifice to save their people. The wonder of Pearse is that he, and others who had paved the way such as Standish O'Grady and Yeats, could infect so many followers with the same idealistic fervour. Even the sensible and pragmatic James Connolly went out on the morning of the Rising saying calmly: "We are going out to be slaughtered."

Another important feature of 1916 for me is the prevalent imagery of Ireland at that time as a demanding mother who expects her sons to give their lives so that she can be free. Yeats fleshed out this image in his play Kathleen Ni Houlihan. Ireland, as personified by an old woman, is suddenly revitalised when she manages to recruit a young man to join her cause. Kathleen (the woman) lures him with enigmatic rhetoric and songs about dying heroes to join the ranks of the rebels. He follows Kathleen rather than staying behind to marry his pretty and wealthy sweetheart. As Kathleen leaves the house triumphantly, with the young man behind her, she is transformed into a girl with "the walk of a queen".

Though not intended by Yeats, the more sinister implication here is that Ireland is a vampire, drawing men from their ordinary loves and joys to the fatal attraction of the role of freedom fighter. Kathleen accepts no half-measures: "If any one would give me help he must give me himself, he must give me all."

Pearse's Old Woman of Beare is another Kathleen Ni Houlihan, while his frequent allusion to the necessity of a blood sacrifice and his personification of Ireland as a mother who demands this of her sons is enshrined in the Proclamation itself:

229

"In the name of God and of the dead generations from which she receives her old tradition of nationhood, Ireland, through us, summons her children to her flag and strikes for her freedom...In this supreme hour the Irish nation must, by its valour and discipline, and by the readiness of its children to sacrifice themselves for the common good..."

The overtones here are religious, in that the notion of inevitable self-sacrifice is paramount, yet the underlying motif of the mother/goddess goes back to pagan times. Then the earth goddess was appeased by the annual slaughter of a young man. His blood was believed to be necessary to facilitate a fruitful harvest. Seamus Heaney draws on these images for his poetry in *North*. Like Pearse and Yeats, Heaney personifies the nationalist cause as a powerful female figure, this time in connection with present day guerrilla fighters for a united Ireland in the North. Poems such as "Kinship" revive the vision of Mother Ireland as some primitive goddess incarnate in the bogland of Ireland. She is a figure who is both awe-inspiring and sinister, the source of life yet still greedy for "the blood/of her faithful":

Insatiable bride./ Sword-swallower,/ casket, midden,/ floe of history
...I stand at the edge of centuries/ facing a goddess
...Our mother ground/ is sour with the blood of/ her faithful
....how the goddess swallows/ our love and terror.

The final implication here is that the psychological impact of this ancient mythic mother's demands continues to hold sway over the nationalist consciousness even today.

Other Irish writers who were contemporaries of Pearse and Yeats relate to the motif of the dying hero and the goddess in different ways. Synge had little time for heroes and goddesses in Irish theatre: "I do not believe in the possibility of a purely fantastic, unmodern, ideal, breezy springdayish, Cuchulainnoid National Theatre..." His Christy Mahon is the antithesis of a mythic hero, being cowardly, selfish and singularly lacking in expertise of any kind. His Pegeen Mike, though stubborn and sharp-tongued, is hardly a powerful goddess, and ultimately she cannot persuade her "hero" to sacrifice himself for her changing whims.

230

Though closely involved with the nationalist movement, O'Casey also preferred to steer clear of "Cuchulainnoid" theatre. Like Synge, his male protagonists, such as Captain Boyle and Donal Davoren, are cowardly chancers whose first concern is their own personal safety. O'Casey's women, like those of Synge, are passionate and strong, but hardly untainted by human weakness either. The reality of the women's powerlessness in the world made and inhabited by their drunken posturing men is eloquently rendered by both playwrights. In Act 2 of *The Plough and the Stars*, Rosie, Bessie Burgess and Jinnie Gogan are literally sandwiched between the inflated rhetoric of Pearse and the inebriated catchphrases of the barflies. While the men tell each other how Pearse's speech has made their blood boil with excitement, it is the hot tempered women who actually have a fight. The men feel less enthusiastic when they are confronted with the reality of a fight.

Though hardly realistic dramatists, Synge and O'Casey wrote about Irish people in a way which did not try to elevate them beyond their human quirks. The often irresistible comic figures which emerge effectively debunk the Celtic Twilight penchant for heroes who will lay down their life for the cause. Nevertheless, the rhetoric of the dying hero and the goddess as employed by Pearse, and to a lesser extent, Yeats, persuaded a great deal of ordinary Dubliners like O'Casey's Fluther Good to give up their lives for the vision of an independent Ireland. Yeats was to ask himself after the Rising: "Did that play of mine send out /Certain men the English shot?" Pearse was never an onlooker; he had no doubts about the fate to which he led his followers, and certainly no misgivings. He saw himself and his men bathed in the fame and glory of heroes dying in the service of the goddess:

"Such is the high and sorrowful destiny of the heroes: to turn their backs to the pleasant paths and their faces to the hard paths, to blind their eyes to the fair things in life...and to follow only the far faint call that leads them into the battle or to the harder death at the foot of a gibbet."

TWO HURLERS ON A DITCH

Edward Mulhall

I stood with the editor of *The Irish Times* outside Donnybrook
Church at Breandán Ó hEithir's funeral. The talk was of
elections. We discussed briefly our own small parts in the
enfolding drama: *The Irish Times* and the Duffy tapes, the
interview with Lenihan on the Six-One news (of which I was an
editor), what it was like being on the other side of a breaking
story, the scene as Brian Lenihan and Bertie Ahearn listened to
the Duffy tape for the first time before going on with Sean
Duignan. But mainly the talk was of that evening's confidence
vote in the Dail, the PDs and the price of their support. On the
fringes of the crowd, which included poets, writers, broadcasters,
politicians and the plain people of Aran and Dundrum, was Máire
Geoghegan-Quinn who had had the "serenity to accept that
which we cannot change" on the formation of the FF/PD
coalition. PD Minister Bobby Molloy had just left for what
turned out to be a crucial meeting with the Taoiseach. On one
thing we were all agreed, Breandan would have loved the
occasion. He would have been on top of the latest gossip, with
detailed accounts of who rang who, who said what to which
soldier, and who drove where in 1982. He would have relished
the ironies of Bobby "Iosagán" Molloy with the Aran Fianna Fail
vote pushing Haughey, Lenihan and the Party to the limits of
their loyalty to avoid a General Election.

Within hours the drama had reached its climax. On that
evening's Six-One RTE political correspondent Donal Kelly
broke in with the dramatic news that having failed to get Brian
Lenihan to resign the Taoiseach had sacked his long-time friend
and colleague. There followed a specially prepared retrospective
on Lenihan's ministerial career: black and white shots of him in

the 60s with Minister for Education Donogh O'Malley, uncle of the PD leader who inherited his seat, Lenihan electioneering in the fields of Roscommon, more recent pictures of him with Haughey on his becoming Tainiste, and his celebrated return to an Ard-Fheis after his illness to introduce the leader's speech. The Six-One ended with the recording of the Taoiseach's announcement to the Dail: "Brian Lenihan had been a friend, a loyal and trusted colleague with whom I have served for over quarter of a century...what I have to do, I do with great sadness and great sorrow."

That "quarter of a century" was recalled by John Healy, in one of his last major articles for a national newspaper on the next day. It was Healy who had christened Molloy "Iosagán" when he was first made a minister by Jack Lynch in the Arms Crisis period, and Healy who had dubbed Haughey, Lenihan and Donogh O'Malley "The Three Musketeers". The era of the three Musketeers was also Healy's era and he was their chronicler, often from the inside. It was now at an end. As he wrote he refused to write Lenihan's political obituary as he had refused to write Haughey's during the crises of the 80s. Yet, "We have known better weeks, better times. Brian Lenihan knew better weeks, better times. They were the days of the Three Musketeers...who, backed by Lemass, got into the business of Nation-shaping, pulling Ireland out of the morass of De Valera and coalition tit for tat politics...Now Donagh is dead, Brian has resigned, and Charlie is left alone to carry on the vision of Ireland which Sean Lemass started and for which he created and used the Three Musketeers." (*Irish Independent*, 1/11/90).

Not long afterwards Healy was dead and the now divided Lenihan and Haughey would be photographed at his funeral, exchanging pleasantries with the new President Mary Robinson in the background. On the day of the funeral a group of friends gathered in a radio studio to pay tribute – Sean Duignan, Douglas Gageby, Ted Nealon, Tom O'Dea and John Waters. They talked of Healy the broadcaster breaking new ground with *Hurler On The Ditch* in the early 60s, Healy the editor of the *Evening Mail*, *Sunday Review* and *Western Journal*, Healy the writer of books like *Nineteen Acres* and *No One Shouted Stop*, but principally of Healy the reporter, and his insider's view of politics.

The deaths of Breandán Ó hEithir and John Healy within a few weeks of each other robbed Irish journalism and Irish writing of two of its major figures. It also robbed Irish political life of two of its most astute and incisive commentators. They were great reporters and yet more than just reporters. In their writing they gave a unique insight into the essence of the Irish character, and an understanding of Irish political culture that has defied many critics and not surfaced in much of contemporary Irish fiction. I bracket them together, not just because of the coincidence of their deaths and the fact that their journalistic careers spanned a similar time and range (the 50s to the 90s and reporting with the *Irish Press* to commentating in the *Irish Times*), but in taking them together, with their differences as well as their similarities, you get a picture of Irish political life from the inside and the outside. Both, incidentally, would have objected to such a linkage. Ó hEithir was often quite vicious in his criticism of Healy and his relationship with the Three Musketeers: "My description of that was that John Healy was very clever to lick his own arse with Charlie Haughey's tongue...what Healy did was write about Healy and Haughey kinda moved through the story." (Interview with David McKenna, *In Dublin*). Healy on the other hand would not have had much time for Ó hEithir's radicalism, his interest in Eastern Europe, his views on the North or his cynicism. But, above all, both were straight men who wouldn't put a tooth in it when it came to expressing what they believed and would have been well able to fight their own corner.

By taking them together we can begin to unlock certain of the enigmas of Irish political life. Take Charles Haughey and Fianna Fail for example. Healy has always understood and admired Haughey, seeing him as the inheritor of the Lemass/O'Malley mantle and sticking with him through the trials and tribulations of the various crises. Similarly Ó hEithir while being closer to the old-style radicalism of early Fianna Fail than the mohair suit brigade, understood the deep-rooted nature of core Fianna Fail support. A support that in defiance of the analysts and pundits has remained statistically loyal throughout this whole period, and a party loyalty that had more to do with family tradition and cross-party antagonism than wider issues or units of socio-economic measurement.

Along with the wider issues of Irish political life both Healy and Ó hEithir reflected on the importance of the GAA in Irish political culture. It was typical of Ó hEithir's interest in the GAA that his book on the games, *Over The Bar*, is the closest he came to autobiography. Appropriate too that the film used on the 9 o'clock news to announce Healy's sudden death showed the Hurler on the Ditch kicking football in Charlestown on his return to film the TV programme *My Own Place*. Their GAA is not just one of sporting endeavour but one of debate and argument, of friction and conflict, of loyalty and enmity, of stories and characters, much as politics was.

It was summed up for Ó hEithir in *Over The Bar* by the story of Bill Doonan heading for Monte Casino. He was a traveller from Cavan and a good footballer. He joined the army but itched for real action so when the second World War started he deserted, crossed the border and joined the British Army: "In the Autumn of 1943 the war in Southern Italy raged and Bill Doonan was a radio operator with his unit. One Sunday afternoon in September he was no longer to be seen... A search was mounted and they found him at last. Even when they did they found it difficult to attract his attention. He was up a tree on the side of a steep hill and seemed to be in a trance. And in a way he was, for after much effort and experimentation, Private Doonan had eventually homed in on the commentary of the second half of the All Ireland football final between Roscommon and Cavan from Croke Park... If anyone asks you what the GAA is about just think of Bill Doonan, the wanderer on the side of that hill, in the middle of a World War... at home."

On the North Ó hEithir railed against the revisionists who would write the violence out of Irish history by pretending it didn't happen. Healy railed against the verbalisers on both sides of the border – "For 70 years... just as in the South... you did not need to have political policies and elaborate political programmes so long as you could motivate the followers with the slogan *Up Dev*, so the Unionists relied on *No Surrender*. You were in business." (*Irish Times* 16/11/85)

They had similar positions on the urban-rural divide. Both Westerners with a strong allegiance to their home patch they rejected the traditional eulogising of the land and the farmer. Although Healy has written with great eloquence of the small farmer in *Nineteen Acres*, the story is of the struggle of the past, of land lost. Healy was essentially a townie and he draws clear lines between urban and rural Ireland in the middle of rural Ireland. This truth belies the simplistic division between Dublin and The Rest, for many of the urban dwellers in so-called rural Ireland have more in common with their countrymen in suburban Dublin than with those living outside the town on farms a few miles down the road. This Ireland, not urban in the Behan sense, and not rural in the Kavanagh/Heaney sense, has been written out of much contemporary Irish literature.

Ó hEithir was a notable contributor to Radio na Gaeltachta, as reviewer, interviewer and panelist. He was a great champion of the station, recognising its power as a local station connecting the people of the Gaeltacht and providing a lively forum for political debate, where at election time the sharpness of the local rivalries made the nation debates tame by comparison. It was in effect the first legal local station and its successes heralded the pattern of success of those stations licensed under Ray Burke's Broadcasting Act. An examination of the JNMR figures will show that success in radio is not merely a question of formula programming. As Century radio struggled with its music format, much as 2FM struggled in its pre-Gerry Ryan days when it was just a music station, so speech-based local stations such as those in Clare, Kerry, South Kildare and North Donegal have flourished, and RTE Radio 1, despite its heavy speech input much criticised by Minister Burke still dominates the market.

Healy recognised the power of the radio chat-shows and often said that he could learn more from listening to them than he would wandering the corridors of Dail Eireann. Often he didn't like what he heard, like the news of the closure of a factory (Travenol), broadcast as the workers were leaving for home before they could tell their families the news. But he recognised its power, how the political debate on programmes like Morning Ireland, Day by Day, This Week and Today At Five was often more relevant than that taking place in Dail Eireann. And how the phone-in shows, the Gay Byrne Show, Pat Kenny Show and Live Line, reflected the changing attitudes of a changing Ireland. Thus, the frank discussions on sexuality on Women Today, the confrontations between the travellers and settled community and the frank attitude to the Pope's visit on the Pat Kenny Show, the daily reports of the Kerry Babies case and the other reports from the courts of the Hidden Ireland on Today At Five, the letters on the Anne Lovett case and the account of the Eileen Flynn case on the Gay Byrne show, and the phone-in during the Divorce Referenda on Live Line all gave an instant picture of a society in flux, and often in conflict, that was unique. Healy listened and was aware, and this helped him call things right.

For no one listening closely to those chat-shows over the two constitutional referenda could have been surprised by the results, or those who heard the grassroots rally behind Haughey, in phone-ins on his leadership, surprised by his survival. Healy, on the panel of John Bowman's Day by Day on the mornings of those "gang' revolts, certainly wasn't. He called it right. Thus Healy began the "On The Airwaves" column in the *Irish Times* for election campaigns. Not before its time, as many of the crucial turning points in the elections of the 80s came on radio programmes. Party leader phone-ins had become a reality with the 1987 election. In that campaign Charles Haughey's remarks about renegotiating the Anglo-Irish Agreement, and his celebrated remark about not knowing the extent of the dissatisfaction with the Health Cuts in 1989 were both made on phone-ins. And, of course, there was *Saturdayview* – Mrs Robinson, her family and Padraig Flynn. Listen to the Plain People of Ireland Healy would say as he guarded his listening post.

Healy's reputation as a political commentator is based primarily on the Backbencher column, *Inside Politics*, which he wrote first for the *Sunday Review* and then the *Irish Times* in the 60s and early 70s. The column was unique in style and content. Its style was modelled, by Healy and his initial collaborator Ted Nealon, on the oratorical style of Paddy Lindsay, the Mayo Fine Gael minister and barrister. As Healy himself said, "Backbencher had

237

seen it all before, had heard it all many times and nothing surprised him. It was the human condition." (*In Dublin*)

What was different about Healy's approach was that it was not just political reporting using information gleaned from patrolling the corridors of Dail Eireann, although it had its share of scoops, but it also offered opinion and insight, argument and prophecy. It took sides, an unheard-of thing in political reporting of the time. "I banished objectivity. It's a cop-out line ... Be fair, it's a better word." It abused and praised in almost equal measure, but most important of all, it redefined the politics of Leinster House as the local politics of the cumann or public meeting, the pub or the football match. Because of this approach Healy's work acts as a running commentary on the politics of the 60s and 70s. Cheering and haranguing from the sideline he charted the triumphs and failures of that generation of politicians which took over from the Independence/Civil War generation.

Backbencher was first with the story of Fine Gael's Just Society document, one of the first attempts to break from Civil War politics. It lifted the lid off Taca and the connections between Fianna Fail and business, an era which old Fianna Failers saw as a corruption of the purity of the Fianna Fail tradition. His close contact with the Three Musketeers led to an inside track on Lemass's government and early warnings on free education and the proposal to merge the universities. But political comment was not just about information, but how it was used, the judgement from experience. Healy was proud of his ability to predict: "A prophecy come true, Lemass is for the country", was how he underlined his success in predicting the 1965 General Election. In subsequent predictions though, it was not just the calling in advance but the why.

Thus talk of how Niall Blaney's milk subsidy would win the 1969 election for Jack Lynch, or of "Corish's men with each man transferring impeccably and fully to his coalition partner" in predicting a Coalition victory in 1977. Healy had no egg on his face, unlike other political correspondents in the election of 1977, but the 20/20 vision of accuracy was to blur during the arithmetic confusion of the 80s − though not in the two crucial referenda, when he predicted pro-life and anti-divorce wins

238

(thanks to Angel politics and Fianna Fail sitting it out). And, of course, victory for Haughey in the heaves of the 80s, "with one great leap our hero is free".

The refusal to write the obituary of Charles Haughey was seen by some as a reflection of Healy's own political bias, but for him it was just an understanding of Fianna Fail and "village values', "Fianna Fail is like a village community. It can have fights within the village but once the next village threatens it or scoffs at its pretensions to be the best village the internal squabbles are forgotten and all join in a band to face down the threat from the outsiders."

It is in his account of the principle figures of that era, Lemass, O'Malley, Lynch and Haughey, that you can see the core values as Healy saw them. He was a believer in strong leadership, in getting things done. In politics with a vision, but a vision rooted in practical reality. He was also a believer in alternative government as the essence of democracy and he welcomed the Just Society and the Labour manifesto of 1969 as attempts to have real opposition. Loyalty was another basic creed. Healy was loyal to his friends almost to a fault. As Ted Nealon has observed he would be slow to criticise those he liked personally, and this loyalty was a quality he respected in politicians. There was also a respect for the Oireachtas and for those who performed well there across all parties. He was a master of the Parliamentary sketch and one of his best pieces, although he wasn't in the chamber, was of Oliver J. Flanagan's vote, in December 1986, to save the Fitzgerald government.

On Lemass he wrote: "The Boss Man was a realist. He never flinched the reality of things... Sean Lemass never talked about patriotism: he never talked about Republicanism: he never talked about his own role in 1916... He wasted no time in talking about the past when he had energy to work in the present for the future. And he wasted no time in talking about how he would do the important things in the future: he simply went and did the important things... Sean Lemass said of his time in politics that he did not encounter any pressures on him from the Church. It was as nice a way as any of saying that if and when some Churchmen sought to twist his arm they were told firmly what to do. Lemass never forgot he was answerable to the ballot box and never allowed his ministers to forget it either. Lemass didn't talk about the possibility of free post-primary education for all: he had his minister overnight make it a reality... Lemass didn't talk of nettle-plucking by going to talk to Terence O'Neill: he did it himself first and talked (briefly) afterwards. No one questioned his Republicanism. No one resigned from the party. There were no splits. There were no rows. There was no crisis. There was only the applause of the plain people of Ireland." (*backbencher*, 15/5/1971)

On Charles J. Haughey:

"Once in the 60s I was asked would I be happy to trust Charles J. Haughey as Taoiseach? My reply was 'yes – providing I am able to patrol him 24 hours a day to save him from his friends'. There was so much of Sean Lemass about him."

On Haughey's confidence vote in Jim Gibbons after the Arms Trial:

"The issue was not one of Gibbons or Haughey: the bigger issue was this, was Haughey loyal to the party or was he not? For Haughey there was no question of what was to be done. The party was bigger than Haughey: he would support the party and prove his loyalty... Now up and down the country in the months which followed, that unswerving loyalty, by the man they would have regarded as a little peacock who would not bow a knee, was to be recognised by the grass-roots and repaid... He has taken most everything which can be thrown at a politician. A lesser man who had made the Taoiseach's office twice might have called it a day and walked away from it all to watch over his wooded acres in Kinsealy or to reflect in the solitary fastness of Inishvickillaun, on a political life usefully lived. The hunger to match Lemass is still there, the driving force." (*Irish Times*, 5/12/84)

On Jack Lynch:

"Jack Lynch, never as I've said a creative leader, did not understand the need to stretch people to give them goals to achieve. He settled for the role of defender. Like the captain of a team with a good lead, he fell back in the full back role. He was the heart and soul of decency, the man with the cocker spaniel soulful eyes, darling of the Reverend Mother circuit, the original Teflon politician... Behind the Honest Jack image was a very tough Cork hurler who knew how to pick his time (when the ref wasn't looking) to put the handle of the hurley into the ribs of a political opponent, run on with the ball to clear it, then turn back to lift the player off the ground perplexed as to how he got to be there.

You do not get to the top in politics by being Mr. Nice Guy. On the hurling field you can take the first dirty dig in the ribs and account it an accident. If a player comes twice or three times, then you know the score...Lynch always knew the score." (*In Dublin*,)

In these assessments and others on the major political figures of that era, 'Little Liam' Cosgrave, Garret 'The Good' Fitzgerald, Corish, Spring, Des O'Malley, 'Iosagán' Molloy, 'Mantis' McGiolla, Healy created a cast of characters which the readers could recognise just as they could the characters in their own town or village. Often too, more mysterious figures strode through the columns: the national handlers, the verbal republicans, the young tigers, the Donnybrook set, the Mercs and perks party, the people of the snipe-grass, even the plain people of Ireland. The conversation was often pub-talk, argument and innuendo laced with jokes and stories. He has told of his first encounter with his friend Donogh O'Malley, having exposed on the front page of the *Evening Mail* O'Malley's appearance in a drunk driving case at one of Haughey's special late sittings (sudden sittings arranged to catch the journalists out), and of O'Malley being carpeted by De Valera for almost missing a vote because of drink. The Taoiseach carpeted him – "they tell me you are drinking again Donogh..." O'Malley cut in on the Taoiseach: "I wouldn't mind them Taoiseach – sure Jaysus they told me you used to sleep with Mary Sweeney and I never believed them." Stories of Lemass offering a ministry to Haughey as Taoiseach but advising him as a father-in-law not to take it. Or of an encounter between George Colley and Donogh O'Malley which led to O'Malley persuading Niall Blaney to enter the leadership race for the Lemass succession and which then caused Lemass to urge Lynch in as a compromise candidate. Stories of kites being flown, such as Brian Lenihan's one on an honours system, or a tax on fur coats, or Ireland re-entering the Commonwealth.

Healy himself often enters the story as a central character – in the Dail restaurant as Lenihan, O'Malley and Blaney set off to launch a leadership challenge, in O'Malley's flat late at night examining the first editions of the papers and their response to his surprise announcement. Being given John McGahern's *The Dark* by Minister for Justice Brian Lenihan to see if it should be banned or not, Healy was surprised by the book and wrote a long piece in Backbencher, but Lenihan later confessed he "wasn't exactly worried about the burning of a masterpiece; there were constituency considerations: the McGahern family lived in his Roscommon-Leitrim constituency where every vote counted. As far as I can recall *The Dark* was banned for a time." Or driving through Anghagower in Mayo with Haughey as Minister for Agriculture explaining the plight of the small holder, his mother's family the O'Donnells and their 19 acres, a journey which would lead directly to Haughey as Finance Minister introducing the farmer's dole.

And it is this last journey that seems the essence of Healy's political outlook. He believed in politics as something tangible, in politicians who could get things done. Thus, in his accounts of Lemass, O'Malley, Haughey and the others he would recite their achievements, the programme for economic recovery, free education, the succession act – to achieve these things the politicians had to master the skills of politics. They needed idealism, and he would laud the Just Society and Lemass's efforts to reform the constitution, and those who stood up to the verbal republicanism of the 70s. But they also needed to be realistic, pragmatic and decisive. They also needed to bring the people with them, particularly their own, and to do this loyalty was all. It was the loyalty of Haughey in voting confidence in Gibbons that preserved his future after the arms crisis. And for Oliver J. Flanagan it was 'loyalty all the way with Oliver J.', a man oft-derided for old-fashioned views and the best example of 'clientelism' in politics, yet Healy wrote "ours is a peasant country and none reflected it more so than Oliver J. Flanagan...

242

He did not do much to conceal his dissapproval of the Donnybrook set and Garret Fitzgerald. And yet on Friday last, Oliver J. Flanagan, Doyen of the Dail, seeing his party was in a minority, insisted on leaving his hospital bed to vote and so ensure it survived and lived out the year 1986. It was his finest moment for he was reminding a House yet again that whatever you think of the leader your first duty is to the House of which you are the Doyen, and your party which sustained you. Loyalty, in spite of all the demeaning, is the name of the game.

The figure is leaner now, the head has to lean forward with the walking aid. It has been a long day since any one person walked through the lobbies of Leinster House as tall as the King of Laois/Offaly." (*Irish Times*, 22/12/1986)

Oliver J. Flanagan also makes a number of appearances in Breandán Ó hEithir's book *The Begrudgers Guide To Irish Politics*. First in the story of Locke's Distillery, the furore surrounding the sale of the Kilbeggan distillery in 1947 which brought to national prominence the young Oliver J. Flanagan (who had been elected as a monetary reform candidate riding a bicycle round the constituency with *Here Comes Oliver* on his front and *There Goes Flanagan* on his back).

Flanagan challenged the sale accusing Fianna Fail, one of whose senators was a partner in the firm selling the property, of selling part of the national assets to 'foreign con-men and their con-ladies', and even of bribery, including a celebrated gold watch to De Valera. On the surface Flanagan didn't come out too well from the tribunal set up to investigate the matter. "We found it necessary to exercise extreme caution in dealing with the evidence of Deputy Flanagan. We found him very uncandid and much disposed to answer questions unthinkingly as though he were directing his replies elsewhere than to the Tribunal. On several occasions he contradicted himself and was disposed to shift his ground when he found that answers already given would lead him where he did not wish to go. He was, on other occasions, in conflict with testimony which we believed to be true." The allegations were dismissed but far from being in disgrace Ó hEithir points out "the result of the General Election in February showed that the people of Laois-Offaly could read the smoke

243

signals even if they could not see the flames or feel the heat of the fire. Oliver Flanagan topped the poll increasing his vote by 5,000 to 14,370; more than the great poll topper Sean Lemass got in Dublin or Eamonn De Valera got in Clare."

One of Oliver J. Flanagan's other appearances in the book is in a Dail exchange with Minister for Education Donogh O'Malley concerning complaints to the TD from his constituents about a text-book *An Anthology of Short Stories,* then on the Inter-Cert English reading list. Deputy Flanagan listed a number of words (3 bastards, a bleeding, a bugger, a for Christ's sake and a Then by God) and he read two paragraphs from a short story which were 'suggestive':

"Quietly she lifted a ewer of water and climbed out of the window and scuttled along the cool but cruel gravel down the maw of the tunnel.

Her pyjamas were very short so that when she splashed water, it wet her ankles. She peered into the tunnel. Something alive rustled inside there. She raced in, and up and down she raced and flurried, and cried aloud, 'Oh gosh, I can't fit it' and then at last she did. Kneeling down in the damp she put her hand into the slimy hole. When the body lashed, they were both mad with fright. But she gripped him and shoved him into the ewer and raced, with her teeth ground, out to the other end of the tunnel and down the steep path to the river's edge."

In reply Minister O'Malley asked if Deputy Flanagan had read the whole story. When he replied that he had from cover to cover, Ó hEithir quotes the minister's reply:

"I would also point out to the Deputy that if he had read the story he would see this young girl is going into the tunnel to catch a trout and not to catch anything else. If these ideas which the Deputy is putting in Irish minds, which no doubt, as on the last occasion, will be widely published in tomorrow's papers, are all he can find in O'Faolain's, *The Trout,* which has also been described as O'Faolain's finest story, then I can only say 'God help us'... I know that Deputy Flanagan possibly has ambitions in another sphere and he hopes one day to be leader of the Knights. If that is so, I agree that Deputy Flanagan is quite entitled to aspire to such a great office, though anyone using the Catholic

Church for his own material or other advancement makes me vomit."

The Begrudger has the attitude of many in Irish society – who have a "deep and abiding doubt about our ability to run our own affairs as well as others might run them for us. Our country, the manner in which it is run and those who run it are a constant disappointment to the Begrudger... his keen realism has triumphed over his idealism and brought him into direct conflict with received wisdom ... his stock in trade consists of the slur, innuendo and guilt by association; a fault he shares with some contemporary historians, politicians and more particularly those who market politicians through the media for consumption by the public... he has a grasshopper mind cursed with an elephant's memory... with the Begrudger you always know where you stand, even though his stances change with baffling rapidity."

How Ó hEithir used the Begrudger to dissect Irish political history is best summed up by his chapter headings like *We will in our arse have our own gentry; WT Cosgrave, the Pope and God's Granny; I solemnly swear that this oath is not an oath; De Valera, the gold watch and 60,000 gallons of whiskey* and *Hit me now with my mother and child in my arms.*

Ó hEithir's approach is not that of Healy's. It is not one of lunches in the Russell or drinks in the Dail bar, there is no cosiness with politicians and there is a different perspective.

On Lemass:

"It has been truly said of him that he came to power too late and left it too soon. He was a lucky Taoiseach... his coming to power coincided with a period of world growth and economic recovery ... he was not afraid to reverse policies he had previously preached and implemented ... it must be said that in the particular kingdom of darkness that was Ireland in the late 50s the man who produced a white stick would be acclaimed as a wonder worker. Lemass produced a stick and a seeing-eye dog and the rising tide that floats all ships can be thanked for the rest of a recovery which was only temporary and fraught with fatal flaws. But at least the ship had been refurbished, refitted and caulked and it did float free of the dismal mud-flats ... Try as one may, one cannot have Lemass, the convert to free enterprise, the man who reversed the flow of emigration, architect of the New Ireland, welcome antidote to the embroidered fainne on Dev's cloak – all that and more you cannot have without accepting TACA, the vulgarisation of Ireland, the destruction of Dublin and the failure to develop the country's real resources apart perhaps, from tourism which is always a mixed blessing in any civilised country." (*Begrudger's Guide*)

On Jack Lynch:

"...he was straight out of the 'laughter of comely maidens' scenario...he was Narcissus who was in love with the idea of having power, not to do anything on God's earth with it if he could help it, but to make sure it was not snatched by the wrong hands...there would be a Munster Final every week in Jack Lynch's Ireland – 2 or 3 at Christmas and Easter if things were going well: if there were no unseemly strikes, if all injuries had been inflicted accidentally and all disagreements settled on the field out of the referee's sight..."

On Haughey:

"Why shouldn't Charlie Haughey lead the Fianna Fail party – he was probably one of the best ministers this country ever had. What I'm afraid of is that like Lemass before him I think he may have come to power too late. He showed great indecision when he did come to power. Admittedly he would say he got power at a particularly bad time...he certainly has a very cynical attitude...he resents that people have learnt to use PR more effectively than he did himself. And he's far too strong a personality to allow himself to be handled as Garret is handled."

Ó hEithir's own cynicism permeates his work as a commentator in that book and in his columns in Irish in the *Irish Times*. "The country's too small. And Haughey took George Colley's father's seat. And these things are very important in a tight society. All the fighting in Fianna Fail was about personalities really. It had damn all to do with any principle except that people couldn't get on, they couldn't bear other people." (*In Dublin*)

But these were not top of the head prejudices but born out of the insight of someone steeped in the politics of the grass-roots. And in some of the best political reporting in recent years Ó hEithir went out to the grass-roots for the General Election of 1987, to write a daily column called 'The Hidden Election – what the average voter is thinking'. Ó hEithir at the time had been broadcasting a weekly review of the provincial press called 'The Hidden Ireland' after Daniel Corkery's famous book. Some in RTE objected to the title 'Hidden Ireland' calling it patronising. That, of course, showed a lack of understanding of the Corkery connection where the Hidden Ireland was the hidden treasure of native Irish literature, and to assume that Ó hEithir would have a Hall's Pictorial approach to the provincial press, picking just the quirky and the extreme. This was not Ó hEithir's approach. While always humorous and alert to the unusual, he used the piece to underline various issues and views that might have been ignored by the national press. Thus the picture of the right to life and divorce referenda were very different when viewed from the 'Hidden Ireland', likewise the effect of Winter storms, health cutbacks and emigration.

The approach was similar for 'The Hidden Election'. In Clare it was talk of De Valera, Daniel O'Connell and the Thomas Burke (of the Farmer's Party and later as a independent bonesetter) and a vote for Sile De Valera to honour her grandfather because she stuck with Clare after her little dissapointment the last time. In Galway it was all candidates not issues... and the malice was as soft as the weather but it was real. In Tipperary..."broken backboiler politics and the exchange: *Question – Would you buy a secondhand car from Charlie. Answer – No way, but Garret probably would.*" In Limerick West..."Having an election here is like taking the temperature of someone in the whole of his health. It's pure waste of time and money and can only produce one result. If Fianna Fail lost one of their seats here the older people would take to the hills thinking it was the end of the world." In Offaly..."What do you think of what that ferret-faced little hoor Barry Desmond has done to us now. I pointed out that Barry Desmond was no longer a minister and that John Boland was the present Minister for Tablets. For a man who boasted of having given Oliver J. the first 'stroke' in every election since 1948 he had a powerful command of bad language. John Boland, if he is in the least bit superstitious, would be well advised to walk clear

247

of ladders, red haired women and hares for the next week." And finally when in Kerry where all the children raised their hands when asked if emigration is likely to play a part in their immediate future he sums up: "The practical results of current emigration are everywhere to be seen. West Clare is as sadly affected as Connemara or West Kerry. One hears of almost a full football team from Castlegregory reforming in the USA. In Connemara, one is told of pubs in Boston where nothing but Irish is heard. All these well-educated, energetic and very disillusioned young people have already voted with their feet and this election will concern them only as a contest far less important and exciting than an All-Ireland final. That is depressing and far removed from the world of strokes, national handlers and the abstract mathematics of that morning's ill-tempered debate on radio between Des O'Malley and John Bruton."

It is this concern about emigration that links Ó hEithir back to Healy, for throughout Healy's work there is this forced movement, the movement from the land to the town, from the town to the city, and from the city to Britain, Europe and America. And all because of the failure of the political process to provide jobs to keep them at home. It was the great barometer of political achievement, Sean Lemass turned the tide of emigration and unless Haughey did it he would be made walk the plank by the electorate.

The emigration he writes about was out of need not ambitions. He tells in *Nineteen Acres* of the struggle of his mother's family, the O'Donnells, to hold on to their small holding through a civil war, two world wars and an economic depression. Of how his mother and two sisters emigrated to America, his mother eventually returning with the price of slates for the home-place, his aunts sending the dollars which educated the Healy family. He tells of the agony at home, bringing his Uncle Jim away from his own fireside for the last time:

"Then slowly he looked into the fireplace and said 'There are four fires there'. Slowly the enormity of it dawned on me. His was the last fire in that part of Castleduff and if it was quenched, quenched too were the last hopes of a return to his closest neighbours. It was the old belief and tradition in the power of fire. Where there was a fire there was life and the promise of life. So it was when one by one, his neighbours left for England or America, there would be a wake in the house and Jim or Mary Anne being the last to leave, would take a blazing sod from the last fire in that house, carry it spluttering and sparking across the fields of the hill to place it on their own hearth as part of the rakings. In that way, although the emigrant's house was closed and the hearth cold, the fire which for so long blazed there never really went out. There would be a continuity, for when the emigrant came home again, he (or she) would take a blazing sod from Jim's fire which had never gone out and, with the tongs which he carried it, bring the new blazing sod back to the old hearth to relight a new fire... If this fire went out it was the last living thing which bound the neighbours to return, for he knew the word would go that Jim O'Donnell's fire, the last fire on the hill was quenched..."(*Nineteen Acres*)

This examination of his own roots and how they reflected the pain of the country was born of Healy's own brief emigration in the late 50s. He left out of ambition not of need and he was greatly disillusioned. Rather than the bright America of his dreams he found the emigrant's America a harsh and bleak place. His aunts who had made a great show of their affluence when they visited here were living lives of misery and loneliness. It changed him.

"I realised that never in the 27 years of life, had I, before going to America, used the phrase 'my country'. It had a wonderful ring to it and still has. And so you become an apostle of Ireland. If this is to be my country then I want to have a say in what my country will be and what it will do and where it will go." (*No One Shouted Stop*)

This new determination led to the searing anger of *No One Shouted Stop – Death of an Irish Town*, in which Healy charted the slow death of his home town of Charlestown. A death at the hands of emigration, war, economic depression, consumer culture and apathy – "We in Charlestown saw only our Auschwitz-like trains of dumb emigrants going, but what of the men of Dublin like a monstrous multiplication of those trainloads pulling in and vomiting their pitiful cargoes into the ships at Dun Laoghaire and the North Wall and who stood aside, busily talking about our fourth green field and our ancient heritage, and all the arid cliches of those days... Who can walk away from this town without walking away from his own flesh and blood, his own past, good and bad as it might be, and still say he has a commitment to his country's present and future? And because your country is nothing more than a multiplicity of a thousand Charlestowns, you realise that you do not have a choice: you must stand and fight. And if the odds seem loaded, well the odds were always loaded.

"It would be much easier for everyone if today's enemy came dressed up in the old, too familiar clothes of the conqueror.

"But Apathy does not wear the historically hated redcoat. Indifference does not charge in on a cavalry horse, and Injustice and Uncharity do not come tearing down Barrack Street in black-and-tanned lorries to shoot up a town which is already surrendering to Batman and the poppressagentry and plug boys and the whizz-kidders of the economic jargon boys of Dublin who have assured them that they have no future anyway; and don't call us, we'll call you." (*No One Shouted Stop*)

That was in the 60s. When Healy re-issued the book in 1988, much had changed in Charlestown. Connaught Regional Airport (Knock Airport) was established just outside the town, the shops had bright new fronts, there were new fronts on the perimeter of town. But despite this prosperity, according to a local, things were worse than 20 years ago, "all the young crowd are gone: there's no one at home if they can help it. The best day is dole day." (*No One Shouted Stop*, 1988). The story had come full circle. Healy himself had put his faith in Europe and the benefits of regional policy, but this seeping through as real benefits for the people of Charlestown was more a hope than an expectation.

Ó hEithir also found echoes in the emigration of the 1980s. He watched the emigrants in Paris and London, the graffiti on the walls of a Paris pub 'Aoibhinn bheith in mBeann Eadair' and reflected on the difference between the new emigrants and the old, "most of them have one thing in common, they would much prefer to be in Ireland. They resent the forces that caused them to emigrate much more than those who grew up with little

250

or no expectation of employment at home. For these are the products of an Ireland that seemed to have abolished emigration – the Ireland of free second level education, industrialisation and hope, above all hope, for an even brighter future. There is no need to labour the point, the Ireland of Tom Murphy's *Bailegangaire* is reality. The Japanese factory closing down, the husband sending home the weekly telegram with money but never a letter. The old woman telling a story about how laughter was stolen away. These young emigrants are learning this the hard way and they are also learning that the Ireland the politicians and economic experts told them they were living in was a mirage." (*Sense of '86*, RTE Radio 1)

In one of my last meetings with Healy, at a lunch to launch the Irish Presidency of the EC in January 1990, we talked of the relevance of Europe to the growing tide of emigrants. He had now briefly become a bureaucrat as Press Officer for the Presidency, an expression of his belief in Europe and in Charles Haughey. He remained optimistic and talked of the real practical things that could be done for County Mayo by the EC. I talked of a series of recent reports that Jim Fahy had compiled for Six-One following the workers of the Babygro factory in Mayo who had been made redundant and many of whom were now in London. In the week that Healy died, Jim Fahy had some other reports from County Mayo, they told of the despair of parting as emigrants returned from Knock Airport after Christmas, and the anger of two Bishops that 'no one was shouting stop', and of another 'Irish town', Ballinrobe, where unemployment was growing at an alarming rate, the recession in the US and Britain no longer giving the escape valve of emigration.

The legacy of Healy and Ó hEithir is hard to gauge. They were not father figures of a school of writing and their influence may only have been indirect on those who read them or knew them. But you can find echoes of Healy's approach to politics in the work of what could be termed the *Magill* school of journalism (Vincent Browne, Gene Kerrigan, Colm Tóibín, Fintan O'Toole, John Waters). Ó hEithir himself was a link between the new generation of writers in Irish, the *Innti* poets (Michael Davitt, Liam O Muirthile, Nuala Ní Dhomhnaill etc) and the generation of O'Flaherty, O Cadhain, O Ríordáin and O Direáin. You can find echoes of their work in Tom Murphy's plays (*Crucial Week, White House, Bailegangaire*), in the party poems of Thomas McCarthy, in Sebastian Barry's *Boss Grady's Boys*, in the Plunkets of Dermot Bolger's *The Journey Home*, in the poetry of Paul Durcan. But there are vast uncharted expanses of Irish life which so far Irish literature has failed to examine and some of these get their only expression in the work of Healy and Ó hEithir.

For me, Backbencher was my political education. My father bought the *Indo* or *Press* during the week for their superior sports coverage but on Saturday it was always the *Times* for Healy. As my awareness of politics grew the column informed the reality of the streets outside, the public meetings, the election band wagons. As a publican's son I had an even greater exposure to political discussion and argument. Our regulars were built around a core of people who were my father's generation. They had built up a social club which brought drama, the Abbey Theatre, Lennox Robinson, Jack McGowran and Siobhan McKenna to the town in the 50s. They were strong followers and officials of the GAA. They were passionately interested in politics, principally Fianna Fail, and for a time one was a TD. I remember the by-election in Kildare in February 1965 when FF took the Labour seat on the death of Labour leader, William Norton, the General Election later that year when our TD lost his seat, and the Presidential Election of 1966 when Tom O'Higgins stormed into town. There are memories of public meetings, of Kevin Boland and Niall Blaney battling with hecklers or David Thornley addressing a deserted square, of the slick and professional Jack Lynch entourage with the RTE reporter in the leather jacket. I have direct images from Backbencher from those years of people drinking tea late at night surrounded by newspapers, of someone crouched beneath the cabinet table listening in, of ministers carpeted by the Taoiseach in rooms with high windows and long shadows.

Reading Backbencher attuned you to local reflections of National Trauma, the TD's son who left Labour to join Fianna Fail because of the shift to socialism, the local founder of

Aontacht Eireann and the bitterness of post-Arms Trial politics, the farmers in revolt and on the streets. And further back, my own family's small holding lost a generation ago, the talk of childhood spent on the land and what might have been, as it was distributed by the Land Commission with no-one left to run it. The split in the town over the Great War when more per capita fought than any other place in Ireland. Johnny I hardly knew you. Insurrections, Sinn Fein banners in the attic, celebration and reappraisal when nettles were grasped, the Sinn Fein councillor who was the local grave-digger. My own aunts emigrating, one to England the other to America, as much to escape the burden of taking care of the extended family than economic need. There was a resonance on the national stage of those local difficulties. And just as there was wonder in seeing your town named in a poem as a far flung Mythology (*Lines On A Canal Bank*), or hearing small town life captured in a radio play (Murphy's *Crucial Week*), so seeing the local perspective in the national press stimulated interest.

As always the political talk of the time was mixed with sport, often with even more vigour and energy. There were as many characters, heroes and villians, on the sporting side of the story as on the political, as *Over The Bar* shows. One of the major things that is common to Healy and Ó hEithir is the use of the sporting metaphor. For here sport is not merely recreation but a part of the political culture.

Thus politics and sport are imbued with the same national characteristics: will to achieve, the reward for endeavour, a sense of belonging, loyalty, patriotism, being lifted out of mundane reality by the special. Just as one may support Kildare or Galway or Mayo despite having lived for years in Dublin, you were defined by where you came from, by the values and the prejudices of that background.

It is this theme that is central to Healy and Ó hEithir. They had a sense of belonging to Mayo and to Aran and they understood that many other urban dwellers had this as well. In understanding this and in seeing much of Ireland as a collection of small communities, be it Aran or Charlestown, Athy or Finglas, Dundrum or the North Mon, they could better understand how

253

politics worked. This is not the politics of the parish pump and clientelism, although this is part of it and not necessarily a negative part, but a politics where local values and fears were predominant. This is not necessarily a conservative analysis, just as there is a rural–urban myth there is a myth that rural conservatism dominates political life outside Dublin. One of the lessons of the 1990 Presidential Election apart from the 'loyalty' of Fianna Fail to its own is that there is an urban 'progressive' Ireland outside Dublin, as the pattern of the Robinson vote in that election will show.

So in Healy and Ó hEithir we continually get the twin values of sport and politics. Healy looked for heroes. In championing Charles Haughey he was down to his last hero, a hero like Mickey Walsh in *No One Shouted Stop*. He was a great handballer who emigrated to England and missed the chance to become the great champion he was. "He came back in his middle years and we said that he had left it too late. He played against himself in the ball alley. We were down to our last hero. Then Walsh came out to beat the best in Ireland and became the champion we knew he was all the time."

The last time I met Breandán Ó hEithir was in the foyer of the RTE TV block before he returned to Paris following Cork's double All-Ireland. We talked of travel, of the transformation in East Germany and Czechoslovakia, his visit to his wife's roots in Columbia; of politics, of Robinson's nomination and her trip to the islands and Fine Gael's search for a candidate; of work in progress, the book on Irish murders and a satirical novel on RTE; of the health of our fathers and of sport. We talked of the new dawn for the Lily Whites now that Kerry's Mick O'Dwyer had come to save them, and the World Cup, of Eamon Dunphy, Jack Charlton, the storm that had found its tea-cup and the shame-of-being-Irish controversy. But mostly we talked of the Irish team and that one moment in time when the nation held its breath as David O'Leary prepared to take the penalty that would mean victory against Romania and a quarter-final against Italy in Rome. He talked about the background of the Irish team, the second and third generation Irish. He wondered how many Irish abroad shared that moment, were we a nation for those few

254

seconds, could the epitaph be written? One of the most telling television images of that moment was in Dublin Castle at the European Summit at the end of Charles Haughey's reign as President of Europe. All stood still to watch the shoot-out. Ministers, officials and journalists crowded into the press room as O'Leary took the kick. As he scored, the image that was to last and which was used again and again to reflect that moment was of John Healy, Press Officer to the Irish Presidency, a grown man crying. Healy, the Reporter, understood the moment. Fair play.

WOMEN AND POVERTY

Aileen O'Mara

Every autumn, health centres in the poorer parts of urban Ireland are thronged with women, queueing with slips of paper before the Community Welfare Officer, in the modern form of begging.

They sit in line, with their pieces of paper proving their income, waiting the discretionary decisions of Community Welfare Officers who decide whether or not they get some money towards their bills, telling the intimate details of their personal lives in front of their neighbours to get a few more pounds.

With their husbands on the dole, or with no partner, and living on inadequate social welfare payments, women are there looking for discretionary payments towards the cost of paying for school uniforms, and footwear allowances for their children or simply to put food on the table.

Every other month, and particularly after Christmas, they seek help towards their ESB bills, and school books. Sometimes, they see their children expelled because they do not have the proper footwear deemed necessary by the school. It is not just the social welfare system that women contend with to survive day by day. They meet the moneylenders, they worry about repaying the exorbitant loans. They do the deals. They let the rent and other bills go into arrears in order to put food on the table. They worry about the knocks on the door because it might be the man from the Corporation, or someone else they need to pay. They do without food in order to ensure their children are properly fed. They borrow from their neighbours or family on a Tuesday, and repay them on a Thursday, when the dole is paid. They send their children to do the shopping because they hate seeing all the things they cannot afford.

Increasing research and surveys indicate that women are among the poorest groups in society and that increasing numbers of women fall into poverty through unemployment, ill-health, desertion or single parenthood. Social analysts call this phenomenon "the feminisation of poverty". It has long been recognised in other European countries, in Britain, and the US. Now it is being recognised here in Ireland, as the growing statistics from state and voluntary groups show a rising incidence of poverty side by side with an economic boom.

The European Commission in 1975 defined the poor as "those persons, families or groups of persons whose resources (material, cultural and social) are so limited as to exclude them from the minimum acceptable way of life in the member states in which they live".

Poverty is a state of exclusion.

When the Economic and Social Research Institute (ESRI) published its authoritative report on poverty in 1988, it quantified what many people already knew: widespread and growing poverty in the country. It found that one in three people were living at or below an adult income of less than £48 a week at 1987 levels, lower than the basic minimum recommended by the Commission on Social Welfare in 1986, a report full of commendable recommendations, the central ones of which have been largely ignored since.

Women's poverty in Ireland is effectively hidden from the political or economic agenda, and from public debate. Women are excluded from the decisions that affect their personal lives, their communities, their and their families' futures.

They are living on incomes so low compared to the average income that they are in effect excluded from the ordinary living patterns, customs and activities of this society.

The ESRI figures mean that one in four children are growing up in families in poverty and because of the class and educational inequalities inherent in our society, they have little prospect of escaping this situation.

For example, educational achievement, which has important consequences for future income and employment, is closely related to social class. A recent investigation of the social background of those at third level found that over 50% of boys from professional backgrounds went on to third level, compared to just under 30% of lower non-manual, 14% of skilled manual and 8% of semi-skilled and unskilled. The drop-out rate was highest amongst children whose fathers had manual working backgrounds.

State expenditure on education favours the better off: the top 20% of income earners receive 30% of public expenditure; the bottom 20% receive 9%.

Health expenditure also favours the better off. The top 20% of income earners receive 24% of public expenditure on health, while the bottom 20% receive 17%, according to a 1984 ESRI study.

Living on the margins leads to feelings of alienation and powerlessness and rejection, and a sense of helplessness and dependence on others.

The physical surroundings increase the sense of alienation and powerlessness. Dublin is the best example of geographical segregation of rich and poor, but every town in Ireland has its own example of the marginalised working class estate cut off from the rest of the community.

A comprehensive report on Dublin county's deprived areas highlighted the lack of services coupled with the ghetto effect of concentrating masses of unemployed and low income groups together.

The CODAN reports, published in 1988, compared the choice and facilities available in the affluent suburbs of south County Dublin, with the local authority communities of west Dublin, devoid of adequate shopping and transport facilities. In Fettercairn in West Tallaght, over 3,000 people have only one shop, along with a few visiting mobile shops. There are no neighbourhood centres, the nearest shopping centre is several miles away, and there is no proper footpath for pedestrian access.

The reports profiled the poorer areas of Dublin, where unemployment was almost triple the county average; the proportion of the population with higher education is 7%, while the proportion of the population with primary education only is twice the average.

The proportion of the population aged 15 and under is 40% higher than average, and the ratio of unemployed to employed persons is 2 and a half times the average. In some areas, the rate of unemployment is 70%.

Rent arrears are an accurate indicator of need. In areas of Tallaght, built between 1982 and 1986, accumulated rent arrears are over 33,000.

In Brookfield in Tallaght, over one third of the 700 households depend on unemployment assistance – the lowest welfare payment.

In Brookfield, one in ten is an unmarried mother, and one in 13 is a deserted wife. Yet services and amenities in the area are scarce there. A corporation house is used as a doctor's surgery, a playgroup and a meeting place for local groups.

In the local authority estate of Jobstown, over 50% of heads of households are unemployed; in the neighbouring private estate, the figure was 5%.

The scale of women's poverty is enormous. Extrapolating from the comprehensive survey of income in households carried out by the Economic and Social Research Institute (ESRI) in 1988, the Combat Poverty Agency revealed that there are over a quarter of a million women living in poverty in Ireland.

In 1987, there were 274,000 women living below a line equivalent to £48 a week for one person, compared to 244,000 men: these figures are based on an assumption that income is shared equally within families.

The ESRI data is not comprehensive; it does not include households where women are not the heads, and who do not pay income tax, so it excludes women who are poor in well-off households.

"Women are the poorest of all," said Mary Daly in her book, *Women and Poverty*, quoting from Beatrix Campbell's *Wigan Pier*

Revisited. "Women are responsible for family finances but they have none of the power that goes with possession. Having it in their hands never made money their own."

The most vulnerable women are those rearing children on their own (one in seven babies was born outside marriage last year); vulnerable also are the women in low paid work, traveller women, homeless women, elderly women, particularly those living alone and women caring in a fulltime capacity for the elderly or sick.

They are very often doing this with help from a social welfare system which discriminates against women because they are more often than not treated as "dependents" and are entitled to less than their husband.

There are over 150,000 adult dependants in the social welfare system. The vast majority (an estimated 125,000) are women. They do not receive a payment in their own right, but are included in the "family" payment which is made to the main claimant (the man).

The 1989 Unemployment Assistance rate was between £42 and £47 a week, and between £26.90 and £29 for the adult dependent, and from £10 to £11 for the child. This is what over 62% of the unemployed are receiving – some 22% less than other welfare payments, and significantly below that recommended by the Commission on Social Welfare of £57 to £68 a week for an individual, and between £91 and £109 for a couple.

The adult dependent rate is about 62% of the main recipient, the gap having widened in recent years with the larger proportional increases to the main recipient.

The income of adult dependents is not secure, because they do not get it into their hands. This may worsen poverty amongst women, the Combat Poverty Agency believes, because women do not always get the money. In fact, 4,500 women have had to resort to a system of "split payments", where they get the dependent rate separately, because they were not receiving their share from the husband or partner.

Less than one-third of Irish women earn an independent income through paid work, compared to 60% of men. Over six in ten –

61% – of women who work outside the home are low paid.

The low paid part time workers are mainly women, unskilled manual workers, clerical workers in low grades and shop assistants.

The biggest demographic area of growth is also the one with the highest poverty risk: the single parent family. At least 80,000 such families existed in the 1986 census, most of them headed by a woman. Most of these are dependent on social welfare, or on private maintenance from their husbands or partners. Those depending on private maintenance are particularly insecure: a study of 1,127 maintenance orders made through the courts between 1976 and 1986 found only 13% fully paid up, and amounts awarded were very low.

Women are living longer, and as they get older, the more likely they are to be poor.

And for those with jobs, there is an increased reliance in the economy on part-time and service sector jobs, both categories low paid, and typically associated with women.

Surveys of poverty amongst women point to one central fact: women's responsibility to care for children reduces their access to an income of their own, and therefore heightens their risk of poverty.

As the groups working with women in poor areas have increasingly found, in order to get women out of the isolation of homes and to become aware of their problems and its solutions, the first thing needed is childcare facilities.

These figures measure the extent of financial poverty. They do not measure the extent of the other dimensions of poverty in society, which are clear to anyone who has been in the featureless estates of outer Dublin, the inner city deprivation of run-down flat complexes, who has sat in a crowded and stuffy health centre, queued in a dole office with a leaky roof, or walked long distances because they could not afford a bus.

The physical surroundings of poverty are dismal. The

261

emotional ones can also be deprivatory, the stresses and pressures of coping alone or without support, as well as reducing nutrient intake to ensure that the rest of the family have enough.

Dr Pauline Lee and Dr Michael Gibney of the Department of Clinical Medicine in Trinity College's Medical School, produced startling results in a report on patterns of food and nutrient intake in a suburb of Dublin with chronically high unemployment, published in June 1989.

They surveyed the large housing estate of Fettercairn in West Tallaght, representative of high levels of unemployment and consisting mainly of young families. 50 families were surveyed between November 1987 and April 1988 — 55 women, 42 men and 121 children under 18 years of age were assessed.

86% of the households had gross income less than £150 per week, and 76% were in receipt of social welfare.

Pressure for additional finance (toys at Christmas, Communion or Confirmation outfits) led 52% of families to take out loans with either moneylenders or other agencies, or had sought help from the St Vincent de Paul.

In terms of nutrient intake, women were taking less than men.

The diets of women were characterised by low intakes of fibre, low intakes of iron, low intakes of vitamin C.

Looking more closely at the findings for women, the researchers found a large variation in energy and nutrient intakes with energy intakes being lowest in the group of single mothers and deserted wives, and highest in the group of married women with three or four children. Single mothers, for example, had a considerably lower intake of meat, resulting in markedly low iron and zinc intakes.

With regard to inadequate nutrient intakes, women always fared worse than men, with about three times as many women having less than 75% of the Recommended Dietary Allowance (RDA) for vitamin C. Amongst single mothers, only half the women achieved even half the RDA for iron.

However, no differences whatever were seen between children from single or two-parent families, suggesting that women do without in order for their children to eat properly.

The women at greatest nutritional risk were the single mother or deserted wife, this was especially evident for iron intakes, the study found.

Meat consumption among single mothers and deserted wives was well below average which contributed significantly to their lowered iron intake. Yet there is no evidence that children of single parents or deserted wives shared the nutritional disadvantage of their mothers.

Contrary to popular belief, there was a low alcohol consumption amongst the families surveyed. "Most of the family income was spent on food and necessities for the children who were unquestionably the main focus of attention.

"Parents seemed to be prepared to make any sacrifice necessary to see that the children were not 'short' of anything. Often, however, this meant severe hardship particularly for the mother who usually went without herself", the report said.

The high incidence of smoking was worrying for the researchers – 71% of men, 64% of women.

"A few women gave weight control as their reason for smoking but the majority of people said that cigarettes kept them from 'cracking up' and was their only form of relaxation". Some passed the comment that it was a case of "either cigarettes or Valium" and the former was more acceptable to them.

42% of the unemployed households surveyed went to the Community Welfare Officer for help to ensure their ESB bill was not cut off. The CWO paid half; the balance was made up from the Children's Allowance monies.

"Larger families (with three or more children) where the head of the household was unemployed seemed to be the ones suffering most through lack of money. These were the families who most often needed help with their electricity bill or help from the St Vincent de Paul, and this constant pleading for financial assistance left them feeling very degraded."

Diets were characterised by high consumption of milk, bread and potatoes and a low consumption of fresh fruit and vegetables.

Poor quality beef, mince, sausages, frozen beefburgers, chicken and bacon were eaten; fresh fish was seldom eaten though fish fingers were widely used.

Bread and milk was bought from the local van or shop, often "on account" and paid for on pay day, ensuring that although money ran out the day before, there was bread and milk available. Fat intake amongst the adult males and females exceeded the recommended value.

Children consumed a lot of breakfast cereals, mostly Cornflakes, Rice Krispies or Weetabix, often in the evening time as well as for breakfast.

The survey found that "those found to be at the highest risk of nutritional inadequacy were women in general and in particular women in single parent families."

The study pointed out that social welfare payments for children took no account of their age, and their increasing demand for food was not taken into account.

Catherine's is a typical family, documented by the Combat Poverty Agency to illustrate and highlight the plight of those on social welfare.

Seven years of grinding poverty eventually forced this Dublin family out of the country in an effort to seek a new life in Australia. In a case study of a typical family caught in a cycle of despair caused by constant low income, the family of Catherine and her husband, living on social welfare, encapsulates the experience of women and their families in poverty.

He had worked as a plumber, lost his job seven years ago with no hope of getting anything else. They have five daughters and one son, aged 19 to 8, and the Agency detailed the spending of their weekly income of £142.26.

£107.90 was Unemployment Assistance, £5 Fuel Allowance, £12 for the eldest from an AnCO course, and £17.30 child benefit. Every penny was accounted for.

Despite that, seven times in the past year, Catherine went to her local Community Welfare Officer to seek help with the ESB bill, and for help with the school uniforms, and children's shoes.

Theirs was a typical spending breakdown amongst low income

264

families. Over 40% went on food, of which 42% of that went on bread and milk alone.

She described the experience of poverty: "It's being preoccupied with the pittances for today, tomorrow and next week. It's being nervous about knocks on the door in case it's the man from the ESB, or Dublin Corporation. You stay quiet about your situation in case someone feels sorry for you. You feel guilty about having a cigarette or a drink, and you have to constantly prove your poverty to get discretionary help."

In poor households, women do without the labour-saving devices that reduce the drudgery of housework; they lack the comfort and solace of nice possessions; they are marginalised from the greater community by their lack of income.

Coupled with that, they live and grow up in a society that has become increasingly unequal, with access to education, to the law, to the health and social services, and to economic power, entrenched in a self-perpetuating system of inherited advantages.

In the year of the Dublin Millenium, 1988, the Catholic Social Services Conference, an organisation established in the forties to give food to the poor, wrote a hard hitting report on poverty and its consequences in Dublin.

Called *Dublin: Hard Facts, Future Hopes*, it concentrated on its work amongst the poor in the city, highlighting the growing social and geographical divide in the city that was celebrating its one thousand years.

This year, Dublin is celebrating is designation as European City of Culture. Nothing has changed.

Dublin, unlike other European cities, has its poverty concentrated on particular geographical areas – the result is that children growing up in deprived households and environments, and children growing up in affluent areas never have to meet, mix and understand each other. The main concentrations of poverty are in the huge local authority estates on the edges of town, and in the older flat complexes in the inner city.

It was the CSSC which highlighted the role and experience of women in poverty.

"The particular experience and voice of women tends to be lost in all discussions of public issues," the report said. "This follows from women's position as a group which lacks collective power in the decision-making processes of society."

On the issues of poverty and powerlessness, women are even more invisible – a product of their dual experience of economic independence on welfare or low wages and their subordinate position as women.

"Yet the evidence indicates that women are among the poorest groups in society and that increasing numbers of women fall into poverty through unemployment, desertion, ill-health or single parenthood.

"As well as acknowledging the distinct experience of women in relation to poverty, it is essential to recognise women's role in helping to cope at a personal and family level. Women manage the family budget, take most responsibility for the care and up-bringing of children and support men both emotionally and financially in times of unemployment. This burden of managing on low income takes its toll: women in such situations suffer poor physical health, depression, anxiety and low self-esteem.

"But is important not to paint such women as *victims*. The experience of CSSC has been that the majority of those at the forefront of community activities and support programmes are women. The leadership potential of many women living in economically depressed areas often finds expression in self-help-projects, personal development courses, co-operatives and adult education."

The Combat Poverty Agency, along with other voluntary groups working with the poor, has long recognised the important and growing evidence of community development groups working at local level with the poor. The vast majority of them are run by and for women, and have been very significant in helping to tackle the isolation and powerlessness of poverty, by promoting community participation and involvement, running personal development and self-help courses.

The importance of these women's groups in particular has

266

already been recognised by the Department of Social Welfare, who were overwhelmed by the response to their scheme of small grants to women's groups around the country. This year, £11,000 was given to a myriad of groups.

"These groups are mushrooming all over the place," said Liz Hayes, the author of a CPA study of three women's community projects, in Little Bray, in Ronanstown, in Clondalkin, and in the North Wall in the inner city; all three are based in Dublin.

"Women's groups are becoming the most dynamic thing happening at community level. We are not that surprised by it. It was a feature in the North in the 80s, and is continuing there," said Hugh Frazer of the Combat Poverty Agency.

"They evolved from an urge that women wanted to get together and talk about their problems, to providing literacy and personal development courses. But the evolution from providing personal development courses is slow, to that of looking at a political analysis of society and where they fit in. At the moment, there is quite a lot of interest in establishing a network of the women's groups around the country."

Most of the groups are based in small community centres, or converted Corporation flats, many of them run by nuns from orders working closely with the poor. It is hoped by the Agency and others that a core of community leaders will emerge from these groups, to voice the experiences of women in poverty.

Through the personal development courses, women have found that their sense of isolation and powerlessness is not their fault, and that others feel the same.

The groups have identified areas such as lack of childcare to enable women to get out of the house for some time, the lack of preventative health measures, and lack of access to vocational training opportunities as some of the key issues relating to women.

"There was little evidence of women giving attention to their own health needs in any of the projects," researcher Liz Hayes found. "A constant topic of conversation in personal development courses was how to act assertively with medical professionals. It was suggested that women found it easier to be

267

assertive over their children's health than for themselves."

Ms Hayes records how positive action occurred in the Ronanstown project, when a course on women's health stressed the need for regular cancer smears as a preventative health measure. Participants negotiated with the local health centre to organise a special time when groups of women could go together. As a result, a special clinic was organised one morning a month for women in the area.

The Ronanstown group criticised the Vocational Training Opportunities Scheme, which allowed people on the dole to do the Intermediate and Leaving Certificates, without losing benefits. But because it was for those in receipt of unemployment benefit, the women were excluded from the course.

"The women felt that the organisers of such mainstream education courses did not even see the needs of women on low income, much less try to meet them," she wrote.

The Little Bray management committee actively supported a woman who complained about her treatment in the Garda station when she reported an alleged violent incident in her own home. The committee helped her to send her details to the Director of Public Prosecutions, to the Minister for Justice and other politicians.

Many of the projects ran welfare rights groups, to inform people about their entitlements, but also to help them assert themselves when they faced the officials in the dole office or health centre. Increasingly, welfare rights groups are speaking out to the media at the time of the Budget on behalf of social welfare recipients.

The lack of childcare facilities was an ongoing theme in the three projects studied, as it was in many projects around the country. Unless a creche was provided in conjunction with activities, women were dependent on family and friends. Women with partners had equal difficulty as single parents. Women did not recognise that they had the same right to go out as men, felt that they had to organise their home and children first.

"One woman in Little Bray said that she would love to get involved in a campaign to provide more childcare facilities but by

268

the time she had helped out in the centre, attended extra meetings, taken part in a new course and looked after her family she was exhausted and had no energy left for anything else."

The high level of early dropout from education was a consistent feature in the projects, highlighting the fact that the formal education system has failed the majority of women living in disadvantaged areas.

In its report, *Towards a Policy of Combating Poverty Amongst Women,* the Combat Poverty Agency saw that women's groups played an important role in the elimination of women's poverty, in that they provide immediate support and advice for women, they assist them to gain more control over their lives and help them identify causes and solutions to the difficulties they experience.

"The women in the projects are quite definite that they are not feminists," said Liz Hayes. "Many see feminists as lesbians or men-haters. They are clear about not being labelled as feminists." To them, feminists are middle-class with middle-class worries. They see women's representatives looking for better work conditions for women, outlawing discrimination in work.

"The culture of working class women and middle class women is different," said Kathleen Maher, a community activist in Ballymun in north Dublin who evolved from working at community level, to doing a Community Development course in Maynooth.

"The whole powerlessness that we face prevents us from participating in an equal fashion as middle class women," she said. "I think we have a lot in common, but it's not obvious yet.

"Our lack of resources means that we have problems networking, getting a phone, using the bus, getting an office. The contacts are not there. The Council for the Status of Women is there, but it is difficult to get involved in that.

"Working class women don't want to be called feminists because of the whole connotations of lesbian, they don't want to be ostracised," she added. "That view has to be recognised, and faced.

"Also, I think the personal development courses are not getting at the issues of the feminist movement, and women are not learning about the historical background of feminism. There is no discussion of feminist principles."

WHO'S AFRAID OF CHANGE?
Irish Politics in the 1990s

John Waters

During all my fourteen years in school, I only ever won a single medal for sports. All of the sports we played were of the Gaelic persuasion, and I was useless at these. Mostly they seemed to be a cover for legalised violence. I had a fear of leather footballs, especially when wet. When we played football in the field behind the school at lunchtime, I was always the last to be picked, except when there were girls around who wanted to play, and sometimes then as well. Whereas other boys had their mantelpieces well stocked with trophies, mine was bare. But on the final day of term in my Leaving Cert year, I was given one last chance. There was a school sports that day, and I resolved that I would not leave without a medal of some description. I tried the high jump, the long jump, the egg-and-spoon race, the three-legged race and the sack race – all without success. My last hope was the tug-of-war: if I hung in with the right team, I reckoned I had as good a chance as anyone.

There were two teams of ten, picked by a teacher who, like most of his kind, was full of bile, prejudice and bias. When I looked at the line-up of our side, I saw the medal begin to melt before my eyes. I myself was the scrawniest and most spindly boy in the class, and it seemed to me that part of the skill in selecting the team would be to compensate for this by ensuring that some of the fitter, bigger and better-built boys were on the same side as me. I should have known better by then: clearly what the teacher wanted was not a fair contest but a morality play, in which the good, wholesome and virtuous would triumph over the weak, long-haired and morally bankrupt sections of the class. The teacher had somehow contrived to ensure that all the misfits, ne'er do wells and wasters were on our team, whereas the other side had three or four of the strongest and most energised boys in the class.

The contest began. Such was the climate of nihilism on our side that I had been made anchor-man. I wrapped the rope around my waist and braced myself so that when the big pull came on the rope I would at least manage to remain upright. The rest of our team, and all of the other side, pulled hard on the rope in the professional manner. As they pulled, the angle made by each boy with the ground became smaller and smaller until both teams, with the exception of myself, were practically flat out on the ground. The other team was indeed much stronger than ours, and in fact succeeded with the very first pull in taking us right up to the line. The teacher stood at the line with whistle poised in front of his lips, ready to greet the victory of the great and the good over the middling and mediocre.

From my vantage point at the end of the rope, it suddenly occurred to me that, although the other side needed just a little more than a hair's breadth to take them over the line, they could not achieve this without risking losing the ground they had already gained. Like most of our side, they were at full stretch, their heels dug deep in the ground, every ounce of their weight on the rope, but within the breadth of another hair of being flat out on the ground. They had no space to manoeuvre the extra inch of pull that would ensure their widely-predicted victory. From my anchor-man position it occurred to me that if sufficient pull could be applied to the rope from my end, both teams could now be pulled as if dead weight. I shouted to our team to hold the line and then began to jerk on the rope for all I was worth. The sudden jerking, as opposed to the continuous pressure they had become accustomed to, sent the opposition team into total confusion. They scrambled around seeking a fresh grip, while at the same time trying to coordinate their pull to prevent their advantage being eroded. I pulled hard on the rope and shouted to our team to get up off the ground, which they quickly did.

Too late the opposition began to see what was happening. They tried to lie down again and reassert their pull, but their confusion was too great even to protect the ground they had already won. Our bunch of morally bankrupt misfits pulled them half the length of the field before we let go. I still have the medal to prove it.

I write this in the Spring of 1991. For the past six months – in fact from around the time when the 1990 presidential election got into its full swing – I have had the same feeling about Irish politics as I had at that crucial moment of the tug-of-war almost eighteen years ago. Irish politics are now at a point where they can change out of all recognition, where they will yield to whatever pressure we choose to apply.

The word "democracy" is one of our great sacred cows. To attack "democracy" is a bit like kicking a blind man in the street. Democracy, after all, is government by the people, and it would be a low class of animal who would argue with that. And so, no matter what kind of crude or primitive system of elected government is cobbled together, it is placed beyond reproach by the simple expedient of calling it "democracy". In the past couple of decades, almost everybody in Ireland who is not a member of a political party has come to be less than enamoured of Irish politics. People do not see the political process as reflecting either themselves or their interests or aspirations. When you ask people what they dislike about politics, they almost invariably reply along the lines that "all politicians are on the make", or "they're all the same". If you analyse what people say, you come to realise that what they mean is that Irish politics are undemocratic.

We may have elections every couple of years, but for most people this means a choice between candidates towards whom, at best, they feel only slightly varying degrees of indifference. As far as the public is concerned, the candidates are chosen for them, just as arbitrarily as the teacher picked the tug-of-war team. You support a "team", not because of its personnel, or because of its particular strengths, but because you believe – you have been led to believe – that it is *your* team, and that it is capable of winning.

People – as people – have little or no capacity to influence government policy in the way it affects their own lives, never mind in terms of planning to ensure the security and prosperity of future generations. Moreover, for well over half a century, the Irish political system has been in the stranglehold of the Fianna

273

Fail/Fine Gael duopoly, which has sustained itself by maintaining an illusory tension based on spurious divides such as derive from outdated definitions of nationalism, and "moral issues" like divorce and contraception. Because of this, an odd dichotomy has developed whereby many of the matters which provide fodder for debate and movement within the political process no longer have the same currency in the world outside that process; and, conversely, the issues which *do* affect real people in a real way are slow to be integrated into the game of politics.

For years, commentators in the media have been haranguing the Irish electorate for its lack of sophistication. They have accused the Irish people of being politically backward, of treating politics as a kind of blood sport, of failing to make the imaginative connection between the ballot box and the way in which they are governed. The leader columns of our newspapers have railed against the politics of tribalism, clientalism and the parish pump. There is little in this with which I would have argued up to six months ago. I now believe that these charges are no longer justified, that they are outdated, and that, moreover, those who continue to make them are now themselves among the most backward people in Irish politics.

Oddly enough – or perhaps not – these very commentators are themselves even more resistant to change than the most backward or conservative politician. Since the presidential election last year, I have written about this on a number of occasions in *The Irish Times*, and have noticed that ideas like these provoke a very odd reaction among journalists who write about politics. Most of these with whom I come in contact seem anxious to impress on me that I am mistaken about there being any major changes afoot in Irish politics right now.

It has been most interesting to observe the fallout of the presidential election in the pronouncements of several of our leading political pundits. Without exception they appear to have the greatest difficulty with the notion that the Irish electorate actually *meant* what it said in the presidential election, that it is now, more than ever before, disposed towards making the kind of connections which many of these very same pundits have long despaired of its being able to make.

Cynicism is catching. One of the most corrosive aspects of Irish political life these past few years is the cycle of cynicism which has developed in relation to almost every utterance by a politician. For the reasons already mentioned, the political parties themselves must accept a great deal of the responsibility for this, but so too must those who have allowed their perspectives to be defined by their antagonism towards particular political personalities. It is a peculiarity of Irish politics that "outstanding" politicians have tended to create a kind of mirror image of themselves in the antagonism of their adversaries, whether in the politician's own party, in another political party, or, as frequently happened also, in the media.

In fact, the grudges tended to last longer in the bosoms of journalists than in those of politicians, who frequently were able to subjugate their personal animosities in the interests of personal survival.

Thus, while such a, shall we say, "controversial" politician continued to occupy a prominent place in Irish life, much of the political discussion and debate of the time tended to be related to questions of his personality, history, mistakes, rather than to the wider issues of public concern at the time. Certain political columnists and correspondents created whole careers for themselves out of this process, maintaining their dogged opposition to an individual politician long after his credentials had ceased to be an issue of any great importance for the public. Often, reading the writings of such columnists, you got to wondering why they bothered to write about politics at all, such was their inability to break out of the rut of hostility towards particular politicians. They did not seem to like politics or politicians very much, and any idealism they might have had in the past had long since been corroded by cynicism.

In actual fact, for all their moralising, most of these columnists seem actually to *like* the idea of Irish politics being backward, corrupt, or whatever – it gives them a constant supply of ready material and allows them to feel superior both to the politicians and the people who continue to vote for them in spite of everything. The odd paradox about political commentary in this country is that, in order to be successful at it, you have to become

275

adept at reading a political scene which fills you with fear and loathing. Almost all of our political writers are people who subscribe to a different form of politics than that which they earn their livings writing about.

Most of them, for example, would much prefer if Irish politics yielded more willingly to a left/right divide. They refuse to see Ireland as it is: as a nascent democracy, a post-peasant political culture coming to terms with self-government. It is a source of constant irritation to such people that the Irish electorate has persistently refused to be press-ganged into their neat little view of the world.

But, being pragmatists all, they have managed to accommodate to our odd little ways. Given a choice between what they *want* to happen and what they can *safely predict* will happen, they will plump for the safe option every time. Pundits like certitudes more than they like dreams. In fact, they need political certitudes – far more than do the rest of the population: they depend on them to maintain their meal tickets. It is actually in the interest of the average commentator on Irish politics – much more than in that of the average politician – that nothing very much should ever change, and certainly that change should come about in an ordered and predictable fashion. When an electorate begins to throw up radical results, the pundits have a vested interest in defusing and translating them back into a language which conforms with their own analyses. It is also of vital importance, regardless of how much events may outwardly seem to differ from what they predicted, to retrospectively rearrange the furniture in a manner which makes clear that they were actually correct in their original pronouncements.

This can be amusing, but it can also be dangerous. Politics is very much a group activity; it depends on a constant interaction between the process and the electorate which sustains it.

For this to work properly requires a constant flow of communication in both directions. This communication needs to be as pure as possible. People need to be told what they have done, what the effects of their choices have been, what *really happened*. They do *not* need to be told what the political correspondent wants to persuade them they *actually* meant. They

276

need constant affirmation of the impact of their vote, because that is all they have.

Thus, because Mary Robinson's victory in the presidential election was not foreseen by a single political commentator, we have for the past few months found ourselves playing on a pitch with goalposts sticking up in all the wrong places. The retrospective analysts, variously and depending on their particular standpoint, declared that the Robinson win was a triumph for liberal values, a victory for public relations, a personal endorsement of the candidate herself, indicative of an appetite for socialist values, a gain for feminism, a rejection of socialism... Whatever you're having yourself, actually – just so long as it's on the menu laid down by the pundits.

It does not appear to have crossed anybody's mind that the Robinson victory was an expression of the very values for which the commentators have been calling for years. The word "expression" I use advisedly: as I've said in the past, it is important, when considering the implications of the presidential election, to distinguish the dancer from the dance. Mary Robinson did not create the mood which elected her: she merely materialised in the right place at the right time, saying the right kind of things, to enable her to tap into what was there already. She did not begin the process, but merely displayed the truth of its existence.

There is very little to be gained, therefore, at least in so far as understanding what is currently happening in Irish politics is concerned, from contemplating the personality or politics of Mary Robinson herself, although it has *some* relevance, as we will see later on.

An awful lot of nonsense has been talked about Mary Robinson's victory – both by those who welcomed it and those who did not. I have said it before, but it's worth repeating: Mary Robinson's election as President of Ireland was not a victory for applied left wing politics, nor for "liberal values" as commonly understood in this country, nor for feminism in the normal sense of that term; it was an expression of a deep and rapidly escalating mood of radicalism which is rooted firmly in real issues and the actual state of life as lived by real people in this country. For the first time, a majority of the Irish electorate raised a hand to draw the Irish political bandwagon to a halt. When we look back at the 90s from the next millenium, this is what we will mean when we speak of the great changes which came at the end of the 20th Century. In the 90s the Party will die, to be replaced by the cult of the gifted amateur, which in turn will give way to the integration into politics of real people, their wishes and aspirations. The old system, whereby the electorate was faced with a choice between candidates chosen by anonymous men in smoke-filled rooms – and about whom, if they really thought about it, the public had no real feelings – is almost dead. The new politics will be "democratic" in the truest sense: they will be about electing our own kind to represent us in public life. Despite the efforts of those with a vested interest in its survival, Hobson's Choice Politics is dying fast.

Why did Mary Robinson win? Mary Robinson won the presidency by appealing to the ignored and forgotten people of Excluded Ireland. It's as simple as that. I was born in Castlerea, County Roscommon, and lived there for much of the past thirty-five years. In that time I have had to watch my home town being destroyed by forces which it was unable to understand, forces which were brought to bear on it from outside, and which, as the late John Healy said, "come tricked out in the fleshy seducing clothes of progress". In the past twenty years or so, the entire *raison d'etre* of towns like Castlerea has disappeared. Their world had literally turned upside down. From being net producers of goods, catering for most of their internal needs as well as those of their immediate hinterland, they have been reduced to anonymous suburban centres which now seem to exist primarily to absorb the produce of mass consumerism. With a savage irony, traditional "market towns", such as Castlerea was, have been deprived of their status by "market forces". Because the political process is devoid of ideas, and because there is no political virtue in honesty, nobody has the heart to turn off the life support system, or even to point to the writing on the wall. The politicians and the system they operate simply opts out; it leaves the fate of these places to market forces, so the life just drains away in the form of the emigration of the younger generations.

If you drive west from Dublin, in the direction of Galway, Westport or Ballina, you will within a short time become conscious of something very seriously amiss. At a point somewhere around an hour's drive from Dublin, the entire tone, mood and sensibility of the country changes in a manner which at first is difficult to pin down. You pass Kinnegad and begin to hit towns like Tyrellspass, Moate, Ballinasloe, Ballymahon, Loughrea, Lanesboro, Craughwell, Roscommon, Castlerea, Ballyhaunis, Balla, Ballaghaderreen, Charlestown. It will take a few towns, maybe even a few journeys, a few years, for the penny to drop. In one town you will see a couple of old age pensioners huddled in a doorway, in another you may have to blow your horn at a couple of youngsters in danger of running onto the road in pursuit of a ball. Be assured, however, there will be no traffic jams. You will see nobody between the age of eighteen and twenty-five. I wrote about this recently in *The Irish Times*, describing it as The Land Where Every Day Is Like Sunday. For a day or two afterwards I found myself being stopped constantly in the street by people who came from such places and who wanted to tell me that I had articulated exactly what they had been feeling for years but had not been able to express. I told them that I suspected they had already expressed it very well, much more eloquently than had I: in the vote they gave to Mary Robinson in November 1990.

All across the country, but particularly in what we know as "rural Ireland", there are hundreds, thousands of communities who feel themselves under threat, who feel surplus to requirements in their own birthplace. We have lived, over the past thirty years, in a country which led us to believe that the things we feared most – the destruction of the lives of individuals and families by unemployment and emigration – belonged to the past.

In the optimism of the times through which we lived, the 60s and 70s, politics were just a form of entertainment, an occasional diversionary sideshow. For the past few generations, we entered into the spirit of Irish politics, believing that politics was the icing on a heavily-cherried cake. But when we bit into the cake, we found it to be mouldy and bitter to the taste. The cherries were fakes and dissolved on our tongues.

I detect a great anger at large in this country over the past couple of years. It takes different forms in different places, but it has a common root. Over the past ten years, the economic "bottom-line" has come to have an almost religious significance for politicians, managers and media people – almost all of whom spend their lives in Dublin.

I am talking, yes, about Dublin 4. To be of Dublin 4 does not necessarily entail actually living in a particular part of Dublin, or even, strictly speaking, living in Dublin at all. To be a Dublin 4 "type" you require only to think in a particular way, which essentially is to think only of yourself and your own immediate interests. Dublin 4 types are left wing on social issues but right wing on economic issues. Over the past decade, Dublin 4 has used these issues to provoke war after war with what it perceives as the backward forces in Irish life. In reality it is conducting a war among forces which it itself has created, which have little currency outside its boundaries. In a sense, because Dublin 4 people are at most one generation removed from the country, the war is waged against the D4 type's own roots and background. They are people embarrassed about not having emanated from a culture more in keeping with their present position, and take their impatience out on those they perceive to be too backward to climb the same ladder as themselves. Everybody could be like them, they insist, just so long as we agree to do things their way.

Inevitably, the Dublin 4 type is hated by the rest of the country, with the result that, even when D4 occasionally comes up with good ideas – as occasionally it does – the very fact of its sponsorship ensures the roundest possible rejection by the population at large.

Dublin 4, however, has had one famous victory in recent years. In the early 90s, it became the official sponsor of the drive to – as the expression had it – "reform the nation's finances". As a result of our troglodyte political practices, we were told, the country was on the brink of bankruptcy. We had, in that famous phrase of the time, been "living beyond our means". Through the medium of the Doheny & Nesbitt School of Economics, Dublin 4 succeeded in feeding its ideas about the economy intravenously into the political system. Fiscal rectitude became big in Irish politics, and close links were forged between politicians, economists and journalists, who between them succeeded in hijacking the entire political and social agenda and making it a vehicle for the views which, though they ensured the immediate survival of those who promoted them, had little to offer in terms of the long-term well-being of the country as a whole. Such was their power and influence, that no politician or political party seemed willing to break with this self-imposed consensus. Cutbacks became the order of the day and the catchcry of the time. Needless to say, most of the cutbacks occurred in places far removed from the habitats of Dublin 4. Ignoring the obvious contradictions under their very noses, these people insisted that all activity outside Dublin not just pay for itself, but be *seen* to pay for itself. They seemed wilfully blind to the obvious fact that, as an agricultural nation, we required, first and foremost, a vibrant rural life. Dublin may make a pretty cherry on top, but if there is no cake to hold it up, the cherry will roll off and end up in the dustbin.

The Dublin establishment, including the government, the opposition parties and the media, has become absorbed in a view of the country's economic condition which to most of its people is a fiction. The establishment congratulates itself on the latest inflation rates – proof, we are told, that the policy of fiscal rectitude is bearing fruit – but gives no thought to the cost of this abstract gain to the lives of the people who populate this economy of ours. Each percentage point of a decrease in the rate of inflation can be measured just as surely by a widening of the silent greyness which is enveloping rural Ireland in its cold embrace. We celebrate our "recovery" from our recent bite of economic frostbite, softening our focus to obliterate the loss of vital limbs and organs which have resulted from our choice of "cure".

Ironically, Dublin 4's view of the economy was most vigourously pursued by the man whom they most fervently wished to do down. From 1987 onwards, Charles Haughey enforced a policy of fiscal rectitude which proved more successful on its own terms than previous efforts had been. This stuck a bit in Dublin 4's craw, but, pragmatic as always, it learned to live with the man it loved to loathe. The economy, we were informed, was "back on track". Economists whom we had not seen for several years now arose and appeared to many. The country was "back on its feet".

This was news to the country. Just as in the past people had had difficulty in remembering a time when they had "lived beyond their means", now they found it hard to appreciate that they had "never had it so good". They became confused, then angry, then determined.

There is a great anger abroad in this country at the present time. In some places about straightforward matters like health cuts, or the effects of years of a disastrous industrial policy, or the threatened closure of sub-post offices. But the anger is such that putting right any or all of the above will no longer be enough; because the common root of this anger is the belief that this country is being run by a set of people, and according to a set of "principles", which takes no account whatever of the true nature of life in this country or of the needs of the majority of its inhabitants. Mary Robinson, as though inspired by a guardian angel, left Dublin 4 and travelled among the people of Ireland making the right noises about emigration, unemployment, community development and the failure of politics. And the people of Ireland made her President. I do not see how we could possibly have made ourselves more clear.

In the course of the campaign, Mary Robinson was careful to avoid talk of divorce or other elements of what might be described as the liberal agenda. And yet, the only significant issue which was extrapolated from her victory by the main political parties or the media was the issue of divorce, which we were told was "back on the agenda".

The people of Ireland may or may not want divorce. They may or may not want the right to judicial separation, to annulment, the right to any unlimited number of possible formulae for living apart from one another. But what they want much, much more than that is the right to live, first of all, *together* – with the people they love, reared or grew up with. The greatest anger of all in this country today is among the families who have reared their

282

children for export. Half a million young people left Ireland in the 1980s, most of them the people who would have changed this country regardless of the politicians or pundits. The political process, while paying lip-service to the "tragedy of emigration", is in reality quite happy to have the possibility of sudden and dramatic change filtered off by emigration. But nobody bargained on emigration having a radicalising effect on many of those who remained: Mary Robinson got the votes of Irish emigrants by proxy – their parents and friends voted in their place.

This is something of which many politicians and commentators have long despaired, and yet, now that it is happening, they seem anxious only to explain it away, to dismiss it as a once-off, a freak, an aberration. For all its hectoring, the political process has failed the people of Ireland. It has lamented their backwardness, and yet presented them time and again with Hobson's Choice. A people get the kind of politicians they deserve, we decide, conveniently forgetting that they get, first of all, the kind of politicians they are offered.

A classic example of this has been the behaviour of Fine Gael, during and in the aftermath of the presidential election. Under its previous leader, Alan Dukes, Fine Gael seemed to have embarked upon a totally new course in Irish politics. With the politics of the Tallaght Strategy, Dukes made the first of what was to be a series of moves towards this new model. A thoughtful if uncharismatic politician, he correctly identified most of the social and economic difficulties of modern Ireland as arising from the nature of Irish politics. He pledged himself to eradicate the malignant growths of expediency, party self-interest and short-term thinking from the body politic. Under Dukes, Fine Gael backed off its traditional role of opposing for the sake of opposing. It gave the Fianna Fail government of 1987-'89 the space to breathe in order to carry out the surgery which the entire political process had by now decided was necessary. According to Dukes's reading, much of the groundwork in shifting the public perception of the function of an opposition had been achieved. But in the media and within Fine Gael itself, there were people who were not as keen on the notion of change.

In the run-up to the 1989 election, a number of articles began to materialise in the newspapers questioning Dukes's political judgement and speculating as to the likely duration of his leadership. The party's difficulties were understandable: many of the Fine Gael grassroots and public representatives had put in a lifetime attacking Fianna Fail. For them it was the only reason to be in politics: as a cat chases mice, their role in life was to make things difficult for Fianna Fail. They longed for the old days, when Garret and Charlie were synonyms for good and bad.

Dukes remained cool under pressure. Rather than alter the course of policies which did not seem to be in either his own or his party's immediate interest, he simply stated and restated the underlying message: change or die. Dukes believed that, by refusing to give in to the expediencies of the present moment, he would in the longer term show that his kind of Fine Gael had the stuff to become the natural party government of Ireland.

But Dukes was not given the time to implement his longterm strategy. Fine Gael panicked and reverted to type, dumping Dukes in the process. Here too, the presidential election provided the crucial moment. Fine Gael interpreted the fact that the campaign was going badly for them as a public indictment of both the Tallaght Strategy and Dukes's leadership, when in fact it was merely a reflection of their failure to run the right candidate. (This doesn't mean that Austin Currie was the "wrong" candidate: he just didn't happen to be called Garret). In a sense Alan Dukes helped bring about his own downfall by acquiescing to the hounding of Brian Lenihan in the infamous Jim Duffy tapes affair. Conscious of the three-years of withdrawal symptoms which his party had suffered following the Tallaght Strategy, Dukes probably reckoned that a quick fix of the old gung-ho politics would keep the grassroots content for a while longer. But once a dog is let loose you can't tell him who to bite, and the outcome probably did more to undermine Fine Gael's integrity than Brian Lenihan's. For all of Dukes's wholly admirable rhetoric, here he was resorting to the very form of politics he purported to despise. In a sense, he deserved what he got; though from another perspective his demise may be looked back upon as one of the great tragedies of modern politics.

This episode clearly shows how the process and those who live off it have a vested interest in the continuation of Hobson's Choice politics, and how, like a living organism, it moves to protect itself from external correction. This is why, whenever we, the mere voters, say we want something different, the process redirects our request through the prism of its own self-interest and gives us back what it thinks we will endure.

A different kind of example of this is to be seen in the left wing parties who helped to get Mary Robinson elected. Neither Labour nor the Worker's Party seem able to come to terms with the fact that the Robinson victory may be just the turning point for which they have waited all these years. Since November last, they have shilly-shallied on the margins, like a coward on the edge of a dancehall fight tearing off his jacket and pleading to be held back before he kills someone. Mary Robinson won 25 of the 41 constituencies, and yet neither of the two left wing parties has made any real effort to offer the electorate in these places an alternative to Hobson's Choice.

Instead, by this Spring of 1991, we have Fianna Fail strutting about in the "social democratic" finery which delivered Mrs Robinson to the Park, while those who helped to put her there scramble in the bottom drawer of socialism attempting to cover their embarrassment before presenting themselves to the public. The rhetoric of the two left wing parties as we approached the litmus test of the annual party conference season gave little reason for optimism that either party had come to terms with the outcome of the Presidental election.

As I write this, neither of the two left wing parties has given any sign that we can expect any immediate building to be done on the admirable singlemindedness they displayed in the presidential campaign. Both talk of using "long spoons" when dealing with the other, and, ironically too, talk the same language of ideological claptrap. Both seem intent on avoiding real change and confining themselves to fatuous and irrelevant gestures.

The Labour Party has replaced its historic Starry Plough logo with a red rose, and declared that it will henceforth be a "democratic socialist" party. The party's new constitution marks the abandonment of traditional Labour policies, such as the

285

nationalisation of banks and the achievement of democratic control of industry. Instead, the talk is of more generalised aspirations, like the "equitable distribution of wealth", the "elimination of poverty" and the "promotion of justice".

The Worker's Party has likewise plumped for "democratic socialism" – perhaps because the alternative was the "social democracy" route charted by Eoghan Harris in his infamous pamphlet of last year. If mine enemy says white, then the answer must be black. Party leader Prionsias De Rossa has, like Dick Spring, confined himself to vague generalisations about the party's commitment to "social ownership" and "democratic planning".

I don't think any of this is what potential supporters of both of these parties are waiting to hear. I think that what they want to hear is a harmonious left wing voice which has the air of success about it.

Left wing policies, as such, are not the problem: I know of an awful lot of sensible people who are totally in favour of the nationalisation of banks (some of them are "right wing" economists).

And why is it that almost everyone, including many on the Left, continues to insist that it will take the left wing parties several generations to reach the levels of support achieved by Mary Robinson in November? The answer, I believe, is that the Left is in love with losing, or is at least conditioned to defeat. If this is true, they have nothing to worry about, for losing is a self-perpetuating condition.

In the aftermath of the presidential election, eyebrows were temporarily raised at the so-called "anomaly" that, whereas Mrs Robinson could command 43 per cent of the popular vote, support for Labour and the WP had, if anything, diminished since previous opinion polls. Then it was decided that Mary Robinson's victory had "no implications" for left wing politics. The fact that this view was shared by many on the Left is indicative of the inability of such people to contemplate the notion of victory.

There were, on the Left, two broad responses to this "anomaly". One argued that, since Mary Robinson had been a "liberal" or "centrist", rather than a "left wing" candidate, the

286

dichotomy was not surprising; another held that the gap could be marginally narrowed by modification, adaptation and persuasion.

Both views are wrong; there is no anomaly. Nor is there a problem with "socialism" per se. In an interview I conducted with Mrs Robinson some two months before the election I asked her about her previously professed socialist views, which had by then been sublimated into her emerging campaign persona, but which would subsequently be the focus of hamfisted Fine Gael attempts at a "red scare". "I find", she replied, "that 'socialism' is a word that excludes dialogue and understanding. I think I'm very conscious of language. If I talk about issues that would be totally compatible with a socialist view of society, but I don't use the word 'socialism', then heads are nodding and it's acceptable. But if you use the word 'socialist', people withdraw in fear. They don't know what you mean; but they know that it's communism and Russia, and it didn't work."

Mary Robinson won the presidency, not because she was a socialist, nor because she *wasn't* a socialist, but because people realised that she *could*. Left wing parties languish at single figure levels of support, not because they are left wing, but because they languish at single figure levels of support.

Mary Robinson began her campaign with roughly the same level of support as the combined totals of the two left wing parties. In the early stages of her campaign she added to her vote in ones and twos, and if that was all there was to it she would indeed have taken a couple of generations to reach the magic 40 per cent line. But sometimes in an election campaign, a candidate is offered the opportunity to transcend the mere arithmetic accumulation of support. This point occurs when, by an almost magical process, the candidate and the electorate begin to smell victory together.

Mary Robinson won because she *could;* because she *believed* she could; and because she succeeded in *communicating* that belief to large numbers of people. She created a magical moment at which her accumulation of support shifted from the mere arithmetic to the geometric. This is Robinson's Law: the left wing support in this country is the square root of its own potential, which when multiplied by the possibility of success equals the realisation of the

287

impossible.

There is, throughout the entire political process at the moment, a palpable fear of the electorate. Nobody – and certainly no political party – seems to know what the people want. Perhaps I can be of assistance: what the people want is the democratic realisation of their own wishes through the political process. That's *it*. The people who might vote for the left wing parties are not interested in the internal wranglings, wordplays or standoffs. What they want is a united Left which holds in its sweaty paw the possibility of an alternative government.

This will mean these parties having to change, but not the kind of tinkering which is being undertaken. The problem for the Left is that, acclimatised to opposition politics and a minority position, they never imagined that when change beckoned it would entail them having to change themselves. They thought they had just to sit and wait to inherit the Earth, so misused and abused by right wing parties. Like other forces in Irish politics, they had created for themselves a cosy little niche which, for all their posturing, they hate having disturbed.

Walls have come down in Irish politics. Unlike those in Eastern Europe, they fell silently, as in a movie without sound; but they *did* fall and they will resist every attempt by the system to rebuild them. The Right tried to persuade us that Eastern Europe meant the end of socialism, when in fact it meant the death of dogma – of both Left and Right. The Left tried to persuade itself that it was merely a problem of semantics – that an overhaul of the language would allow the socialist chariot to career on to the winning post. As might have been expected, the problem has proved much more profound.

In fact, the Western Left was spooked much more by the capitalist triumphalism which followed, than by the events in Eastern Europe themselves. Unable to decide whether to drop socialism or merely change its name, the left wing parties ended up doing neither and both. They tinkered with combinations of the words "socialism" and "democracy", hoping that everything would die down and they could get back to normal. But language was only a part of the problem: remember that the terminology of Left and Right translate almost as direct opposites in East and West. If you walk into the offices of the Civic Forum in Prague, the people you meet there will strike you as having much more in common with the left wing parties of the West than with the right wing parties who were so quick to adopt them. They wear jumpers and T-shirts. The men sport bushy beards; the women are in charge. The main point of difference is that for Civic Forum, "social democracy" is a tautology and "democratic socialism" a contradiction in terms, whereas for their counterparts in the West these terminologies have now been exalted into sacred cows. Because of this very obsession with language, the western Left has allowed a situation develop whereby it both perceives itself, and is perceived, as the ideological opposite of people in movements like Civic Forum.

In their anxiety to protect their own ideological territory, left wingers forgot the fundamental point that they, in their own societies, were in a precisely analogous position to the revolutionaries who overthrew the socialist regimes of the East, and that the liberation of people – anywhere, anytime – is *never* a problem, and *always* an opportunity, for the underdog.

It has been quite astonishing over the past year and a half, to observe the contortions of the Left here in Ireland in the wake of the revolutions in Eastern Europe. The leaderships of both Labour and The Worker's Party have made regular sacrifices of core values and become almost daily communicants at the altar of The Market, albeit with the occasional ejaculation of socialist piety as they beat the red roses on their lapels. Among the rank-and-file, not surprisingly, the confusion has been even more acute. One prominent Labour party left winger of my acquaintance has taken to greeting people in the street with felicitations along the lines of, "That Boris Yeltsin is a fucking terrible gobshite, isn't he?" Czechoslovak President, Vaclav Havel, likewise, has been a regular target of left wing frustration in the West, the usual gibe being that he is "too good to be true". In fact, President Havel has dealt much more efficiently with the semantics of post-Eastern European leftism than any of the local mob that I have had to listen to. Like Mary Robinson, Havel had in the past called himself a socialist, but had ceased to do so because of the difficulty with definitions. "I stopped calling myself a socialist without changing my politics," he has said; and on another occasion elaborated: "God created me in such a way that my heart is on the left side of my chest. And I will not deny my affiliation with the, let's say, liberal minded international intellectual community, which is called by some left wing."

I am on Vaclav Havel's side, whatever he chooses to call himself. The Irish Left, also, needs to decide which – or, more correctly, *whose* – side it is on. If it continues to see itself on the opposite side to those who strive for change in Eastern Europe, then it will perish like the apparatchiks of "actually existing socialism" in the East. It would do better to strive for the same ideal as such people: for a society in which the genuine dreams and aspirations of the people can be transmitted through the political process. I think it's called "democracy". Both here and in Eastern Europe there remains a need for the human values of socialism, for justice, egalitarianism, altruism and the concept of the community. If the Left can bring such a society about in Ireland, they will be entitled to call it what they like.

But in the end, I suspect, it will be left once again to Fianna Fail. There is a perception in Irish politics that radical change must come either from the "right" or the "left", but this ain't necessarily so. There is an equal, perhaps greater, possibility that the present system will simply reform itself in response to the new mood of the people, and that much of the running will be made by those who have done most to perpetuate the kind of politics which the people are now in the process of rejecting. With Fianna Fail on forty-odd per cent of the popular vote, it is difficult to foresee a model of Irish politics which would not include them. It seems to me that by far the quickest and most effective way to change Irish politics is to change Fianna Fail. There are already signs, as I have pointed out before – and been dubbed a Fianna Fail apologist for my pains – that the person who has taken most out of the electorate's message in November last is Charles J, Haughey.

It has got to the stage in Irish politics where it is considered better to despair of change than allow of the possibility that it might be brought about by Haughey and Fianna Fail. This does not seem to me to be either a sensible or a realistic position, and if pointing this out makes me a "Fianna Fail apologist", then so be it.

As I wrote at the time, in his Ard Fheis address in March of this year, Charles Haughey appeared to be going the furthest distance of any of the current crop of political leaders towards meeting what I perceive to be the wishes of the electorate. Although Haughey appeared to be speaking in the usual manner to the assembled delegates in Dublin's RDS, although he paused from time to time to accept their applause, and although he sprinkled his speech with the inevitable reassurances about "our national traditions", "the men of 1916", "our forefathers" and "the great objectives of our party", he seemed for the first time in a long time to be talking, not to the party faithful, but to the rest of us, the *un*faithful people of Ireland. It was as though he had finally twigged that he had led Fianna Fail into a time-warp and had decided to lead it out again. It is easy to be cynical about Haughey's motivation: at this stage, you might say, he has little to lose and perhaps a whole new political lifetime to gain from coming on as the Great Progressive of Irish politics. But politicians can often be at their most useful when they have nothing to lose. Moreover, the vision and ideas articulated in Haughey's speech would, if implemented, mean a far different and better Ireland. We have heard these ideas delivered with far more passion and conviction than Haughey will ever be capable of. But we have never heard them from someone with such means at his disposal to turn them into reality. What he was offering was a total perestroika of Fianna Fail, which could amount, in effect, to a new era of politics in Ireland.

He may not, as I say, be doing this for what you or I might think of as idealistic motives, but most of us will be able to live with that, just as we can live with the fact that Haughey, whom we elected to lead us, has for the past four years been implementing the wishes of a small and unrepresentative section of the electorate. We can live with a lot – just so long as we are allowed to live.

There are none of us getting any younger, so our leftist friends will have to indulge our lack of patience with their debates on the fine distinctions between social democracy and democratic socialism. The old politics is on its arse on the ground and we have to take what chances we get to pull the ground from under it.

Even if this messes up the well-laid plans of the parties and the political commentators, we want change, and we want it now. We, at least, are not afraid.

THE IRISH FAMILY
The Gallaghers and Ireland

Mary Raftery

"Steadfast Susan Tightens Her Belt" — this was one of the headlines which greeted the news of Patrick Gallagher's conviction in Northern Ireland for fraud offences. The Susan referred to is Gallagher's wife, and this type of coverage was fairly representative of the attitude in the South to his conviction. It summed up in many ways the peculiarly sympathetic attitude which we have to the well-heeled stroke-puller within our society — in this case Patrick Gallagher, one of the most flamboyant of them all. It also clearly showed that in spite of everything, the glamour never left the Gallagher family.

The reasons for this kind of attitude have much to do with the history of the Gallagher family through its last two generations. The fortunes of the dynasty have closely mirrored developments within Ireland since the 1940s and an examination of the Gallaghers paints a revealing picture of Ireland over the last 50 years. It is the story of the accumulation by the family of vast wealth and power, and of the collapse of the empire they so painstakingly built up.

The dynasty began in Tubbercurry, County Sligo with a small farming background. A large family, most of the children emigrated in the 1940s, following the flow of Irish who went to rebuild Britain after the war. The Gallagher boys worked on the building sites of London for the best part of a decade. And there they made their fortunes.

Matt Gallagher, father of Patrick, returned to Ireland in the late 1950s, and founded the Gallagher Group of construction companies. James, Hubert and Charles Gallagher formed the Abbey Group, an equally powerful collection of construction and manufacturing companies active in both Britain and Ireland. The two groups, however, were from the beginning completely separate with no connecting links of any kind, and there is no suggestion here to the contrary.

Matt Gallagher had returned to Ireland just ahead of the posse. The country was on the verge of the economic boom of the 1960s. As emigration ceased for the first time in the history of the independent state, there would be a need for low-cost private housing. A new middle class was being created which was willing and able to pay for shelter.

Matt saw the potential, and began to amass a vast land bank throughout the country. And then he built — row upon row of Gallagher houses throughout Dublin, Cork, Limerick, Waterford and Galway.

It was during the 1960s that the enduring links between Fianna Fail and the building trade were forged. Fianna Fail had created the conditions for the success of the handful of big builders in the country. And Matt Gallagher, one of the biggest of them, was the archetypal Fianna Fail builder.

It was entirely natural that Matt should be close to Fianna Fail. In the euphoric optimism of the 1960s, they could feel that together they were literally building the country — Fianna Fail and Lemass by allowing the building boom to happen and Matt by providing the bricks and mortar.

There was little question of rules and regulations at the time. In terms of building and development, the country was virgin territory, but ripe enough for fortunes to be made by those in the right place at the right time. During the 60s, Matt Gallagher could frequently be seen dining in Dublin's Russell Hotel, favourite haunt of mohair-suited Fianna Fail stalwarts, with maps of the city spread on the table, deep in discussion with among others, one Charles J. Haughey. The Gallaghers and the Haugheys were close family friends, with the heads of both households buying and selling land from each other.

The other branch of the Gallagher family was also close to Fianna Fail. James Gallagher had returned to his roots, and in 1961, on his first attempt, was elected Fianna Fail TD for Sligo-Leitrim. He remained politically active during the following twenty years, for most of which he was also Chairman of the Abbey Group.

The confidence derived from the booming success of the 1960s was passed on by Matt Gallagher to his son and heir, Patrick. Matt died in 1974 — he was only 57, his son a youngster of 22. The knowledge that he belonged to a dynasty that had literally built Ireland meant that Patrick, like Matt before him, felt he could not fail. That confidence dictated the way Patrick was to run the business, which was to have a devastating effect on the country over the next two decades.

Matt Gallagher died at a crucial time in the Irish economy. The oil crisis of the early 1970s and recession was beginning to bite, nibbling particularly at the heels of the building industry. That recession induced a perceptible change in attitude towards wealth among the Irish business classes. That change was mirrored in the two generations of Gallaghers.

Matt Gallagher had certainly amassed a fortune through his business, but there was a sense at the time that what he and his like were doing was useful to the country, it had a purpose — by employing thousands of people and filling the need for new middle-class housing, they were contributing to progress.

But the new generation had little use for progress. With recession came a new hardness. Patrick Gallagher reflected the changing climate in the country by shifting the emphasis of his father's business. He began to sell off the vast land bank, and to concentrate on the top end of the housing market. It was a calculated and cynical gamble. At the time, he said: "We felt that in every recession there were people who would make it through, this time they were the civil servants, the accountants the airline people and so on, so we simply catered for them."

Patrick then proceeded to remove the Gallagher Group from its traditional building business altogether. He laid off thousands of building workers — instead of actually doing the building, the Gallagher Group discovered that there was more money in simply providing the land (complete with planning permission and so on) to other companies.

The next step was entirely logical in the Gallagher scheme for the pursuit of profit. Pure property speculation, untrammelled by the need to do anything useful with that property, became the primary activity of the Gallagher Group from the late 1970s on.

The Gallagher Group would now have been almost completely unrecognisable to any of Matt's business associates, most of whom had by this stage retired from the Group. The sophisticated and tricky seventies had well and truly supplanted the simpler and more straightforward sixties. The Gallagher Group now comprised almost fifty companies. At the centre of this sprawling labyrinth lay a controlling company — conveniently registered in the Cayman Islands to keep it safe from prying eyes.

The fact that ownership of all the Gallagher companies lay with a foreign-registered company was to have peculiar repercussions at a later stage. Companies registered in places like the Cayman Islands can effectively keep their ownership details completely secret — they are not obliged to reveal any detail of their operations. So it was not possible to obtain proof positive that Patrick Gallagher owned the Cayman Islands company which owned all of the Gallagher Group companies.

The net effect of this was that coverage several years later of Gallagher's dubious activities both north and south of the border was hampered by a legal situation where Patrick Gallagher could not be described as owner of the Gallagher Group. He was Managing Director, he clearly controlled it, but no mention was to be made of actual ownership. This serves as one small example of the slightly ludicrous effect of the combination of weak company law in Ireland and powerful libel laws.

Patrick Gallagher was a huge success as a speculator. He bought and sold landmark properties around Dublin at a great rate, apparently making millions on the transactions. The press couldn't get enough of him. To them, he epitomised the new, dynamic face of Irish capitalism — young, brash, successful, with no deal too big for him to handle. At various stages, he was quoted as saying that he would expand his business abroad. Completing the circle of the two generations, he could now choose to export his success, whereas his father and uncles had had nothing to export but their labour.

Newspapers and magazines gushed about his having 'the Midas touch'. Gossip columnists hung upon his every word. He was the man who couldn't fail. His excesses were in some way seen as a measure of his, and by extension the country's, success. When he outbid an oil sheik for a horse at Goffs, it seemed that Ireland had somehow made it in the international money league. What people latched on to was not the obscene amount of money paid for the horse, but the fact that an oil sheik, no less, had been put in his place.

Trade unionist Michael Mullen objected, outraged that anyone could pay over £1 million for a horse, particularly when bloodstock transactions were not taxed in this country. His was a lone voice. Gallagher, it seemed, was above criticism as far as the bulk of the press was concerned.

The newspapers were full of tales of how he was spending his money, of the latest horse or stately mansion he had bought. Between them all, he and his family bought up a good number of the ascendancy homes around Dublin. He himself acquired the biggest and best of them — Straffan House in Kildare represented ostentatious wealth on a truly grand scale. He installed his mother and some of his sisters and their families in mansions around the capital. His younger brother Paul, in the business with him, bought a huge castle in Wicklow. From a small farm in Tubbercurry a mere handful of decades previously, the Gallaghers were now the new ascendancy. And fully in keeping with the image, Patrick was a familiar sight, complete with top hat, in the owner's enclosure at the Epsom Derby.

This is not to say that Patrick had lost touch with reality at home. He kept in close contact with his father's friends in the republican party. He was one of very few businessmen invited to the celebrations in honour of new party leader Charles Haughey in 1979. Anyone who had at one stage owned no fewer than almost thirty properties on or near St Stephen's Green was a valuable asset to the ruling political party, and indeed vice versa.

An example of how far Patrick had brought the business from the early construction days of his father and the 1960s was to be found in the fate of the Gallagher gallery in Ely Place. Matt Gallagher, perhaps like his friend Charles Haughey, had seen himself as a patron of the arts in his later years. He had promised to finance and build a gallery for the Royal Hibernian Academy,

297

which would of course be named after him. But it was only half finished when he died.

His son clearly did not share his father's interest in either the arts or indeed in posterity. There was no profit in art galleries, and so the building remained a shell, inhabited only by stray cats. Eventually, a few years ago, the other wing of the family surfaced to finish the job. The Abbey Group's Charles Gallagher, a brother of Matt's, donated the money to build what is now known as the RHA Gallagher Gallery.

As Patrick Gallagher bought and sold his way through Dublin, the cost to the city was devastating. He was ruthless in his dealings. In the case of two prized Victorian buildings on the corner of Dawson St and Molesworth St, he demolished both, brushing aside all protest by threatening to lay off his building workers unless the demolition was allowed to proceed. At one stage during the occupation by students of the old buildings, in a scene straight out of Hollywood, Gallagher arrived to negotiate with them from the back seat of his black Rolls Royce. But this was the new Ireland, and his popularity with the press was not so much as dented.

Much of the Gallagher Group trade was in derelict sites, and speculation ensured that they remained derelict. It was simply more profitable to buy and sell the land than to do anything useful with it. Under the tyranny of this kind of uncontrolled greed, the 4-acre Gaiety Green site at the top of Grafton St had become a monstrous eye-sore. Another 4-acre site opposite the National Concert Hall on Earlsfort Terrace had been equally shamefully treated. Patrick Gallagher had bought both sites; it was in the attempt to sell them on, to make the quick killing and his usual fast buck that the tycoon finally came to grief. It was April 1982, and Gallagher was 30 years old.

The shock was severe, catapulting the building and property industry into serious recession. It was also totally unexpected, probably most of all to the Gallagher family itself. They were all in the middle of doing up their mansions at vast expense — Patrick had only just moved into the magnificently renovated Straffan House, and costly building work was rudely interrupted on Dollanstown House in Meath, where Patrick's mother lived.

The family had had a sure sense of its own infallibility. After all, everyone said that Patrick had the Midas touch.

This belief in his own propaganda came easily to Patrick, reared at a time when it seemed the most natural thing in the world that his family should make money out of the growing prosperity of the country. His pedigree — coming from the family that built Ireland — meant that he could do no wrong. So right up until days before the collapse of the Gallagher Group, the family simply didn't believe it could happen. To them, it had the dreamlike quality of a chapter from the book of GUBU, with Patrick like his friend the then Taoiseach, the victim of unfathomable forces outside of anyone's control.

The truth was, as always, slightly more mundane. The Gallagher Group had simply overstretched itself, and become too exposed to the banks, who were owed a total of £30 million. Patrick had succumbed to the greedy gambler's temptation, and had done one deal too many. And as far as the public was concerned, that was the end of it — at least for the next six years.

After the dust had settled, Patrick Gallagher went the way of his father and uncles before him, and disappeared to England. With financial help from Irish business associates he set himself up in the British property market, and continued to speculate as he had in Dublin. But in 1988 came the second major blow to the family — Patrick was arrested in London by the RUC and charged with fraud offences committed in connection with a Gallagher Group bank based in Belfast.

Although the Belfast bank represented only a tiny part of the Gallagher operation, it was the Northern Irish authorities that had doggedly pursued him over a period of six years. The authorities in the South gave no indication of similar activity or even the slightest sign of interest.

RTE subsequently revealed that Patrick Gallagher had committed offences in the South similar to those to which he was pleading guilty in Northern Ireland. He had essentially been using money deposited by ordinary account holders in the Gallagher-controlled banks (both North and South of the border) for his own business purposes. In the collapse, those depositors had lost all of their money.

These revelations unearthed a can of worms within the Irish legal system. In spite of enormously detailed documentation provided by the liquidator of the Gallagher bank in the South, the authorities simply did nothing. The Garda Fraud Squad had been sitting on the file for over five years. It seemed they had neither the staff nor the expertise to proceed with the investigation. Even RTE's attempts to publicise the affair had run into trouble. The Director of Public Prosecutions intervened, the broadcast was postponed; it might interfere with some future trial at some future date, he said.

Eventually, some months later, RTE did broadcast the details of Gallagher's illegal banking activities. But still no prosecution resulted. The Director of Public Prosecutions announced that there was insufficient evidence to bring charges. Sources within the Gardai made it clear that they disagreed. Public representatives and even a Government minister (not a member of Fianna Fail, however) expressed consternation. But at the end of the day, nothing has happened. It is fashionable these days in Ireland to revile 'British justice'. But if the Gallagher case has shown anything, it has made clear that in this area at least, Irish justice is virtually nonexistent.

The Irish system lacks a modern legal framework designed to tackle corporate and business fraud. For whatever reason, the political will to introduce such a framework does not appear to exist. The bulk of Irish law governing financial malpractice comes from the last century — the most up-to-date fraud legislation dates from 1916, and devotes most of its energies to dealing with the theft of livestock and to the activities of clerks and servants.

In Britain, the laws had been continually up-dated in line with changing business practice. But in this country, we were too consumed by the headlong rush towards the promise of modern prosperity in the 1960s to bother about such minor things as rules and regulations. The combination of archaic laws and a hopelessly undermanned Fraud Squad forces one to conclude that Irish business can make up its own rules. That conclusion is reinforced by the frequent boasts of improvements in the pursuit of a different type of financial abuse — namely social welfare fraud. Attempts to illegally claim the small amounts handed out on the dole are severely dealt with, but to make off with millions while carrying on your business is ignored. Ireland has clearly shown that it knows how to appreciate the Midas touch.

LETTERS ON A NEW REPUBLIC
(Three Open Letters to Three Presidents, Jacques Delors, Mary Robinson, Gerry Adams)

Richard Kearney

Dear Jacques Delors,

The present European situation offers, I believe, a unique opportunity to reconsider the problem of Northern Ireland. Is it not time for the Community to supplement internal Anglo-Irish initiatives with a broader European arrangement? If the Community has deemed it appropriate to address the German question on its Eastern periphery, might it not avail of the current redrawing of the European map to also help resolve the Irish question on its Western periphery? If Germany required a European solution, as the twelve member-states agreed, is this not equally true of Northern Ireland? Surely the growing prospect of a federal Europe has momentous implications for a divided Belfast as well as a divided Berlin?

I propose accordingly that you, as President of the EC Commission, seek approval from Ireland, Britain and the ten other member-states, to include Ulster in future discussions on political and economic union in Europe.

The Germans left no doubt about their willingness to subsume their national agenda of unification into the transnational process of European integration. Dr Kohl conceded after his Paris

---

NOTE: These Open Letters are edited versions of three articles which were published, respectively, in *Fortnight* (July/August, 1989, Whatever Became of the Rights of Man?); *The Irish Times* (May 18, 1990, The Implications of a Federal Europe on a Divided Belfast); and *The Irish Independent* (Nov 9, 1990, The Tide Turns for Citizens of a New Society).

meeting with Mitterand on April 26, 1990 that "German unity and European unity are two sides of the same coin". And Hans-Dietrich Genscher was even more explicit in his Luxembourg statement on March 23, 1990 that the process of German unification be sought "in the context of EC integration...and the creation of a pan-European order". Endorsing both Gorbachev's vision of a Common European House and Mitterand's proposal for a European Confederation, he went on to say: "We Germans do not want to go it alone...we want to take the European path. We seek dynamically evolving stability for the whole Europe".

Clearly, we cannot have stability in the *whole* of Europe until we have it in Ulster too. The denouement unfolding plot of the recent German drama should also bring the Irish question onto centre-stage. Is it not time, at last, that it be ushered from the wings of Anglo-Irish affairs into a wider international dialogue? Is there not a crossroads where the choice must eventually be made between 1) the old separatist path of exclusive national sovereignty and 2) the new federalist path of an integrated Europe? We now stand at that crossroads here in Ireland – as in the rest of Europe.

Beyond all the high-flown rhetoric of unification there lurks, however, an unresolved ambiguity. A gap still divides the official internationalism of the German government, for instance, and the gut nationalism touched off in recent election campaigns there. Ireland, too, has a considerable way to go in overcoming the rhetoric of ambiguity. And here I believe that a critic like Fintan O'Toole should be heeded when he writes that "if we really want to use modern Europe as an argument for Irish unity we have to weigh both sides at once, the overcoming of division *and* the power of nationalism to create barbarism" (*Irish Times*, April 25th, 1990). Every Isaiah needs a Jeremiah. Particularly at a time when we appear to be witnessing both the end of East-West divisions and narrow nation-statism on the one hand, and the resurgence of ethnic nationalism in the East European and Soviet Republics, on the other.

But while attending to such warnings, it is important to credit recent signals of readiness, on both sides of the Irish sea, to pool national sovereignty. The inclusion of Joint-Authority as one of the three Forum for a New Ireland proposals (1985), followed by the signing of the Anglo-Irish Agreement (1987) and the Single European Act (1988) by both governments, revealed a willingness by Dublin and London to embrace a "new totality of relationships" exceeding the traditional limits of nation-state sovereignty. The fact that this totality now extends beyond the two islands to include the Continent augments the movement towards *shared* sovereignty.The political union of Europe is the next logical step in this process.

But will the parties to the ancient quarrel of Ulster finally agree to such a solution? Though many might have doubted Mr Haughey's readiness for European integration in the past, his handling of the EC presidency in the first part of 1990 signaled a new openness. Moreover, his acceptance of the "12 member-states...pooling their sovereignty" in regard to key functions and in tandem with EMS & CAP committments (*Irish Times* interview, May 12, 1990) was also highly significant. His Ardfheis committment in 1990 to a European solution to an Irish problem may eventually be observed: "A new Europe is emerging. Are we in Ireland to be left behind, caught in a time warp, standing aloof and unmoved by these great movements...?"

But what of the British Conservatives? Here, too, there is room for sober optimism. In spite of her Bruges speech and delaying tactics at EC summit meetings, it was often forgotten that Mrs Thatcher actually signed the Anglo-Irish Agreement and the SEA, both of which committed Britain to a significant sharing of sovereignty. And her successor, John Major appears more open to a pan-European stance — in spite of the Gulf setback. Indeed, it was his own Conservative predecessor, Churchill, who actually proposed in 1940 that Britain and France should become "one government, one nation, one people, one parliament": which goes to show that even the most nationalistically-minded British Conservatives are capable of transcending the traditional confines of nation-state sovereignty when it comes to the crunch. Indeed, it could be argued that it was because the Lady said no to Europe that her own Conservative party finally said no to her.

So what of the parties in Northern Ireland itself? Regarding the leader of the nationalist community, John Hume, one would be hard put to find a more committed European. His oft repeated dislike of the term "nationalist" together with his advocacy of a Europe of Regions (*EC Report on Regional Policy*, 1987, and *Across the Frontiers*, 1989) and his stated willingness to embrace a new agreement superceding the terms of the Anglo-Irish Agreement, are evidence of his enthusiasm for a European solution.

Which leaves the unionists. The historic tragedy of Ulster has been that the unionist claim to a United Kingdom and the nationalist claim to a United Ireland are mutually exclusive. The last 20 years of violence is a symptom of these irreconcilable claims to nation-state sovereignty. If, however, the separatist model of nation-states is substantially altered in a new European federation, the conflict of sovereignty claims may be rendered redundant. This would also answer the timely call by the New Ireland group (May 4th, 1990)) to both the Irish and British governments to withdraw their territorial claims on the province. A call given renewed energy by the election of Mary Robinson as President of the Irish Republic in November 1990 and the subsequent open debate on articles 2 & 3 of our Constitution in Dail Eireann in December 1990. It is now, surely, but a matter of time before some constitutional arrangement with our northern neighbours is reached. It is no longer a question of *whether* but of *when*. A joint initiative at European level taken by you together with the leaders of the respective parties in Britain, Northern Ireland and the Republic would be most welcome at this point in time.

Deeply rooted passions will not disappear overnight of course. And certainly one of the most urgent tasks will be that of addressing the fundamental question of cultural *difference* in a new Europe. The Protestant poet, John Hewitt, had much to say for his Ulster community here when he spoke of the necessity to balance European and regional identity. He had no difficulty in resolving his own dual identity at *national* level (Irish-British) by declaring additional allegiance to Ulster at *regional* level, and to Europe at *international* level. European regionalism, as Hewitt no less than Hume realised, offers the best solution for both communities of a divided Ulster. It points the way beyond the nationalist/unionist endgame of exclusive sovereignty.

Once again events in Germany offer suggestive parallels. As Erhard Eppler, a leader of West Germany's Social Democrats, stated not long ago in the Bundestag: "The question of identity no longer necessarily connects to nation-states...And it may even be that the European nation-states are being overcome from both sides at once: by the EC, and from below, by regional cultures". An auspicious statement this and one echoed by Eppler's colleague and compatriot, Peter Glotz, who writes: "At the end of the 20th century, the nation-state is ecologically, militarily and culturally out of date". For real democracy to succeed, Glotz argues what is required is a "pan-European federation" with a dual movement of power "down to regional autonomy and up to trans-national structures"; which is another way of confirming the pioneering line taken by David Martin, Scottish MEP and Vice-President of the European Parliament, that in the new Europe "the nation-state, as we have known it for the last 200 years, has become too large and too small to effectively deal with local and global realities" (22 Sept, 1990, John Wheatley Centre Conference, Scotland).

But the question remains – how to strike the right balance between a new internationalism and a new regionalism? The *EC Report on Regional Policy* (October 1987), together with Article 23 of the SEA, already offer provisions for a Europe of equal and interdependent regions. And your own espousal, Mr Delors, of a European triad of *region-nation-federation* (*Antenne 2*, January 24th, 1990) has, I am convinced, radical implications for the Ulster situation. May I add, indeed, that on this matter I was personally most encouraged by your response to our discussion of a Europe of the regions in *Across the Frontiers* when you wrote: "The main point that you and the various contributors have made is how important the very notion of *region* is likely to become within the European Community and, for that matter, in Ireland. Let me tell you how close I feel to your common dedication to the promoting of regionalisation policies in

306

in Europe" (letter, April 25, 1989).

Now that the Northern log-jam shows signs of loosening, might I suggest the time is ripe to consult with political leaders in Belfast, Dublin and London, in order to prepare resolutions on the Ulster question for a future Inter-governmental Conference on European Union? Could not such a European move supplement and subsume the existing Anglo-Irish initiative? Is there not a compelling logic to the notion of Ulster as a quasi-autonomous region relating, inter-dependently, to other regions on the *island* of Ireland, the *archipelago* of Britain, and the *continent* of Europe. This tri-lateral allegiance to the concentric circles of Ireland-Britain-Europe would surely enable both the nationalist and unionist communities to put their historic quarrel behind them and work together for the common good of their region under a "common European roof".

Might we not, moreover, think of this new "totality of relationships" as a new kind of Republic – less nationalist than internationalist; less absolutist and exclusivist in its sovereignty than shared and interdependent; less a conventional centralised republic of the nation-state (a relatively modern invention of the last two hundred years) than a decentralized "postmodern" Republic of regional republics, each with a maximum of devolved self-governing parliaments? Is such a goal of an integrated Europe of local participatory democracies not indeed what your enlightened compatriot, Voltaire, had in mind when he advanced his dream of "one great Europe made up of parts each corresponding equally to the other"?

Ulster is an Irish problem and a British problem. But it is also a European problem. Ireland's historical divisions are, in significant measure, European in origin. We often forget that the Viking invasion was plotted in Norse; the 12th century invasion in Anglo-Norman; the battle of the Boyne in Dutch; the Great Armada in Spanish; the 1798 landing in French; the 1941 blitz of Belfast (where 500 died in one raid alone) in German. We are no foreigners to foreigners. Ireland is also a *European problem requiring a European solution*.

The reconciling of divided communities, in Ireland no less

307

than in Germany and other European countries, can no longer be confined to isolated nation-states. The last best hope, I submit, lies in a federated Europe.

Yours,

Richard Kearney

Dear Mary Robinson,

Your election to the highest office of this land was a good day. I do not share the views of our more cynical commentators that your election was no more than a passing fad, a media-managed mirage, a rhetorical fling with a dream-famished electorate, a change of style but not of substance. I believe it marks a significant, indeed irreversible, sea-change in the life of this small Republic of ours. The tide has turned. And I have no quarrel with those who say that this is all *symbolic*. I don't consider the symbolic less real than the real. Symbols matter more than most things. They are our chosen means of storytelling. And the story we are telling ourselves and others in electing you as President is that we are not just natives of an ancient land but citizens of a new society. We have come of age. We have performed a rite of passage from past to future.

Inside every Irish person there is a native and a citizen battling it out. The battle is between tradition and modernity. Where the native in us sees identity as something given, the citizen sees it as something to be made and remade.

The Rights of the Citizen, as your legal mind knows well, were pioneered by the European Enlightenment and inscribed in the Proclamation of the French *Republique*. They guaranteed the right of each individual, and of each people, of a Republic to choose their own society. Political culture was no longer merely inherited; it was henceforth considered to be something of our own making. Or to put it in Joycean terms, it was no longer a "nightmare of history" but the "uncreated conscience of the race."

Your election has endorsed this transition from outworn piety to a more enabling sense of possibility. The young – and women in particular – have decided that they want a modern enlightened Republic where each citizen enjoys equal rights and responsibilities. And they have shown they want it now.

What we have been witnessing is nothing less than a national psychodrama. A play between opposing parts of ourselves – one part that longs for tradition, security, continuity and another part that wants to come clean, to break the old icons in the name of something different. But if Irish politics has become something of a national drama, Irish theatre has, for its part, come to reflect our inner political struggles.

To cite but one example. A new play by Seamus Heaney opened in our National Theatre on the eve of the Presidential election. The theme of the play, *The Cure of Troy*, bore an almost uncanny relevance to the week's happenings. It staged the choice that must be made by a young citizen *Neoptolemus* between different archetypal figures: *Philoctetes*, the wounded and forgotten campaigner of yesteryear, abandoned on an island and now being recalled to wage another battle for the nation; *Odysseus* who is prepared to use any ploy and deceit for the sake of his tribe; and the energetic and wise female *Chorus* who point the way forward in terms of mutual respect and healing. They look towards a time where "hope and history rhyme."

But if these are the dramatic rites of passage, what of the realities? What lies behind the symbolic choice of you, Mary Robinson, as President? What does it tell us about changing attitudes in Ireland to *religion, party, nation* and *women*. What, in short, does it tell us about our image of ourselves.

A significant feature of this Presidential election – in contrast to recent referenda for example – is that the Church was conspicuous by its absence. I do not recall either of the two main party candidates playing the "Catholic card." And, curiously, when you yourself formally described yourself as a "practising Catholic" this did not sound like a bid for ecclesiastical endorsement (some hope!). You seemed to be saying that one could be critical of one's church and still remain a member of it. There are many on this island – including myself – who share this view.

Voicing clear opposition to the Church stance on the ordination of women, contraception, divorce, homosexuality, or the right to information on abortion, did not prevent you from equally clearly identifying with those in your Church struggling for a more just and caring society – Sr Stanislas Kennedy, Fr Peter

310

McVerry and the like.

Such a statement is surely unprecedented for an Irish political candidate seeking election – not to mention election as President, the highest office in the land. But the surprise is not so much that someone like you had the courage to make this claim. It is that the Catholic Church did not rebuke you for making it; and furthermore, that you did not, apparently, alienate the Irish electorate by so doing.

What it means, I think, is that young Irish people are not prepared to leave religion to a patriachal hierarchy anymore. They are declaring it possible to be a believer *and* a dissenter at one and the same time – surely a promising prospect for the reconciling of Protestant, Catholic and Dissenter on this island?

The fact that a reactionary sect of pre-Vatican Two Catholics (accompanied by one or two Fianna Fail deputies) did circulate a shameful smear against you during the campaign does not represent majority Catholic thinking on the matter. Although one doesn't have to think too far back to days when it might have. Moreover, the election of Cahal Daly as Catholic Primate of Ireland in the same week as you were elected as Ireland's highest secular leader, may well betoken a shift towards a more tolerant post-sectarian Ireland.

What, after all, is one to make of an Irish Catholic Primate who declares that "the real British presence in Northern Ireland is that of a million unionists who identified themselves as British...but had every right to claim Ireland as their home"?

When two of Ireland's most influential figureheads – President and Primate – are prepared to show such generosity to what the majority would have historically considered the "traditional enemy", it is hard to deny that the times indeed are a-changing.

The unprecedented voting pattern across *party* lines is also a new departure in Irish politics. While accepting the candidature of the left-wing parties, your support extended well beyond the party vote. This is the first time in Irish history, to my knowledge, where an independent candidate belonging to no political party (it was almost five years since you left the Labour party) has polled so highly.

What it means, quite simply, is that many Irish citizens today want to be represented by somebody who, like you, is her own person. Which presumably means they identify themselves as persons with *their own minds*.

The fact that the *women's* vote played such a decisive role in this election is also hugely significant. And surely another first in Irish political history. It must signal a deep change in our traditionally male-dominated society. You have broken with the old disabling stereotypes of the Irish woman. You are, if I may say so, representative *par excellence* of equal status for men and women — and therefore of *all* the people.

You are a woman not subordinate to men, a mother enhanced by motherhood, an active woman committed both to the privacy of family life and the public good of political life.

As a symbol of identification for Irish women your election promises the advent of a more enabling relationship between the sexes in our society. Gone are the days when Irish women identify with the *cliché* of Mother Ireland calling on her sons to spill their blood for the fourth green field, or the Sean Bhean Bhocht passively bemoaning her destitute state. You, Mary Robinson, are no Cathleen Ní Houlihan, but you still have "the walk of a Queen." A green Queen with a red rose. An Irish Queen. Something we haven't seen since the days of Queen Maeve of Connaught. Ballina is on the rise again. The West's awake.

Finally, I believe your election betokens a new kind of thinking about what we mean by the *nation*. A Northerner, Austin Currie, was chosen as the candidate by the Republic's second largest party. Brian Lenihan proudly cited his key role as Tanaiste in the implementation of the Anglo-Irish Agreement (although his own party in opposition had initially opposed it, presumably because it acknowledged some sharing of sovereignty with Britain over the North).

And you, for your own part, stated your principled committment to an even wider agreement which would, ideally, take in unionist as well as nationalist opinion. Though I myself think you were somewhat mistaken to oppose the Anglo-Irish Agreement for these reasons, they were of the noblest kind: the kind required in a new Republic of a new Europe, committed to

312

surmounting divisions between nationalist and unionist, to safeguarding the universal rights of each and every citizen.

Mary Robinson, as person and President, you can transcend the border dividing the two nation-states of Ireland and Britain. You are our first genuinely post-partitionist President. And you are also a symbol of real Republicanism. Not that travestied by the Provos; but that which guarantees civil and religious liberties for all. The kind of Republicanism proclaimed in the European revolutions of the eighteenth and nineteenth centuries and invoked here in Ireland, almost two hundred years ago, by the Protestants, Catholics and Dissenters who founded the *United Irishmen*.

This is the only kind of Republicanism young people in Ireland today will endorse. Universal rather than sectarian; European rather than provincial; open to all Irish citizens, not just the members of one tribe.

The vote which put you in the *Aras* was a vote for someone who has served the Irish people both at home (in the Senate and courts) and abroad (as an active member of the International Jurists). We are talking about an act of faith in another kind of Ireland – one where civil war politics is replaced by civic rights politics; where neighbouring nation-states are no longer locked in bitter quarrel; where the glaring gap between rich and poor may be narrowed; where social inequality may be supplanted by social democracy – of a *participatory* kind; where the new communications technology can link together local and global cultures; where educational and financial exchanges traverse multiple frontiers; and where our best artists, film-makers and musicians represent an innovative mix of native and alter-native culture – bringing what is richest in our indigenous traditions to a wider international community.

Let me end where I began – with our writers. There is a passage in Seamus Heaney's *Station Island* where the poet is visited by James Joyce, who offers the following advice:

That subject people stuff is a cod's game...
...Keep at a tangent,
When they make the circle wide, it's time to swim

313

out on your own and fill the element
with signatures of your own frequency,
echo soundings, searches, probes, allurements,
elver-gleams in the dark of the whole sea.

Your election has shown that Irish citizens have taken such advice on board. The sea-change has occurred. There is no swimming back. Thank you for taking the plunge.

Yours,

Richard Kearney

Dear Gerry Adams,

I write to you as a fellow Irishman committed to Republican ideals. What I wish to put to you here is that your interpretation of Republicanism – and that of your fellow-travellers in the IRA – departs radically from the original principles of those who first introduced Republican thinking into this island: I refer in particular to Wolfe Tone and the United Irishmen who were established in Belfast and Dublin in the 1790s.

My main question to you, as President of Sinn Fein, is this: whatever has become of the Rights of Man? Whatever happened to that enabling heritage of civil liberties proclaimed first by the *Republique* of the French Revolution and later again by the various Republican movements which swept through Europe in the ensuing centuries, furnishing the political principles of emancipation for most modern European Republics – including, in part at least, our own Republic here in the South of Ireland?

The Republican legacy of rights includes, I admit, the right to free speech. And for that reason, if for no other, I oppose the existing broadcasting law in these islands which prevents people of your own (and other paramilitary) persuasion from having access to the airwaves. I personally think this takes from our political ethos as a Republic. It curtails the right to freedom of expression – no matter how abhorrent the views expressed. But it also serves to make martyrs of your paramilitary comrades and thereby exacerbates the existing threat to the most fundamental human right of all – the right to *live*: a right which your political movement has sacrificed to sectional, sectarian, and ultimately, tribal interests.

I have always shared the view that lines of communication should be kept open – even with those, like yourself and the IRA, who do everything to keep them closed. Your bombs and bullets can interrupt train and road travel between both parts of this island. But they will never succeed in terminating efforts to communicate another view of things to you and your fellow assasins. It was because of this conviction that I took the decision as co-editor of *The Crane Bag* in 1978 to include an interview with the then IRA Chief of Staff, Seamus Twomey. It was published along with articles by several other commentators, including Conor Cruise O'Brien, in a special issue of our journal on Northern Ireland. Our decision met with the disapproval of not only Conor Cruise O'Brien but also of the Northern Irish Arts Council who suspended all subsequent grants to our publication for the next sixteen issues (in fact until we ceased publication in 1984).

It is therefore in a spirit of libertarian faith that I submit this Open Letter to you – in the hopes that you may listen and perhaps, someday, respond in kind. If what follows reads a little like a "history lesson", please bear in mind that I am addressing these thoughts to you in the bi-Centenary year of the French Revolution – the singlemost seminal event of modern Republicanism. I do not wish to preach, merely to state a point of view, argue a case, and if at all possible persuade.

A signal feature of the French revolution was the conviction that the "rights of man" and the "rights of people" are mutually inclusive. Although the original *Declaration of the Rights of Man and of the Citizen* in 1789 made no explicit reference to the rights of the people, the French constitution of 1791 made up for this omission: "The French nation renounces any war undertaken with a view to conquest and will never use her powers against *the liberty of any other people*."

The principle was ratified and reformulated in the Jacobin constitution of 1793. Article 118 read: "The French people are the friend and natural ally of all *free peoples*..." This constitution proclaimed the equal and inseparable legitimacy of the rights of *man* and the rights of the *people* (or what soon became known as "the principle of nationalities").

Napoleon's campaigns did, of course, inject a dose of pernicious ambiguity into this principle – in so far as his conquests of other nations were frequently carried out in the name of liberation. But this did not prevent later revolutions invoking the French declaration of the rights of peoples. This was particularly true of the revolts which swept through Europe in 1848, intense popular

316

agitations for national democracy and independence. So widespread was this movement for national self-determination that 1848 was christened *le printemps des peuples*.

The legacy of this double declaration of the rights of nations *and* of man was not confined to Europe. It extended to the continents of Latin America, Africa and Asia where, well into our own century, peoples have been rebelling against monarchic or despotic regimes in the name of democratic national liberation. These Siamese twins of individual and national rights were given a universal dimension in 1948, in the *Universal Declaration of Human Rights* by the United Nations General Assembly.

Some of the nations which have been most valuable in support of human rights – France, Britain and America – have undeniably also been guilty of colonial and imperial campaigns against smaller nations over the last two centuries. But it would be disingenuous to ignore the extraordinary appeal of the "rights of man" and the "rights of the people" for nations struggling against despotism and for self-determination. After Hitler's invasion of Paris in 1943 the first action by Alfred Rosenberg, principal idealogue of the Nazis, was to declare war on the ideas of 1789.

What impact did this twin legacy of individual and national rights have on our own island? How did the French revolutionary principles of 1789-93 influence the ideology of the United Irishmen in 1798, and later the 1916 rebellion? Has Irish republicanism been historically capable of sustaining the delicate but indispensable balance between the "rights of man" and the "rights of the nation"? And what, finally, is the republican heritage of rights in Ireland today?

Have the rights of the Irish nation served to safeguard the corollary rights of its individual citizens and minorities – in keeping with the original pluralist agenda of Republicanism? Or have they instead served to subordinate them? When we speak of Irish Republicanism are we talking about the rights of the people *versus* the rights of man, or in accordance with them?

One thing is certain: Sinn Fein and the IRA have no proprietorial claim to the Republican heritage of rights. While you proclaim the right of the Irish 'people' to self-determination, you utterly ignore the attendant rights of man. You also refuse in

317

practice, to acknowledge that the right of the Irish 'people' involves a conflict of rights between the different *peoples* inhabiting this island – nationalist and unionist, Catholic and Protestant.

By contrast, the United Irishmen did recognise this diversity when, in one of their founding manifestoes in 1791, they spoke of Ireland as "separate nations met and settled together, not mingled or convened". Their aim, as Wolfe Tone made clear, was to unite these diverse nations and denominations into a "whole people" under the "common name of Irishman". But this unity could only be achieved, he argued, by establishing a non-ethnic and non-sectarian Republic where the right of the Irish people would not be reductively equated with the right of *one* of its constituent peoples.

By identifying the rights of Irish Republicanism exclusively with the Catholic-nationalist community, you, as President of Sinn Fein, and the IRA have betrayed the common name of Irishman. Admittedly and regrettably, most unionists have, for their part, identified exclusively with their own Protestant-loyalist community. But at least their exclusivity is consistent with the conviction that majority-rule in Ulster is based on a sectarian head-count. They no longer even lay claim, as some of their Protestant and Dissenter ancestors did, to the pluralist Republicanism of Tone and the United Irishmen – a Republicanism which took its tune, in part at least, from the enlightenment principles of universal rights which inspired the French revolution. The idea of a Protestant parliament for a Protestant people and a Catholic parliament for a Catholic people would have been anathema to Tone.

The Societies of the United Irishmen set up in Belfast and Dublin in the 1790s invoked the universalist philosophy of the French *Republique*. Appealing to its members as "citizens of the world", a seminal manifesto of the Dublin society, founded in December 1791, endorsed the double legacy of rights. It asked its members to "swear to maintain the rights of their nature as *men* and the right of Ireland as an Independent *People*".

The spirit of enlightened universalism was again apparent when this same document hailed Voltaire and Franklin – founding

318

fathers of the French and American Republics – as "fellow citizens of the world". It went on to celebrate the initiation of the French revolution on July 14th with a "libation to European liberty and eventually the liberty of the world".

What characterised the French revolution's *Declaration of the Rights of Man* was its claim to legislate equally for *all* citizens and peoples, not just the French. In this it represented a marked advance on both the English Bill of Rights of 1689 and the American Bill of Rights of 1789. It would appear obvious that this *universalist* appeal of the French revolution, which so informed the original Republicanism of the United Irishmen, has been utterly traduced by the sectarian campaign of the IRA against the Protestants and Dissenters of Northern Ireland.

One has good reason to believe that Tone himself would have upheld the inseparability of the "rights of the nation" and the "rights of man". Though a separatist nationalist in his determination to break the colonial link with England, Tone was also an enlightened republican committed to the universal principle of the rights of man. His concern was not to establish Ireland as an isolated nation defined by ethnic or confessional exclusiveness. His quarrel with England was a genuinely Republican one. Like Jefferson and Franklin in America, Tone rejected English monarchy as an oppressive regime which did not acknowledge all its subjects equally but privileged the subjects of the colonising nation.

Tone's resolve to break with England was fired, in significant measure, by a cosmopolitan vision of a Republican alliance between the enlightened peoples of Europe. In this he shared Voltaire's project for Europe as "one great Republic divided into states each corresponding equally with the other". Tone's nationalism was tempered by universalism. And it is surely no accident that one of his closest intellectual allies during his stay in Paris in the 1790s was Thomas Paine, author of the *Rights of Man* and a firm believer that any Republic which betrayed the universalist vision of the French revolution was dishonouring its name.

That Tone would have observed the universalist and pluralist agenda of the rights of man in reality, had the 1798 revolt succeeded, is of course hypothetical. But there are significant indicators that he would. On the religious question, he was entirely opposed to sectarian tribalism as he was to the notion of a single state religion. His goal was a secular republic where church and state would be separated and no denomination allowed privileged position.

On violence, Tone could be held to account. But the oppression and misery suffered by the vast majority of the Irish population in the 1790s (most of them Catholics) was of inhuman proportions. The eyewitness accounts of Humbert's officers as they marched through Connaught make for horrifying reading. All three "nations" that made up the island's population – Catholic, Protestant and Dissenter – had legitimate grievances against the English Crown, grievances denied any adequate parliamentary redress, especially after the failure of 1782. And needless to say, then as opposed to now, there were no local councils, national assemblies, judicial inquiries, Anglo-Irish agreements or European parliaments and courts where reform could be pursued through peaceful and democratic means.

Under such unpropitious circumstances, Tone accepted the inevitability of armed insurrection as the only means of expressing the will of the majority of the inhabitants of Ireland. But he did so reluctantly. Tone's Paris journals show his hostility to blood-letting. He abhorred the manner in which the Terror in France had filled the Pantheon with dead bodies, vowing that such a precedent would never be followed in Ireland. And he expressed singular admiration for General Hoche, leader of the French expeditionary force to Ireland, for his "humane temperament" and overt disapproval of the slaughter which succeeded the French revolution. "I am humane myself," said Tone, "and trust we shall be able to prevent unnecessary bloodshed in Ireland."

Can you or those other Irish Republicans who invoke Tone's name today to justify a campaign of sectarian violence against your Protestant neighbours honestly pretend to honour such scruples? How can you square the monthly death-toll with the universalism and anti-sectarian agenda of the original Republicanism of the United Irishmen – a Republicanism committed to the belief of the French revolution that the particular "right of a people" must never be separated from the universal "rights of man"?

It is not a matter of deifying or demonising Tone and the United Irishmen. It is a matter of deciding critically what is their heritage *now*. Just as the bicentenary of 1789 invites us to discriminate between its positive legacy of liberties and its bloody legacy of terror, so too you and your contemporary claimants of Irish Republicanism in the IRA are obliged to discriminate between the enabling and disabling heritage of 1798.

I would suggest that such discrimination has been inexcusably lacking to date; that the disablng heritage has had the upper, and only, hand in your campaign of violence. Is it too late to begin again? To revise one's vision? To reassess one's interpretation of the Republican origins and ideals? To commit oneself to a Republic for the living rather than the dead?

Yours,

Richard Kearney

INTRODUCTION

I was a seven year old schoolboy in 1966 when the fiftieth anniversary of the Easter Rising was celebrated. Looking back now it is extraordinary how many vivid recollections I still retain of those events – images like that of Joe Lynch as Cathal Brugha in *Insurrection*, the culture shock of seeing familiar streets on the television replacing the grey icons of America. Even more extraordinary is how those same recollections are frequently shared by so many of my generation. Memorials were unveiled, speeches made beseeching God that in her hour of need Ireland would find such brave young sons again. I doubt if the dignitaries making those speeches believed a word of it, I'm sure the businessmen paying for the monuments certainly didn't; but we, in short trousers and cropped hair, did. I was still in school a few years later when the body of Frank Stagg the hungerstriker was brought back from England, escorted by armoured cars across Ireland and buried in the West under concrete, like contaminated nuclear waste, this time not with a guard of honour but an armed guard watching his grave day and night to prevent him being dug up and buried as he had wished. Schoolchildren may not always understand too much, but they know when somebody, somewhere along the line, has been lying to them.

My generation, born at the very tail-end of the 1950's and raised before the bombs began to explode on Derry's streets were perhaps unique in being left so quickly in the curious limbo of being taught certain songs at school one year and seeing them banned from the radio the next. Children born only a handful of years later were raised, at least officially, on a different set of attitudes. In the same way as the Rising meant

323

one thing to my generation and a different thing to those who came immediately afterwards, I began to wonder was this the case with other generations who have grown up since 1916.

Although the events of Easter week are seventy years past, this curious ambivalence in public attitudes means that the Rising is still, and possibly more so than forty years ago, a controversial topic and one in which people are often left in a no-win situation. If you think the Rising good then in popular opinion (depending on the last atrocity) you may be a provo willing to murder women and children first; if you think it was bad you are a West Brit lacky.

Writers, it is hoped, are able to move beyond clichés. This pamphlet takes sixteen Irish writers in chronological order, chosen to hopefully represent a fairly broad spectrum of opinion and ranging from those like Francis Stuart and Mervin Wall who remember the actual events, to those who grew up in the 1960s in the almost iconoclastic shadow of the leaders' images. It naturally cannot represent the whole range of views, or indeed non-views, on the events and repercussions of Easter Week, but still hopefully it can be broad enough to examine the truths, myths and contradictions not only of the Rising and its aftermath, but of our reactions to it today.

Demot Bolger,
Finglas,
October, 1988.

Biographical Notes

Fintan O'Toole was born in Dublin in 1958. His books from Raven include *The Politics of Magic — The Work and Times of Tom Murphy* and *A Mass for Jesse James*. A columnist with the Irish Times, he is currently Artistic Adviser at The Abbey Theatre.

Colm Tóibín was born in Co Wexford in 1955. His books include a novel, *The South*, and two travel books, *Walking Along the Border* and *Homage to Barcelona*. His Selected Journalism 1980 — 1990, *The Trial of The Generals,* was published by Raven in 1990.

Michael O'Loughlin was born in Dublin in 1958 and now lives in Amsterdam. Chairman in 1990 of the inaugral EEC European Translation Prize, his books from Raven include three collections of poems, translations from the Dutch and a volume of short stories, *The Inside Story*.

Ferdia Mac Anna was born in Dublin in 1955. A former rock singer (as Rocky De Valera) and journalist, his first fiction appeared in *Raven Introductions 4*, and his first novel, *The Last of the High Kings* will be published by Michael Joseph in 1991.

Katie Donovan was born in Dublin in 1962. She has taught at The University of California at Berkeley and in Hungary and now works as a journalist and creative writer in Dublin. Her poetry and stories have been widely published in Ireland and abroad, including a selection in *Raven Introductions 5*.

Anthony Cronin was born in Wexford in 1925. His books include novels (*The Life of Reily*), biography (*No Laughing Matter*), a memoir (*Dead as Doornails*), and two celebrated collections of essays (*Heritage Now* and *An Irish Eye*). His poetry from Raven include *New And Selected Poems* and *The End of the Modern World*.

Edward Mulhall was born in Athy Co. Kildare in 1956. A former radio producer and assistant head of radio features and current affairs, he is now a Television producer and the editor of the RTE television Six-One News.

Aileen O'Mara was born in Offaly in 1960. A former staff journalist in *The Sunday Tribune*, she won the News Category of the A.T. Cross Women Journalist of the Year Award in 87 and the Social Affairs catagory of the National Journalist of the Year Award in 1989.

John Waters was born in Castlerea, Co Roscommon in 1955. A former editor of *In Dublin* and *Magill*, he now writes a column for *The Irish Times*. His first book will be appearing from Blackstaff in 1991.

Mary Raftery was born in Dublin in 1955. Formerly a freelance journalist, notably with *In Dublin* and *Magill*, she is now a producer with RTE television. She received a Jacobs Award for her *Today Tonight* special on Patrick Gallagher.

Richard Kearney was born in Cork in 1954. A co-founder of *The Crane Bag*, his many books include *Poetique du Possible* and *Modern Movements in European Philosophy*. His first long poem, *Angel of Patrick's Hill* was published by Raven in 1991.

Dermot Bolger was born in Dublin in 1959. The author of five collections of poetry, his novels, *The Journey Home* and *The Woman's Daughter*, are published by Viking/Penguin who will be publishing four of his plays as *A Dublin Quartet* in 1991.